Springer Studies in Alternative Economics

This book series offers an outlet for cutting-edge research in alternative, heterodox and pluralist economics. It features scholarly studies on various schools of thought beyond the neo-classical orthodoxy, including Austrian, Post Keynesian, Sraffian, Marxian, Georgist, Institutional-evolutionary, as well as feminist, radical, social, green, and ecological economics. It aims to promote pluralism of economic ideas, methodological approaches, and topics.

The series also welcomes works that seek to develop alternative visions of the economy, economic structures and new approaches that aim to serve society, for example by embedding the economy within the ecosystem, or to enrich economic thought by advancing diversity, gender, race, and social equality. All titles in this series are peer-reviewed.

Thomas Gries • Carina Burs • Veronika Müller

The Economics of Ideologies

Belief Systems and Ideologies in Rational Decision-making

Springer

Thomas Gries
Economics
Paderborn University
Paderborn, Germany

Carina Burs
Economics
Paderborn University
Paderborn, Germany

Veronika Müller
Economics
Paderborn University
Paderborn, Germany

ISSN 2731-5908 ISSN 2731-5916 (electronic)
Springer Studies in Alternative Economics
ISBN 978-3-031-93513-8 ISBN 978-3-031-93514-5 (eBook)
https://doi.org/10.1007/978-3-031-93514-5

This Springer imprint is published by the registered company Springer Nature Switzerland AG
The registered company address is: Gewerbestrasse 11, 6330 Cham, Switzerland

Contents

List of Figures

Chapter 1
Introduction, Outline, Discussion in a Nutshell

Political polarization has become a key feature of today's democratic societies. The views and narratives discussed in public, and especially on social media, are often very contradictory and dogmatic. In many countries, we are seeing society becoming increasingly divided into extreme political camps. This polarization is not only driven by the spread and reinforcement of extreme ideologies, it is increasingly contributing to a climate of confrontation and hostility.

One of the main causes of political polarization is the dogmatization of ideological ideas. Ideologically extreme narratives are propagated as the only possible worldview that need to be enforced to the detriment of all other ideas if necessary. Another reason for the polarization we are observing is the way in which today's media works, the media from which we obtain our information. This polarization within the information system, both traditional and online, means that news and information are presented in a way that also fuels the political polarization of media consumers. Sensational journalism and the emphasis on conflict reinforce the perception that political opponents have irreconcilable differences and that dialog is pointless. This creates a spiral of polarization in which people increasingly take extreme positions in order to distinguish themselves from "the other side".

However, the rapid and wide reach of social media is at least as important for this development in traditional media. Social media spread and reinforce extreme positions as well as fakes and propaganda. By connecting the world, information becomes easily accessible, which has both positive and negative effects. On the one hand, it enables people to be better informed and to form their own opinions. On the other hand, though, it can also lead to filter bubbles, disinformation, and opinion leadership through targeted disinformation, propaganda, and a distortion of the truth. This sometimes selective dissemination of information, propaganda, and disinformation by ideological organizations reinforces existing polarized opinions and makes dialogue between different political camps more difficult.

Extreme ideologies therefore play a decisive role when it comes to exacerbating political polarization. These extreme ideologies are often characterized by the

T. Gries et al., *The Economics of Ideologies*, Springer Studies in Alternative Economics, https://doi.org/10.1007/978-3-031-93514-5_1

attitude that there can only be one valid interpretation of reality. They propagate dogmatic convictions and are averse to compromise. People influenced by extreme ideologies tend to see their political opponents not just as people with different opinions but as enemies. This leads to a climate of intolerance and mistrust, which puts a considerable strain on political discourse and sometimes makes the possibility of democratic compromise impossible.

One example of the consequence of extreme ideologies in political polarization is the rise of populism in many countries. Populist leaders tend to offer simple but often also extreme solutions to complex problems. These dogmatic narratives create an atmosphere in which compromise is seen as betrayal and political debate is reduced to emotional appeals to the grassroots. Populism thus creates a highly polarized political landscape in which the middle ground disappears and the room for moderate voices shrinks. Another factor that contributes to political polarization is social fragmentation. In an increasingly individualized society, people often seek out groups that share the same identity and beliefs. This creates the so-called "filter bubbles" on social media and other online platforms where people with similar views interact and reinforce each other's beliefs. This lack of diversity in social circles reinforces the polarization, as people then have no contact with other perspectives and opinions.

As economists especially in economic decision theory and political economy, we should not remain silent when we observe these phenomena attacking the roots of democracy as a place of balance and compromise between different views. We ought to understand what is happening in order to develop appropriate solutions so that democracies remain a place of controversial but peaceful debate where solutions can be found for the benefit of all in society. Therefore, this book seeks both to bring an economic perspective to the discussion of these phenomena and to recognize the limitations of the traditional economic perspective, and then to incorporate findings from other social science disciplines into *The Economics of Ideology*. This polarization toward dogmatic, ideological beliefs that people follow with great conviction and enthusiasm is difficult to explain to economists, who have the notion that individuals act very rationally. Ideologies, as a set of believed narratives, appear to many economists to be a nonrational phenomena. So are all those who follow these ideological, even polarizing, narratives irrational, or even cranks? Does the existence of belief systems and ideologies and their influence on us and our decisions indicate that our rationality is not what it is cracked up to be? Are rationality and ideology possibly even mutually exclusive, or are beliefs, belief systems, and even ideologies meaningful elements of human decision-making behavior? What connections exist between ideologies, the phenomenon we refer to as the "human information problem", and the desire to make the best possible and probably mostly rational decisions for our well-being?

These are the questions we address in this book. We want to understand the role of belief systems and ideologies for our individual choices by using tools from economic decision-making.

Thus our questions depart from, and go beyond, a central area of microeconomics, the standard theory of rational choice. But what is a rational decision?

Economists are very clear on the answer: A decision is made with a specific goal in mind. So you want to get as close to that goal as possible, to achieve it as well as possible. At the same time, however, each decision-maker is constrained by his or her limited resources. Because of these limited resources, the goal can only be achieved to a certain extent. A decision that allows the best possible achievement of the goal given these limited resources is then considered rational. Thus, there is no other decision that will lead to this best possible outcome or an even better one. If we were to make any other decision, we would call it illogical and irrational. Formally, we describe this decision problem as maximizing an objective function under resource constraints:

$$\begin{aligned} \text{max} &: \text{objective (activity)} \\ \text{subject to} &: \text{constraints of the activity} \end{aligned}$$

The decision thus follows a formal, mathematical logic, the same as a machine would do. It is well known that humans are not machines, and yet the idea that humans do not systematically make irrational decisions makes sense. The ability to act logically and rationally, to draw logical conclusions, to plan ahead, and to act strategically and purposefully has given humans their special place in evolution. At the very least, there is no species that does this better than humans. This does not mean that we make every decision in this way; many real decisions are more random – some would say spontaneous, intuitive, or based on good feeling. On the whole, however, we do not systematically leave our decisions to chance. Even if we do not solve an optimization problem each time we take a decision, in the aggregate we act ‘as if’ we do (Friedman, 1953). If we learn from individual, perhaps random, decisions, correct ourselves, and make sure the next decisions we take are better, we will approach the theoretical optimum. The economist’s homo economicus is thus a construct, an artificial character that can implement, in a simple form, the idea that we ultimately make decisions guided by rationality. The idea of the rationality of decisions, the idea of “rational choice”, is thus initially meaningful under the restrictions mentioned in the above. But if people are indeed rational and act and make decisions rationally, why are there so many different worldviews, belief systems, and ideologies that people follow? Believing means not knowing. People follow beliefs and ideological defaults even though they do not really know whether it is really right and good for them. They follow the interpretations, judgments, and rules of the belief systems and ideologies they adhere to and make decisions against that backdrop. People even follow the guidance of their ideologies and belief systems that leads as far as catastrophic wars and violence, including the concomitant risk of their own death. Does the existence of belief systems and ideologies and their influence on us indicate that our rationality is not all it is cracked up to be and that we do not make rational decisions? Are ideologically motivated decisions irrational anyway? Are rationality and ideology mutually exclusive? Or, are we rational, but not in the sense of the truncated, simple framework described in the above as rational choice? Why do belief systems and ideologies exist at all? What functions do they serve? Perhaps belief systems and ideologies serve important functions even for rational people. And perhaps we simply need to better understand the functions of ideologies in the context of our rational choices. Answering these questions is the task we have set ourselves in writing this book. We want to show that worldviews, belief systems, and ideologies are important decision-making tools even for rational people. 'Belief' is part of rational decision-making. Different beliefs can lead to different goals and different ways of achieving those goals. Therefore, what we believe can lead to actions and outcomes of very different qualities, good results but also disasters. This is especially true for the paths proposed for achieving a particular desired goal system. In the following paragraphs of this introductory chapter, we will present the basic ideas set out in this book, that is, we provide an overview and summary of the main issues by way of an intuitive reasoning.

The Human Information Problem (Chap. 2) Since we are writing about the economics of ideologies, in Chap. 2, we return to economic decision theory. People always seek to achieve a given objective as well as possible under various given resource constraints. This is the basic task we want to consider in light of a standard problem, such as the optimal consumption decision. In a simple consumer decision, the goal is to maximize consumption utility. This will also be our starting point here. However, we want to look at a central problem that is not considered in most modeling of decision problems, and that is that the decision-maker usually has a massive information problem.

In the standard models of economic decision theory, the assumption that is usually made is that the decision-maker has complete information. At first glance, this assumption seems innocuous, since in our textbook examples the decision concerns simple quantities of certain goods to consume. When it comes to the purchase of apples and pears, the information problem is obviously not very big, and the information cost of such a decision appears very small. So it is plausible to disregard information costs. But things are already different when we look at differentiated goods. In the case of differentiated goods, we consider a whole set of known or even unknown characteristics. When it comes to unobservable quality and hidden characteristics, we as economists have already recognized that the information problem can have a significant impact on the decision. In such cases, the decision environment is already more complex because we are dealing with characteristics that are not immediately apparent. So if we need information to make a decision – because in the reality of that particular decision the assumption of perfect information does not hold – we would have to somehow get that information. But information does not come for free. Each step in the further information acquisition process comes at a cost. And so our first question is this: How do decisions change when we do not have free and complete information to make our decisions? To answer this question, we start with the benchmark of a choice under perfect information.

However, this is an unrealistic benchmark. To find the realistic case of costly information acquisition, we need to describe the process of information acquisition.

We use Bayesian Learning (BL) as a suitable process. In this information acquisition process, the decision-maker must evaluate, step by step, whether it is worthwhile acquiring further information at the given cost or whether he or she wants to make a decision based on the available information. This process of Bayesian Learning leads to optimal information acquisition but not to complete information acquisition. That is, in the presence of information costs, it is optimal to decide under incomplete information. However, this means that, according to these simple considerations, we make a decision based on what we call Bayesian Beliefs (BB), which are the results of Bayesian Learning. They are the best we can get from learning about reality up to a given point. But we still do not have complete information about reality. We use a belief, albeit the best possible belief, based on the available information. Bayesian Beliefs are the best possible idea we can get from the information we have so far, even if they have to be and will be corrected by further information. Applying a Bayesian Learning mechanism, a decision-maker can gradually acquire the information needed to make an optimal decision. Thus, this process addresses the information problem. And so we study the fundamental modeling and mechanism of this process.

Consumer Choices Under Imperfect Information (Chap. 3) However, we still need to answer the question of how decisions change when we do not have free and complete information to make our decisions. We have used the benchmark of perfect information and can now integrate the need for information acquisition into a standard approach to rational decision-making.

We consider the choice between two consumer goods as product variations about which we have very little initial information. That is, we have little information about the product characteristics of the two goods under consideration. This means that for an optimal consumption decision we not only have to make an optimal choice between the two goods, we also have to solve the information problem in an optimal way. To do this, we use the Bayesian Learning procedure. This shows that information costs lead to the optimal conclusion to this information acquisition and the decision ultimately being made under incomplete information. Even if Bayesian Learning leads to the acquisition and processing of information, thus improving the information set by adding new facts, this learning process and the approximation to reality will be limited. We do not reach reality, but – after this optimal information acquisition process – we settle for a best possible belief, a Bayesian Belief. We believe that reality is close to what we have just learned. It is the best we can do given the information we have gathered. But even if the information set is optimal it remains incomplete. Now, since the result of our Bayesian information gathering still leads to a belief (incomplete information) – even if it is a Bayesian Belief – we can imagine other ways of solving the information problem. There is much evidence in the behavioral economics literature to suggest that people use heuristics to make decisions under incomplete information and in complex situations. Heuristics are often based on plausible narratives and empirical rules. Thus, there is some empirical evidence to suggest that heuristics can be useful for decision-making. Under incomplete information, not only is a Bayesian Belief rational, belief in a heuristic can also be rational. This is especially true when information acquisition to improve a Bayesian Belief is costly and the heuristic is accessible at almost no cost. Both optimal information acquisition and the use of a heuristic can be rational.

No matter how the information problem is approached, the question remains whether the decision is different than one taken in a situation with complete information. This question can now be answered in this chapter. As is to be expected, in general, the decision outcomes are initially different in the case of incomplete and complete information. The loss of information affects the outcome of the decision. That is, even if we make the best possible decision, the result is not perfect in the sense of complete information. The information problem can only be solved optimally, not perfectly.

This result, namely that we have to trust a Bayesian Belief or a heuristic belief even for a simple consumption decision, already points to our later line of argumentation. When we move from reasoning about simple individual consumption decisions to reasoning about complex societal issues and decisions, the information problem becomes much more serious. Bayesian Learning at this complex social level requires a much greater effort. Therefore, the information costs for these social and political issues are even higher, making the application of a heuristic attractive again. As a result, political proposals for action are repeatedly based on statements that cannot initially be substantiated in the sense of Bayesian Learning. They are heuristic plausibilities or, in other words, simple beliefs. Thus, if we want to make good decisions about social and political issues, we again have a significant information problem. However, what can we do in our individual and, above all, societal decisions when we have little information and further information is only very expensive to obtain? We can use heuristics that are available with little effort. Belief systems and ideologies provide heuristic solutions to the general information problem in the individual such social situations. Worldviews, ideologies, and belief systems are possible solutions to the incomplete information we have to live with. Belief systems and ideologies fill this information gap. We are guided by assumptions, hardly justifiable assertions, and narratives because we face this massive information problem.

The information problem however is not the only flaw in the traditional rational decision-making model. The traditional economic optimization model often reduces decisions to purely material motivations; it is primarily material needs that are considered. Non-tangible needs such as safety, control, autonomy, belongingness, and many more are undoubtedly also existing psychological and thus human needs. We will therefore expand the set of needs and preferences to be considered in Chap. 4. We establish the connection between these needs and the adoption of belief systems and ideologies in Chap. 6 and work out in Chap. 7 how these belief systems influence daily decisions and thereby also serve psychological needs.

Needs and Preferences: An Extended Concept (Chap. 4) In standard economic theory, the needs which are considered are primarily consumption preferences for goods and services. These material goods are then optimized either in relation to each other or in relation to immaterial goods such as leisure or risk. Especially in the case of immaterial needs, the economic discussion lacks essential elements that are known in other disciplines, especially in psychology. For the economics of ideology which we want to study, intangible psychological needs play an essential role. Therefore, in Chap. 4, we also look primarily at those needs which have been identified in other disciplines. In this chapter, we argue that people have other categories of needs that are essential for them. That is, if economics is concerned with serving needs in the best possible way, then we need to look at more than just consumption needs. People also have a variety of psychological needs. Extensive work has been done on this in the fields of psychology. After reviewing nearly 600 studies on needs in Müller and Gries (2024), we can divide these mental or psychological needs into three clusters: existential and epistemic needs; relational needs; and agency needs. Existential needs are needs such as, e.g., safety, security, order, and others; epistemic needs are, e.g., control, ambiguity avoidance, etc.; relational needs are needs such as belongingness and social approval; and agency needs are needs such as autonomy and self-determination. There are, thus, a large number of important needs other than the consumption needs that economists look at. Serving these needs undoubtedly benefits human well-being and is thus part of human utility. Our well-being increases when we are protected and feel safe and secure, when we have control, when we belong to a group and are socially included, and when we can act autonomously and independently. Therefore, if our well-being is the goal of economic activity, then we must include these needs in our system of goals. This is not an easy task because these needs are not concrete goods that can be exchanged for other goods, but abstract states that are desired. These abstract states must be produced. They are part of our living conditions. For example, we can live in a country where we largely have autonomy of action. The freedom to live a self-determined life is not necessarily a given; it can also be restricted to a large extent. If that is the case, the need for a state or condition that allows autonomy of action and self-determination is not fulfilled, or only to a limited extent. The property that fulfilling these abstract needs requires certain states means that we have to add another layer to our concept of utility, and that is the layer of desired states. People not only want to consume certain goods (flow concept), they also desire certain living conditions and states in which they live (state concept). Both layers can be integrated into a comprehensive utility concept. In the discussion of psychological needs and the debate around belief systems and ideologies, however, the focus is on the state layer. This layer must now be developed and implemented in analogy with the flow concept of consumption decisions.

People have needs that relate to social conditions and social organization and to the social and political system. This means that each individual can evaluate the match of their needs with the conditions and states found in this society to see whether they are suitable for serving their own needs. Freedom and agency are examples. Agency refers, first, to individuals themselves, whether they can exercise it, and, second, to others, whether and how they are coordinated between individuals. Do the states of society and societal rules allow for exercising freedom and serve agency needs? The desire for order is similar. The state of order not only means order in the personal sphere but also social order. The same applies to the other states we mentioned in our catalog of psychological needs, such as security, control, predictability, identity, and identification, i.e., all possible areas of the categories of needs mentioned in the above. They are needs and desires we have for social conditions and states and are experienced as a kind of public good. And so these psychological needs represent the desire for the provision of these kinds of public goods. We would like to have a social design that meets these desires. Since we have different need structures, we also have individual demand structures for different social designs. A person whose need for self-determination is particularly strong but who places little value on control and security will prefer different social arrangements than a person whose priority is the need for security and order. This is the demand side. But what about the supply side? As we will see in the following section, ideologies fulfill this task.

Belief Systems and Ideologies, and Their Functions (Chap. 5) While we can identify a wide range of preferences and needs, and, thus, to use the economic jargon, demand for conditions and states, the question is this: What do we see on the supply side? What can address and serve these needs? The answer we propose is that belief systems and ideologies are on the supply side. Belief systems and ideologies address and serve the above-mentioned needs. Worldviews, belief systems, or ideologies, and their narratives, perform functions that address and serve the need structures described in the above. They say something both about social conditions and states that meet these needs and about how to achieve these social states. Worldviews, belief systems, and ideologies thus usually convey the following: First, a particular set of goals, including a value system closely associated with them, and, second, a suggested path to achieving those goals. If a person has certain needs, and if an ideology appears to be a suitable means of addressing those needs through its narratives – i.e., its interpretations, explanations, and proposed solutions – then the ideology is an instrument that serves specific needs. Individuals seek to match their individual need structure with a belief system or ideology that addresses and serves that very structure. But what is a worldview, belief system or ideology?

A belief system or ideology is a largely consistent set of narratives and beliefs. A belief system or ideology[1] is usually shaped by an organization. This organization dominates the current interpretation of narratives, beliefs, evaluations, and attitudes. Thus, a belief system/ideology and its organization provide permanent interpretations, evaluations, visions, and, possibly, utopias about society, it formulates goals, and proposes strategies and actions for achieving these goals. Thus, belief systems and ideologies fulfill certain functions for human beings. We can identify five such functions and will briefly introduce them in the following.

---

[1] Ideologies and belief systems are basically two different matters. In the context we are discussing here, however, they usually have very similar functions. Therefore, we use the terms mostly interchangeably, i.e., if we only use the term ideology, a similar statement usually applies to belief systems. Therefore, to make reading more convenient, we will usually use only one of the two terms.

1. Belief systems help to solve the human problem of imperfect information. Belief systems are a consequence of the fact that humans have only incomplete information about their environment and understand it only incompletely. This aspect is discussed in detail in one of the following sections. Humans are able to think logically, gather information, theorize, and possibly understand the mechanisms that shape their environment. This ability enables them to develop technologies and improve their living conditions. Although science has helped to uncover some of the mechanisms at work here, we are still far from truly understanding our complex environment. This is especially true of our complex social and economic systems, although we have made some progress in explaining the underlying mechanisms. Although humans have a major information problem, they still have to make decisions that will help improve their lives and well-being. But how can we make beneficial decisions under conditions of incomplete information and imperfect understanding? We look for tools that can help solve this information problem. Since the cost of information and real knowledge is high, we believe in plausible narratives and rely on heuristic rules (Burs & Gries, 2022). The available ideological narratives are a substitute for the great effort and high costs associated with a complex, real analysis of social and economic systems. When "rational choice" models in economics often assume perfect information, they neglect the human information problem and therefore ignore one of the functions of beliefs. This simplification in rational choice models is indeed a very fundamental assumption. Neglecting the information problem might be methodologically sound if it makes no significant difference to the decision (e.g., if information costs approach zero). However, in a world with complex alternatives and high information costs, doubts must be raised about the justification of this simplification. In the case of complex decisions, a truly "subjective rational choice" must include solving the information problem (Burs & Gries, 2022). The first function of a belief system, then, is to provide support when trying to solve the unsolvable human information problem. In other words, belief systems and ideologies provide a low-cost solution to an otherwise unsolved information problem. That is, belief systems and ideologies provide a set of norms, values, and narratives that help individuals process incoming information, explain circumstances, and make appropriate choices.
2. Belief systems create a coherent worldview. They consist of a coherent set of norms, values, and attitudes shared by an identifiable group. This ontological function means that belief systems provide interpretations and explanations of reality, i.e., the social, political, and economic environment and human existence. In other words, belief systems provide narratives that enable individuals to understand and connect the past, present, and potential future, and to integrate this coherent story into their own lives (and existence). Such integration and understanding of (life) events, circumstances, and information form coherent patterns of reality that create stability and a sense of meaning.

   In addition, belief systems provide a basis for identifying with other people. For example, if a group of individuals shares the same historical narrative that explains their cultural or religious existence, they can form a common identity. Sharing similar values, norms, beliefs, and attitudes and adopting similar narratives about one's identity creates a sense of belonging and unity. Thus, belief systems can help unite individuals in a community and shape collective thinking. However, if taken to its extreme, this mechanism can degenerate into group favoritism and group hostility.

3. Belief systems provide a viable reconciliation option to meet psychological human needs. Ideologies and belief systems provide systems of meaning that address people's existential, epistemic, relational, and agency needs. They explain how people can reconcile them. However, belief systems do not address or serve people's psychological needs in a symmetrical way (for a detailed discussion, see Jost et al., 2017). For example, ideologies that are commonly referred to as "conservative" or, in more extreme cases, as belonging to the "traditional right" of the political spectrum, emphasize the fundamental values of tradition, social order, maintenance of the status quo, role assignment, and acceptance of inequality (maintaining the organic structure of society). Conservative belief systems thus defend established institutions, social orders, and values, thereby providing security-oriented individuals (with stronger existential and epistemic needs) with a sense of stability, order, consistency, and control over their lives. Empirical studies show that individuals who choose a conservative belief system have stronger needs for order, control, consistency, and ambiguity avoidance (e.g., Jost et al., 2009). They also tend to perceive the environment or the unknown as potentially dangerous, or individuals or events that disrupt the traditional social order as in some way threatening. In addition, conservatives place significantly more value on tradition, conformity, loyalty, and group cohesion.

   In general, we find a wide variety of individual needs profiles in society. For some people, existential needs such as security are fundamental, while others have a stronger need for autonomy. Still others may be more focused on belonging and identity. Each person is thus unique in terms of their needs, and we can describe a whole range of people with different dimensions of needs. Each belief system provides a particular mental meaning system that addresses a particular set of basic needs, and people adopt the belief system that best fits their basic need structure.

4. Belief systems or ideologies establish essential forms of togetherness in a society. An example for such an essential principal of togetherness is trust. Belief systems or ideologies can create/destroy interpersonal and/or intergroup trust. In a complex world with imperfect and incomplete information, trust is an effective means of reducing complexity and information costs. The difficulty in evaluating unknown situations makes it necessary to accept information whose truthfulness is unclear. Even a simple exchange of goods is a complex activity. For example, when buying a used car, not all of the car's features are immediately apparent. While the seller knows whether the car is reliable, the buyer knows nothing about it. In a world where mistrust prevails, the buyer might try to have the car inspected beforehand, or demand contractual provisions that make it less likely that the seller will misrepresent the car. However, both a report from

an expert or special contractual arrangements and the potential legal disputes would lead to significant transaction costs. This changes when the two exchange partners can trust each other. If the seller provides information to the best of their knowledge and the buyer trusts this information, the characteristics of the car become transparent and the transaction and information costs are significantly lower. Trust reduces complexity and lowers transaction costs.

Belief systems can convey a general attitude to trust as well as a specific attitude about which groups can be trusted. The way trust is managed between in-group and out-group individuals is significantly influenced by their belief system.

5. Belief systems provide orientation for everyday decisions. Complementary to the second point, ideologies not only provide general and sometimes abstract orientation and an understanding of the world, they often also provide very concrete, detailed rules and recommendations for everyday behavior. Thus, belief systems help individuals process information, understand reality, and organize their values and beliefs. They help explain why people do what they do and how to evaluate specific conditions when making everyday decisions. Individuals can thus rely on their belief systems to help them behave, cope with life's problems, and deal with threatening and uncertain situations (e.g., Jost, 2006). But where do these ideological narratives come from? In most cases, there is an organization – sometimes several organizations – that claim sovereignty over the narratives.

   In the realm of ideologies, one critical aspect often goes unnoticed: the pivotal role of ideological organizations. These entities exert an immense influence over the shape and direction of ideological narratives. Such organizations determine a particular ideology's objectives and strategies as well as the current narrative that represents its interpretation. This narrative can be authentic (representing the ideological core), but it can also be a strategic tool, a facade masking the organization's true intentions. A constant communicative presence is pivotal for ideological organizations, enabling the recruitment of new adherents and the engagement and mobilization of existing ones. Proactive communication on the part of the organization further reduces potential followers' search costs for information about ideologies, which is especially attractive to those with limited resources.

Choice of an Ideology (Chap. 6) Ideologies can thus, in principle, address and serve essential universal needs that we have as human beings. However, even though these needs are universal, they are not in fact weighted equally by every human being. The same is true of ideologies. Ideological narratives vary greatly. Therefore, in Chap. 6, we look at how people with different need structures evaluate and ultimately adopt different ideologies. We describe how to think about the match between individual need structures and ideological narratives. The narratives of different ideologies serve individuals' different preference structures. Therefore, one ideology addresses a particular need structure, and another ideology addresses another need structure. Since people have different need structures, the different ideologies reflect these need structures. This matching of individual needs and ideology, and an individual's subsequent adoption of an ideology, can be described as a simple static choice, as in other well-known economic models. However, the adoption of an ideology can also be represented as a dynamic process by a Bayesian Learning procedure. By acquiring more and more information about different ideologies, an individual learns which narratives the different ideologies have and which need structures they address. Ultimately, an individual learns which ideology matches his or her own need structure and can thus provide a worldview and interpretation of the world in relation to his or her own need structure. We also presume that the structure of needs is not completely rigid. Needs (or their weightings) can potentially change, especially when significant events occur in people's lives. The choice of ideologies can then also change with the weighting of needs. The choice is therefore not completely static but can change when the preference changes. Where an ideology fits the individual's need structure, this leads to the function that ideologies serve human needs, each with their individual structure.

Ideologies and Everyday Decisions (Chap. 7) Ideologies guide people in their everyday choices. Consider the simple example of a consumer decision. Take someone who is an adherent of ecologism. Organizations that represent and stand for this ideology issue the rule that adherents should only consume organic food. For the followers of this ideology, this means they will be guided by this recommendation and will try to consume organic food whenever possible. In their daily shopping decisions, they will try to limit the number of conventionally produced food they purchase and instead buy more organic products, even if they cost more. They are faced with the decision conflict/problem of following their ideology and buying organic or else buying cheaper, nonorganic food and thus potentially being able to buy more goods. Other examples can be taken from the "occupational choice" or general political decisions. When people make their occupational choice, they not only look at the wage they can earn, but also at the kind of work they do. They evaluate what they do, they reflect on the meaning of their work or whether it is useful for others or for society. Political decisions are also often guided by ideological beliefs. It is unlikely that a politician standing for a libertarian world view will suggest drastic regulations. All these examples show that decisions are codetermined by psychological effects that guide our everyday behavior. Individuals do not make decisions based on purely physical preferences. Their decisions are also influenced by the rules and values of the ideology they have adopted. Why and how can ideologies, that is, pure beliefs, influence a rational decision-maker? This question is addressed in Chap. 7.

After a separate discussion of each of these functions of ideologies, we can now turn back to the question how these functions combine to help humans in their decision-making: Since humans do not have perfect information either about the details of their individual decisions or about the complex social mechanisms, people look for orientation – a heuristic, if you will – to find their way in a complex world. Thus, ideologies serve the function of providing general orientation in the world and interpreting what has just been observed. People believe the world works the way their ideology describes it does. Because an ideology addresses, matches, and reconciles their needs, they trust the narratives presented by their ideology. Thus, followers of an ideology are provided with a system of rules by which they can be guided in concrete situations. The rules the ideologies give orientation in all situations in life. They provide assessments and guidance for making new decisions about how to act. Because adherents adopt an ideology because it matches and reconciles their own needs, they are also willing to mitigate their everyday information problem by following the rules of the organization that represents the ideology. This is true in the abstract, universal sense – for example, in social and political positioning – as well as in concrete individual decision-making situations (Burs et al., 2023). Following the rules indirectly serves individual needs, thereby helping to determine the decision-making behavior of individuals. An ethical action in the sense of the ideology's maxims, norms, and rules is a rule-conform action. Thus, with ethical action, we partly serve our needs. Following the rules and norms of a particular ideology in making decisions creates consistency, order, and meaning in life.

Thus, to recapitulate: We want to make good decisions for ourselves. We have chosen an ideology that suits us. Guided by this ideology, we develop an attitude in all areas of life based on the rules this ideology suggests to us. This partly determines our decisions. These decisions are individual, subjectively rational decisions because it is rational to be guided by an ideology (heuristic) under conditions of imperfect information.

The Quality of Ideological Guidance (Chap. 8) Not every ideology is a good guide. The question then is which is a good ideology to follow because it leads to "good" decisions, and which is not? We thus look at the quality of everyday decisions that result from the guidance provided by ideologies. What is "good guidance"? To understand what "good guidance" is, we first need to summarize our reasoning up to this point. As indicted in Chap. 2, we have a massive information problem when we want to make good everyday decisions. The world is too complex to know completely and to understand fully its mechanisms. We do not have complete information, either about all the relevant facts or about the mechanisms of action. This is true for decisions that affect us as individuals, such as consumption decisions, as well as for decisions that need to be made in relation to social processes. The perfect solution to this information problem would be to systematically discover all the facts and explore all the relevant mechanisms. We will learn about the process for doing that as a scientific learning process, so to speak, in Chap. 2 the Bayesian Learning process. We can thus try to understand reality as it really works.

However, systematic Bayesian Learning has only be around in the social sciences for about 250 years. Even though progress is clearly visible, it remains partial, as is the case in the natural sciences. We are learning in very small increments how societies and economies work. But to make good decisions, we need an understanding of a system that we still do not have – and certainly did not have when the first ideological narratives emerged. In the vast majority of decision-making situations, whether individual or societal, we do not have a firm understanding of the real facts or the real mechanisms. The systems we are dealing with are too complex, and we constantly live and act with incomplete information. And so, when we reach the limits of our existing knowledge about facts as well as how things actually work, we have to be content with plausible explanations, narratives, and sometimes even fakes. These sets of narratives are condensed into consistent sets of plausible intuitive relations and causalities and thus become ideologies. That is, because we have – considering information cost – nothing better, we are often ultimately guided by a belief system or ideology. They are, considering cost, the only and therefore often the best choice we have. This is a heuristic solution to the information problem, as we are guided by the norms, rules, and narratives proposed by the ideology we have adopted. Ideologies are the heuristic solution to our information problem. There is much evidence in the behavioral economics literature to suggest that people follow heuristics when making decisions. Heuristics are often based on plausible narratives and rules of experience. Thus, there is some empirical evidence to suggest that heuristics can be useful in decision-making. As we will illustrate in Chap. 3 for a simple consumption decision, belief in a heuristic can be rational. This is especially true when the cost of acquiring information to improve Bayesian Beliefs is high and the heuristic is accessible at almost no cost.

It is therefore subjectively rational to use the heuristics of an ideology to make decisions. It is also subjectively rational to choose the ideology that seems best suited to serving one's need structure. This does not mean, though, that even if we act subjectively rationally the results of such a subjectively rational decision guided by our chosen ideology will ultimately be good. The quality of everyday decisions is determined by the quality of ideological guidance. Depending on the quality of the ideology, it can lead to excellent decisions as well as catastrophically wrong decisions. This is due to four problems that are associated with relying on an individually appropriate ideology.

First, there is the normative problem of what "good guidance" is: What can humans consider as good? We base this discussion on the notion of sovereignty and human dignity and argue that sovereign agents would agree on a set of principles, which we suggest are norms, to evaluate ideologies and their core narratives. Hence, we discuss whether there are criteria by which ideologies can be classified and compared. Can we use specific features to characterize ideologies and classify "goal narratives" and "implementation narratives" in such a way that we can achieve better transparency about the suitability of ideologies for shaping a good future?

Second, there is the information problem about ideologies: Our individual choice of a particular ideology is in itself an example of an information problem. How do we find out which belief system or ideology actually suits us? This process surely begins in the family. Young people first come into contact with worldviews and values through their experiences in their family. They learn what their parents' narratives are, what value judgments are communicated, and what belief systems or ideologies their parents adhere to. In adolescence, however, this view is challenged. The independent search for a suitable worldview begins. This means that a worldview is sought that fits an individual's needs. The result of this search not only depends on whether a suitable ideology is available, but also on whether the adolescent learns about it. He or she needs information about what different belief systems and ideologies there are in order to get a picture of them and then to judge which of them fits him or her best. The more information a person has about a belief system's narratives and pathways, the better he or she will be able to match it with his or her own needs. But even this search, which is necessary before being able to decide on a belief system or ideology, has information costs. Therefore, even this process of learning about belief systems and ideologies will not lead to complete information. Thus, the adoption of a particular ideology occurs under incomplete information about that ideology, as well as about all the others that were available. One may adopt an ideology that does not actually fit one's needs as well as one had hoped. The lack of information leads to choosing the wrong ideology, even if that choice was the best possible and, hence, subjectively rational. That is, we refer to the term *subjectively rational choice*, if the decision-maker cannot do better under the subjectively given conditions and costs. A lack of a good working information system and a lack of true information about an ideology's real goals and implications can lead people to follow ideologies that do not actually serve their needs. This problem is even more severe the more people are exposed to fake news, propaganda, and disinformation. If the political information system does not work well, the choice of a best matching ideology does not work well.

Third, there is the problem of deception: Ideologies are often dominated, led, and shaped by an organization. The ideological organization and the ideological narrative are closely related. The ideological organization determines the ideological narratives as well as goals and strategies associated with that ideology. Thus, the ideology's narrative can be used strategically. It may tell something different than what the organization actually intends to implement. For example, an organization speaks of a prosperous economic future in which as many members of society as possible should share in its wealth. In reality, however, these narratives are only used to attract followers or to gain approval from followers, and the ideological organization is used primarily for the purposes of a few of its officials. The ideological narrative is a strategic tool for enriching a few individuals. How can such a strategy of deception be implemented? Very simply and remarkably straightforwardly: An organization continuously spreads false or only partially true interpretations of the world, which distort both the public's view of the organization's actions and of the realities of the world. The reach and control of communication media can facilitate this manipulation. This is especially easy when the organization has a high level of access to, and presence in, or even control over communication media. A well-functioning information system is required for a good guidance by an ideology. Generally speaking, a permanent communicative presence is central to an ideological organization. Communicative presence enables the continuous recruitment of new followers and the retention and mobilization of existing followers. Proactive communication is particularly important because it lowers followers' information costs of demand for ideologies. In choosing an ideology, individuals seek information. If an ideology provides such information at a low cost, it will reach individuals who have few resources to devote to this search and information-gathering process. This is true regardless of whether the information provided is true or false.

Fourth, there is the problem of suggesting the appropriate instruments to implement the goals of the ideological narrative: Ideologies establish values and design a system of goals. In addition, they also make suggestions as to how this system of goals is to be achieved. These suggestions can be good or bad, but they should be able to shape reality. That is, it should be possible to implement the proposed instrument in reality and affect the reality in the desired way. While the ideological narratives may be idealized, organizations' implementation strategies have to use mechanisms that hold up in reality. And this is where also these ideological organizations come up against a factual information problem, because they too have incomplete information about the facts and mechanisms. At best, they try to design strategies with the best-known working mechanisms and facts. This is a knowledge-based approach (Bayesian Beliefs approach). In the worst case, organizations simply propose and implement policies without extensive knowledge of the facts and without a realistic idea of what effect they will actually have.

The instrument problem also sheds light on another phenomenon that is not unimportant in reality. Two ideologies could address a similar set of needs with their goals and visions. The ideologies do not differ greatly in their goals but can still propose very different instruments for achieving them. As a result, the instruments of one ideology could be very effective in achieving the goals. A second ideology, however, proposes a different set of instruments which is completely unsuitable in reality and will lead the real world in a direction opposite to the desired one. This means that this ideology is not good, simply because it cannot lead reality in a good direction with its bad instruments, even if the original intention was good. That is, of two ideologies that in principle serve the same set of needs, one may functionally lead in the desired direction, the other to disaster.

References

Burs, C., & Gries, T. (2022). Decision-making under imperfect information with Bayesian learning or heuristic rules. *Working Paper, Center for International Economics (CIE)*, Paderborn University, 149.

Burs, C., Gries, T., & Müller, V. (2023). The choice of ideology and everyday decisions. *Journal of Organizational Psychology, 23*(1), 134–153.

Friedman, M. (1953). *Essays in positive economics*. A Phoenix book. Business economics. University of Chicago Press.

Jost, J. T. (2006). The end of the end of ideology. *American Psychologist, 61*(7), 651–670.

Jost, J. T., Federico, C. M., & Napier, J. L. (2009). Political ideology: Its structure, functions, and elective affinities. *Annual Review of Psychology, 60*(1), 307–337.

Jost, J. T., Stern, C., Rule, N. O., & Sterling, J. (2017). The politics of fear: Is there an ideological asymmetry in existential motivation? *Social Cognition, 35*(4), 324–353.

Müller, V., & Gries, T. (2024). *Ideology and the microfoundations of conflict: From human needs to intergroup violence*. Oxford University Press.

Chapter 2
The Human Information Problem

Even though ideologies form the core of this book, we will first take a look at the well-known modeling of a household's consumption choice. We start with the standard household decisions because economists all know them well, and it is easy to show, even in this well-known and very simple context, that the human information problem is a serious issue. Later we argue that more complex decisions than simple consumer choices require us to deal with the human information problem and that this directly relates to worldviews, belief systems, and ideologies. More complex decisions address complex issues in which the information problem is even more pronounced and serious. What is the human information problem? Information is an essential component in the decision-making process. However, the way in which information is incorporated into the modeling of decision processes varies greatly, ranging from the notion of perfect information and approaches including information acquisition to notions in which beliefs or heuristic reasoning drive decisions. When it comes to a discussion of efficient allocations, the neoclassical assumption of perfect information is certainly an important benchmark and standard. However, the notion of perfect information is obviously a long way off from describing a rational choice under reasonably realistic conditions. In reality, a lot of important information relevant to decision-making is simply not available or it incurs information acquisition costs. Therefore, optimal decisions are in reality almost always decisions under imperfect information.

2.1 Information and Choices

Addressing the information problem in an adequate model of decision-making has been a matter of debate for a long time. In the work of Hayek (1945) and Stigler (1961), incomplete information and the trade-off between learning costs and decision quality were included in choice problems. When Simon (1955) introduced

T. Gries et al., *The Economics of Ideologies*, Springer Studies in Alternative Economics, https://doi.org/10.1007/978-3-031-93514-5_2

the ideas of *satisficing* and *bounded rationality*, the debate widened. "Satisficing" describes a choice process in which alternatives are investigated sequentially. As soon as an alternative meets or exceeds a certain level of utility – the "aspiration level" – information acquisition stops.[1] Moreover, information acquisition can include costs (Caplin & Dean, 2015; Gabaix et al., 2006; Reis, 2006). Caplin et al. (2011), Wald (1947), Arrow et al. (1949), Reutskaja et al. (2011), and Branco et al. (2012) describe how consumers search sequentially. They stop information acquisition based on to some rule or aspiration level and choose the alternative that is, as Herbert Simon put it, *"best so far"* (Gigerenzer, 2004). In consequence, following this procedure means information acquisition can lead to what appears to be a wrong choice (Chetty et al., 2009; Lacetera et al., 2012) when compared to having perfect information. However, this does not imply irrationality on the part of the decision-maker. It is the best that decision that could be taken under the constraints of reality. Further, even if the active information acquisition process is stopped at a particular point, decision-makers can adjust their aspiration level if a better alternative appears. Thus, the choice improves with additional information or experience over time.[2] Adapting to new aspiration levels and moving toward a higher aspiration level if possible, or choosing a lower, feasible level if the original high level cannot be reached, can be regarded as quite realistic behavior. However, the result of long-term adjustment toward the best feasible alternative is not too far away from interpreting a choice such that agents act 'as if' they were solving an optimization problem to maximize expected utility (Friedman, 1953). However, in Friedman's interpretation, too, the information problem of "not knowing" and the "need" to sequentially collect costly information remains unresolved.

Many papers on the search for information – like Caplin et al. (2011), Reutskaja et al. (2011), or Rubinstein and Salant (2006) – describe the search for unknown alternative goods. Agents search for alternatives to the already (perfectly) known variations in the hope of finding a better one. This results in there being an optimal point at which to stop the information acquisition and choose the alternative that is currently considered to be the right one. Once the alternative has been discovered, all the relevant attributes are immediately available. That is, identifying an alternative product variation includes identifying all the alternative's attributes. Sometimes knowledge about additional attributes even defines the alternative. Bearden and Connolly (2008) use the example of house inspections when buying a house. A house inspection reveals quite obvious attributes that define the alternative, for example, where the kitchen is, where the bedrooms are, and how much light there is in each room. However, we know from the "market for lemons"[3] and the related literature that a product has many attributes that are not immediately noticeable but nevertheless important for decision-makers. In this example, the house may

[1] A recent review of Herbert Simon's notion of satisficing and the subsequent debate is provided in Artinger et al. (2022).

[2] See Artinger et al. (2022) and Selten (1998).

[3] See Akerlof (1970).

have been built using some toxic materials, or it may be located in a flood-prone area without the potential buyer knowing that. Therefore, the decision-maker's information problem is not only a problem of obtaining more alternatives but also a problem of finding out more about the (hidden) attributes of the known alternatives. One contribution of modeling in this respect is Roberts and Urban (1988), who model multi-attribute utility and learning about attributes. Revealing unknown attributes instead of considering new alternatives allows us to directly link up with the benchmark of perfect information in standard decision models and helps identify the efficiency of the information acquisition process. Learning about unknown attributes may lead to the decision-maker knowing the attributes and thus to perfect information about a particular good.

2.2 Individual Preferences and Match Values

In our decision-making setting, people strive to gather information that reveals the characteristics of unknown attributes instead of discovering new alternatives (e.g., Rothschild, 1974). Therefore, we first define how each product can be characterized by its attributes.

Each product variety features a set of characteristic attributes that distinguishes it from other product varieties. We assume that the number of attributes is n. For each considered good $i \in I$, we describe each attribute j by an index number $s_{ij} \in [0, 1]$. Hence, s_{23} describes the attribute 3 for good 2. This index number s_{ij} indicates to what extent attribute j is provided and serves its purpose. If $s_{ij} = 1$, product i reaches a maximum level of serving attribute j. If $s_{ij} = 0$, it does not exhibit this attribute at all, and product i cannot provide the benefit of this attribute.

Further, we assume that each consumer has a set of preferences that correspond to the attributes of the goods. Each preference can be served by one of the product's corresponding attributes. In line with the treatment of attributes described in the above, each element of the set of preferences is labeled by an index number $r_j \in [0, 1]$ that describes the preference for the extent to which this attribute should be provided. If $r_j = 1$, this consumer wishes the attribute j fully provided. If $r_i = 0$, a person has no preference for this feature at all. So, for each attribute, product i can provide a specific degree to which this attribute is served and the consumer has a specific preference for the degree to which it is served.

In a next step, the person has to analyze how well a product's objective attributes serve their subjective preferences. Therefore, we summarize the preferences in a vector $r \in \mathbb{R}^n$ and the characteristics for each good i in a vector $s_i \in \mathbb{R}^n$. The j's component of the vector r represents the desired extent at which this attribute should be provided, and the j's component of s_i represents the level of providing this specific feature by product i. Therefore, for each attribute j, we can measure the difference d_{ij} between the desired extent of this attribute and the actual level of its provision by product i,

$$d_{ij} = |r_j - s_{ij}|. \tag{2.1}$$

However, consumers do not make a choice by examining only one product attribute. They need to determine the aggregate distance d_i between the two complete sets, the set of preferences for providing specific attributes, and the set of attributes provided by a product i. We can solve this problem using a weighted Minkowski distance,[4] so that a large number of attributes can be included. Distance measures were used in the early days of the debate around product variations (Lancaster, 1966). However, these models usually applied Euclidean distances. The more general Minkowski distance enables us to include a parameter of substitution between the product characteristics. Additionally, each feature can be assigned a weight $\alpha_j \geq 0$, as different attributes have a different level of importance for different consumers. Thus, we can measure the aggregate distance between the set of a consumer's subjective preferences and the attributes provided by the product

$$d_i(s_i, r) = \left(\sum_{j=1}^{n} |\alpha_j (r_j - s_{ij})|^{\rho} \right)^{\frac{1}{\rho}} \quad \text{for } \rho \geq 1,$$

where ρ is a substitution parameter. While the distance defines the difference between product attributes and characteristics and preferences, the reciprocal value indicates the degree of matching. Thus, for each single attribute, we measure the degree of matching as

$$m_{ij} = (d_{ij})^{-1}.$$

Thus, a high value of m_{ij} indicates a good match. Analogously, we measure the match for the set of attributes and define the match value for product i as reciprocal of the aggregate distance. The value m_i defines the degree of match of a product and the consumer's individual preferences,

$$m_i = d_i(s_i, r)^{-1} = \left(\sum_{j=1}^{n} \alpha_j^{\rho} (m_{ij})^{-\rho} \right)^{-\frac{1}{\rho}}. \tag{2.2}$$

The higher the value of m_i, the better a product serves the consumer's preferences. In this first scenario of perfect information, consumers know all the attributes and characteristics of each product and the respective match value with their preferences and can make their purchase decision under full information.

[4] The Minkowski distance metric is a generalization of Euclidean distance and Manhattan distance.

2.3 Choices with Perfect Information

Next we will look at the standard example of a household decision for nonhomogeneous goods. That is, product variations are defined by a vector of attributes that characterize the good in question. However, the properties of these attributes and characteristics are normally not fully observable or known. Thus, a consumer will normally have to find out how a differentiated product $i \in I = \{1, \ldots, k\}$ meets their personal preferences. The individual quality of the match between the characteristics and attributes of good i with the consumer's preferences is indicated by the match value m_i. In the previous section, we derived the individual match value of product i, m_i, and why this match value indicates how well this good and its characteristics meet the consumer's preferences for that product variety. Match value m_i times quantity x_i of that product then generates the respective utility of that product (2.3). Therefore, utility

$$\mathrm{u} = \mathrm{u}\,(m_1 x_1, \ldots, m_k x_k) \tag{2.3}$$

of such product variations is supposedly maximized for an optimal choice under the consumer's budget constraints. To establish a benchmark, we begin with a scenario under perfect information in which the match value of each product variation is perfectly known. To explicitly go through the optimization problem, we simplify to only two products and specify exponential utility[5] as

$$\mathrm{u} = \mathrm{u}(m_1 x_1, m_2 x_2) = 1 - \exp(-A\,(m_1 x_1 + m_2 x_2)).$$

The consumer's optimal choice problem under certainty and full information is

$$\max_{x_1, x_2} \mathrm{u}, \text{ s.t. } y = p_1 x_1 + p_2 x_2. \tag{2.4}$$

Utility u is maximized if we maximize $m_1 x_1 + m_2 x_2$. If $\frac{m_i}{m_j} > \frac{p_i}{p_j}$ for $i \neq j$, the solution is

$$\bar{x}_i^* = \frac{y}{p_i} \text{ and } \bar{x}_j^* = 0, \tag{2.5}$$

which implies utility

$$\bar{\mathrm{u}}_i = 1 - \exp(-A(m_i \bar{x}_i + t_L)).$$

[5] We choose exponential utility as this will lead to a simple expected utility function in the next section when the match value is unknown, and we have to handle the information problem.

The solution is not unique if the ratio of match values equals the price ratio, $\frac{m_1}{m_2} = \frac{p_1}{p_2}$. However, we ignore this special case and only use the corner solutions as our point of reference. Thus, in the case of a unique solution, only one product is chosen, as the consumer knows the match value and knows that this good serves his or her needs better than another product such that the other product does not need to be tried.

Why do we consider this benchmark? Because we want to make it clear that access to and the availability of information matters in a person's decision-making, and we will need this understanding for the subsequent discussion of ideologies even if it is provided in the much simpler example of a consumer choice problem.

In the following sections, we describe a process of learning about the match value in a world of uncertainty and imperfect information and examine optimal choice under these changed conditions. We find that in such cases consumers do not always find a corner solution. Instead, they either try both products in order to learn about the individual match values or they randomly prefer another product that they would not purchase under perfect information.

2.4 Imperfect Information and Bayesian Learning

We will turn to look at the more realistic scenario of consumers having incomplete information. Much of the necessary information is not automatically available, yet the best possible decision needs to be made. From now on, we assume that our representative consumer is unaware of the product's attributes and characteristics. They are uncertain about the match values m_i of products $i \in I$. We thus symmetrically go through the choice problem under these changed conditions. Even though they cannot know the true match values, consumers can learn about them in a Bayesian manner. To illustrate the benefits of using Bayesian Learning, the remainder of this section explains two applications of Bayesian Learning and how they can be used in decision-making. We start with a simple application of Bayesian Learning and then study the setting that is needed in our consumer choice problem.

Bayesian Statistics Bayesian inference is a statistical approach that uses Bayes' theorem to rationally update subjective beliefs as more information becomes available. It provides us with a mathematical method that takes into account both prior beliefs and information, or evidence, to form posterior beliefs. Frequentist statistics, by contrast, assumes that the probabilities of random events can be inferred from the frequency with which they occur in repeated trials. Bayesian statistics is applied, for instance, in the field of data science and machine learning.

Flipping a coin is a simple example from statistics. Suppose the probability of an unfair coin coming up heads is to be estimated. In Bayesian statistics, a person has a prior belief about this probability. After each flip, this belief can be updated. In frequentist statistics, there is no subjective prior belief. Probability is estimated by determining the proportion of heads that come up when the coin is repeatedly flipped.

Thus, in Bayesian statistics, two people may have very different prior beliefs about the probability of an event. Furthermore, they may have access to different information and different ways of interpretating that information. Consequently, even after observing evidence, different people will have subjective posterior beliefs. However, the more information they observe and the more they rationally update their beliefs, the more these beliefs will converge to each other and to the true value.

Bayesian Inference Using Bayes' Theorem The idea behind Bayesian inference is that subjective beliefs can be continually updated whenever new information, or new data, is observed. The more new evidence becomes available, the less influence prior beliefs have. This natural way of dealing with stochastic events can be mathematically modeled by applying Bayes' theorem. This works in the following way:

Let $\mathcal{H}$ be a hypothesis, for example, that a coin is fair.[6] This hypothesis is dependent on some information $\mathcal{I}$, also called evidence, or data. In the coin toss example, this information may be the result of a coin toss. Without receiving any information, for example, without flipping the coin, a person can only form a prior belief $\mathbb{P}(\mathcal{H})$ about the probability of $\mathcal{H}$. Furthermore, a model is used to determine the probability of observing the information $\mathcal{I}$, given the hypothesis $\mathcal{H}$. This is called the "likelihood" and is denoted by $\mathbb{P}(\mathcal{I}|\mathcal{H})$ as a function of the information. Finally, the probability of the information, $\mathbb{P}(\mathcal{I})$, is called the "marginal likelihood" or "model evidence".

Decision-makers are interested in the posterior probability, that is, the probability of the hypothesis $\mathcal{H}$ given the observed information $\mathcal{I}$ and is denoted by $\mathbb{P}(\mathcal{H}|\mathcal{I})$. Using Bayes' theorem, the posterior probability is

$$\mathbb{P}(\mathcal{H}|\mathcal{I}) = \frac{\mathbb{P}(\mathcal{I}|\mathcal{H})\mathbb{P}(\mathcal{H})}{\mathbb{P}(\mathcal{I})}. \tag{2.6}$$

In the coin toss example, this is the posterior probability of the fairness of the coin after observing the information, i.e., after tossing the coin and using the outcome.

This process can be repeated whenever additional information is observed using the posterior probability as a new prior probability. Hence, Bayesian inference is a valuable approach to modeling a learning process in which new information is continually observed.

Bayesian Inference for Binomial Proportions So far, we have seen how Bayes' rule can be used for Bayesian inference in general. In this section, we want to analyze a specific example using this approach. We start by examining a Bernoulli trial, that is, a stochastic experiment with exactly two possible outcomes. These are usually referred to as "success" and "failure", and the probability of success

[6] We could also consider an unknown parameter θ, e.g., the fairness of a coin.

is the same each time the experiment is performed. The simplest example is again a coin flip. If the coin shows "heads", this is a success, and if it shows "tails", it is a failure. Sometimes success is labeled "1" and failure is labeled "0". This approach can also be used to model yes-no questions. People face many such binary decisions in their lives (e.g., "Should I open my own business?" or "Should I become a vegetarian?"). To find an answer to such questions using the Bayesian approach, they collect information that shows either that the answer is "yes" or that it is "no". This is used to update subjective beliefs. At the end of this section, we will see how they come to a decision.

In the following, we will review the Bayesian inference for binomial proportions using the example of the fairness θ of a coin. Coin flips form a Bernoulli trial because there are two possible outcomes: "heads" or "tails". We are interested in the fairness of the coin, that is, in the probability of it coming up heads. Before we can formulate our model, we need to make some assumptions. We assume that the coin cannot land on its side, so that each coin flip has only two possible outcomes. Furthermore, we assume that the coin flips are independent and identically distributed and that the coin's true fairness does not change over time. In order to apply Bayes' rule, we need to model prior beliefs, the likelihood, and the evidence or information signals.

We start by modeling the prior beliefs. This means that we have to form a belief about the parameter θ and the probability distribution that determines these beliefs. In doing so, it is important to include the range of values that θ can take. In our coin flip example, we have $\theta \in [0, 1]$. If $\theta = 1$, the coin shows only heads, and if $\theta = 0$, it shows only tails. A fair coin has $\theta = 0.5$. An appropriate probability distribution for this setting is the beta distribution. Its probability density function is

$$f(x) = \frac{1}{B(\alpha, \beta)} x^{\alpha-1}(1-x)^{\beta-1} \text{ for } x \in [0, 1] \text{ with } \alpha, \beta > 0,$$

where

$$B(\alpha, \beta) = \frac{\Gamma(\alpha)\Gamma(\beta)}{\Gamma(\alpha+\beta)} = \int_0^1 u^{\alpha-1}(1-u)^{\beta-1} du$$

is the normalizing beta function. Plots for various choices of α and β are illustrated in Fig. 2.1.

The first reason for choosing the Beta distribution is that it has support [0, 1], and our parameter θ is in this interval, since it is a probability. So the Beta distribution is a probability distribution of probabilities. The second reason is its flexible shape. We will see this in the example provided at the end of this section. When α is increased, the bulk of the probability distribution shifts to the right, which means that θ is more likely to be greater than 0.5, and increasing β moves it to the left and θ is more probable to be less than 0.5. If both α and β are increased by the same number, θ is probably close to 0.5.

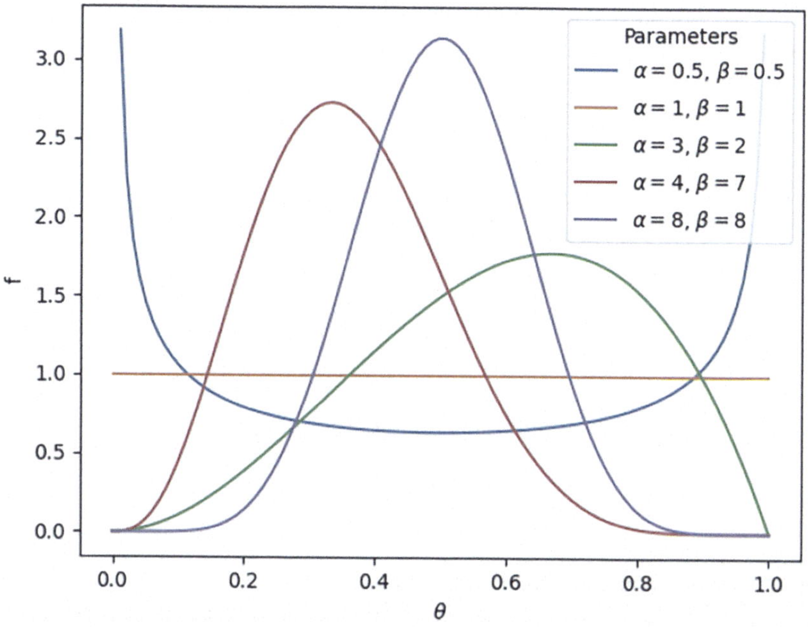

Fig. 2.1 Probability density function of Beta distribution for different parameters

The next step is to choose a distribution for the likelihood. To do that, we have to model the probability of the coin coming up heads, given the fairness θ. This can be described by using a Bernoulli distribution. Let the random variable m denote an observation drawn from the set $\{0, 1\}$ that is $m = 1$ means "heads" and $m = 0$ means "tails". Thus, m represents the information collected by an individual. The probability of a coin coming up heads is

$$\mathbb{P}(m = 1|\theta) = \theta,$$

and the probability of a coin coming up tails is

$$\mathbb{P}(m = 0|\theta) = 1 - \theta.$$

This can be summarized as

$$\mathbb{P}(m|\theta) = \theta^m (1 - \theta)^{1-m} \tag{2.7}$$

for $m \in \{0, 1\}$ and $\theta \in [0, 1]$. If we keep one piece of information m and consider the parameter θ as a continuous variable, then (2.7) is the Bernoulli likelihood function for one piece of information. It is the probability of a fixed piece of information given some value for θ.

Now we extend our scenario to the observation of N independent pieces of information $\{m_1, m_2, \ldots, m_N\}$. For example, tossing a coin $N = 5$ times could give us a sequence of outcomes $\{m_1, m_2, \ldots, m_5\} = \{0, 1, 1, 1, 0\}$.

Given the fairness θ, the probability of seeing a certain sequence of outcomes $\{m_1, m_2, \ldots, m_N\}$ is

$$\begin{aligned}\mathbb{P}(\{m_1, m_2, \ldots, m_N\}|\theta) &= \prod_{i=1}^{N} \mathbb{P}(m_i|\theta) \\ &= \prod_{i=1}^{N} \theta^{m_i}(1-\theta)^{1-m_i}.\end{aligned}$$

The probability of k pieces of information of N for the parameter θ is

$$\mathbb{P}(k, N|\theta) = \binom{N}{k}\theta^k(1-\theta)^{N-k}.$$

This will be our likelihood function for Bayesian updating.

The most useful advantage of the Beta distribution is that it is a conjugate prior for the Bernoulli distribution. This means that the posterior distribution is a Beta distribution as well. Consequently, we can use the obtained posterior as a new prior distribution in the next Bayesian updating process. Thus, if additional information is observed, it can be used in the same way to improve the beliefs even more.

Applying Bayes' rule, we obtain the posterior distribution

$$\begin{aligned}\mathbb{P}(\theta|k, N) &= \frac{\mathbb{P}(k, N|\theta)\mathbb{P}(\theta)}{\mathbb{P}(k, N)} \\ &= \frac{\theta^k(1-\theta)^{N-k}\theta^{\alpha-1}(1-\theta)^{\beta-1}}{B(\alpha, \beta)\mathbb{P}(k, N)} \\ &\propto \theta^{k+\alpha-1}(1-\theta)^{N-k+\beta-1} \\ &= beta(\theta|k+\alpha, N-k+\beta).\end{aligned}$$

The denominator can be ignored, since it is just the normalizing constant that is independent of θ and does not contribute to the form of the distribution. Moreover, it is an integral that is often difficult to calculate.

In a next step, we will explain how decision-makers can use the above process to answer yes-no questions. An example of a yes-no question is whether a person is the right candidate for a top political post, such as president. Let p denote the probability that the answer to this question is "yes". A person receives information that may indicate that the answer is "yes" or "no". Based on this information, they update their beliefs about the probability p. If it is equal to or greater than 50%, the person believes that the answer is "yes". If it is below 50%, they believe that it is "no". An example shows the person's updating process. Analyzing the Beta distribution with parameters α and β further, we know that the expected value is

$$\mu = \frac{\alpha}{\alpha + \beta},$$

and the variance is

$$\sigma^2 = \frac{\alpha\beta}{(\alpha + \beta + 1)(\alpha + \beta)^2}.$$

Choosing a prior means choosing values for α and β. We can rearrange the above equations and get

$$\alpha = \left(\frac{1-\mu}{\sigma^2} - \frac{1}{\mu}\right)\mu^2$$

and

$$\beta = \alpha\left(\frac{1}{\mu} - 1\right).$$

Suppose that a person thinks that the probability of the answer being "yes" is $p = 0.5$. As he or she is not completely sure about this, he or she has a standard deviation of 0.1. Using the above equations, we can determine his or her prior Beta distribution and obtain $\alpha = 12$ and $\beta = 12$. If we plot the density function for this Beta distribution, we can see that it is centered around 0.5 and the width of the curve represents the degree of uncertainty.

Now the decision-maker receives $N = 10$ pieces of information, and $k = 8$ of them suggest that the answer to the question being considered is "yes". Plugging this into the posterior distribution yields

$$\begin{aligned}\beta(p|k+\alpha, N-k+\beta) &= \beta(p|8+12, 10-8+12)\\ &= \beta(p|20, 14).\end{aligned}$$

The above equations give us the posterior expectation value

$$\mu_{post} = \frac{20}{20+14} = \frac{20}{34} = 0.5882$$

and standard deviation

$$\sigma_{post} = \sqrt{\frac{20 \cdot 14}{(20+14+1)(20+14)^2}} = 0.0831.$$

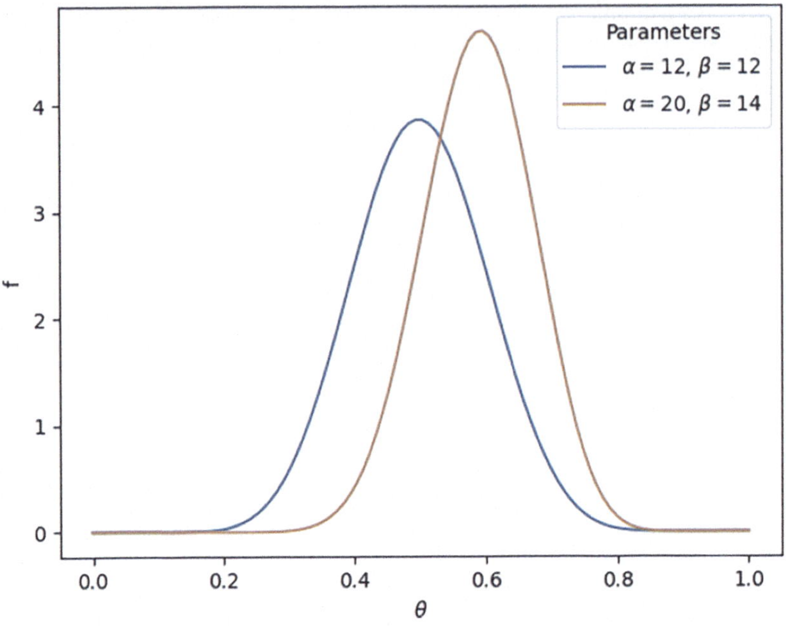

Fig. 2.2 Probability density function of Beta distribution for different parameters

Thus, the probability of the answer being "yes" has increased to 59%, and this can be stated with a standard deviation of 0.0831, which is more certain than the prior belief. As more information is obtained, α and β increase, which reduces the standard deviation, and the posterior beliefs about p become more certain. Thus, this person believes that the answer is "yes".

Looking at the plot of the density function in Fig. 2.2, we see that the curve has a higher peak at 0.59 and a smaller width.

Therefore, we assume that each person starts with a prior belief about the probability that the answer is "yes". Then they receive some more information and update their beliefs. If their posterior distribution has an expected value above 0.5, they believe that the answer is "yes". If it is below 0.5, they believe that the answer is "no".

Following this basic description of the learning mechanism, we can now develop an example that can tell us a little more about the randomness and dynamics of this learning process. We will again take an example from the political sphere. The question is this: Are party A's policies suitable for solving a certain political problem? In our model, the information "yes" is assigned the value 1, and the information "no" has the value 0. The actual probability that the policy is suitable is $p = 0.4$, i.e., it is actually unsuitable. However, the person who wants to assess whether the policy is good or bad does not know this. They therefore start to collect information in order to learn from this information and improve their assessment.

Table 2.1 The development of the expected value μ and standard deviation σ while gathering 10 information signals

N	Signal yes	μ_{post}	σ_{post}
Prior		45.0%	15.0%
1	1	45.5%	14.4%
2	1	50.0%	13.9%
3	1	53.8%	13.3%
4	0	50.0%	12.9%
5	1	53.3%	12.5%
6	0	50.0%	12.1%
7	0	47.1%	11.8%
8	0	44.4%	11.4%
9	0	42.1%	11.0%
10	0	40.0%	10.7%

Before starting to take in information, the person in question starts from his or her intuitive judgment, the prior belief. Let us assume that they hold the prior belief that the probability that the answer is "yes" is $p = 0.45$. The probability is therefore intuitively only 45%, meaning that this person intuitively considers the policy to be unsuitable. Taking this initial value, the following table describes the process of gathering information and what this information means for a person's assessment. This learning process is a process of gradual information acquisition, learning, and re-evaluation until the next information acquisition follows. With every information signal that reality reveals, the person learns something new about reality. Let us look at the process that is described in the following Table 2.1.

The first signal is a 1, i.e., the signal indicates that the policy works and is suitable. Nevertheless, after this first information intake, the person calculates a probability of 45% for success and as an overall assessment at this moment would believe in "no", i.e., no success. The second and third signals also happen to be positive. This means that the information level after signal 3 indicates an almost 54% probability that the policy will be successful. This means that, in this person's perception, they switch their overall assessment after gathering this information. They now believe in the policy's success. This assessment continues for the next two steps of the information intake, even though there were negative signals in between. It is only from signal 7 onward that the now more frequent negative signals will reverse the assessment and reduce it to the actual 40% by signal 10. It is interesting to note that the information, which was randomly positive at the beginning, changed the resulting overall assessment at these points in time. A change in belief is therefore possible not just once but at any time during the learning process. The sequence of signals determines what this person believes about reality, at least temporarily.

Another important observation is that during the learning process the standard deviation and thus uncertainty about the status of the assessment decrease. Information intake thus increases the certainty of the statement that can be made up to that point. This is a significant positive effect of more information, which we will also utilize later on.

Bayesian Inference with Normal Distributions So far, we have examined how Bayesian Learning is used to make binary decisions. However, as we saw in Sect. 2.2, people may also need to learn about certain values like the match value with a particular product they are considering buying. This requires a different distribution for the unknown parameter. A simple choice has a normal distribution.

In our simple model with two goods, consumers have prior beliefs about the match values m_i for each product $i \in \{1, 2\}$ at the beginning of their information acquisition. However, people receive information about the two products with each acquisition step they take and can learn about the value of m_i by observing signals and updating their assessment. We follow Erdem and Keane (1996) who apply Bayesian Learning with normal distributions to consumers' purchase decisions and introduce two independent Bayesian update processes. We can use this procedure to update beliefs about m_i.

We start with a description of how a Bayesian update of new information is done for only one acquisition step. This procedure can then be generalized to multiple steps. We assume a normal distribution for the consumer's prior beliefs about each match value m_i before receiving any information, i.e.,

$$m_i \sim \mathcal{N}(\mu_{i,0}, \sigma_{i,0}^2), i \in \{1, 2\},$$

where $\mu_{i,0}$ is the initial estimate of the expected match value and $\sigma_{i,0}^2$ reflects the initial belief in the degree of uncertainty. Consumers presume that each match value m_i is normally distributed as described above, and we can identify their initial information set for good i as $I_{i,0} = \{\mu_{i,0}, \sigma_{i,0}^2\}$.

As consumers want to make an ex ante decision about the quantity of purchases x_i, they depart from their initial a priori assessment $\mu_{i,0}$ and want to find out more about good i. Consumers collect information to learn about the characteristics of each good i, for example, they read brochures or talk to other consumers. These are two independent observation processes, one for each product, that take place at the same time. However, the piece of received information is incomplete and cannot reveal the true value of m_i. Each piece of information is a fragment, a stochastic signal, and is subject to individual perception. We use N as a counter for each time a consumer receives a new piece of information. Thus, N is the number of information acquisition steps. In each step, a person receives a noisy signal about the match value

$$m_{i,N} = m_i + e_{i,N}$$

with

$$e_{i,N} \sim \mathcal{N}(0, \eta_i^2),$$

where η_i^2 is the variance of the signal, and the interpretation is a measure of the signal's precision. This distribution corresponds to the likelihood function of the Bayesian formula. The advantage of choosing a normal distribution as prior and signal is that it is a conjugate distribution, which means that the posterior distribution is normal, too. Consequently, we can use the obtained posterior distribution as a new prior in the next Bayesian updating process. The posterior normal distribution is given by

$$m_i|I_{i,1} \sim \mathcal{N}(\mu_{i,1}, \sigma_{i,1}^2)$$

with

$$\mu_{i,1} = \frac{\sigma_{i,0}^2}{\sigma_{i,0}^2 + \eta_i^2} m_{i,0} + \frac{\eta_i^2}{\sigma_{i,0}^2 + \eta_i^2} \mu_{i,0} \text{ and}$$

$$\sigma_{i,1}^2 = \left(\frac{1}{\sigma_{i,0}^2} + \frac{1}{\eta_i^2} \right)^{-1}.$$

The posterior expected value $\mu_{i,1}$ is a weighted sum of the prior and the signal. A more precise signal (low variance η_i^2) leads to a higher weight of $m_{i,0}$, which means that the observation $m_{i,0}$ has a greater impact on the updated expected value $\mu_{i,1}$. Moreover, uncertainty $\sigma_{i,1}^2$ decreases after obtaining the signal. Khalil (2011) refers to such an updated perception of the as yet unknown variable as a Bayesian Belief (BB). It is a belief because, according to the information collected up to that point, it seems – that is, we can believe but do not yet know – that the variable has certain properties.

This updating procedure can be repeated with the posterior as a new prior distribution. If a person has made more attempts to collect information and N is the number of received signals or observations, then

$$m_i|I_{i,N} \sim \mathcal{N}(\mu_{i,N}, \sigma_{i,N}^2)$$

with

$$\mu_{i,N} = \frac{\sigma_{i,0}^2}{N\sigma_{i,0}^2 + \eta_i^2} \sum_{s=0}^{N-1} m_{i,s} + \frac{\eta_i^2}{N\sigma_{i,0}^2 + \eta_i^2} \mu_{i,0} \text{ and} \tag{2.8}$$

$$\sigma_{i,N}^2 = \left(\frac{1}{\sigma_{i,0}^2} + N \frac{1}{\eta_i^2} \right)^{-1} = \frac{\sigma_{i,0}^2 \eta_i^2}{N\sigma_{i,0}^2 + \eta_i^2} \text{ with } \frac{\partial \sigma_{i,N}^2}{\partial \eta_i^2} > 0. \tag{2.9}$$

These two equations raise two questions: (1) Does new information that is collected step by step lead consumers closer to the true values they want to find? (2) Can new information reduce uncertainty about the match value m_i that is currently available?

1. To verify whether more information brings the consumer closer to the true expected value, we look at the difference between the updated expected values in one step. We have

$$\mu_{i,N+1} - \mu_{i,N} = \frac{\sigma_{i,0}^2}{(N+1)\sigma_{i,0}^2 + \eta_i^2}(m_{i,N} - \mu_{i,N}), \tag{2.10}$$

   whose sign is determined by the difference between $m_{i,N}$ and $\mu_{i,N}$. The new observation $m_{i,N}$ may be above or below the current expected value $\mu_{i,N}$. Thus, $\mu_{i,N+1}$ is either greater or lower than $\mu_{i,N}$, and the amount of the increase or decrease depends on the factor $\frac{\sigma_{i,0}^2}{(N+1)\sigma_{i,0}^2+\eta_i^2}$. This factor is smaller for a higher N. This means that the more information is collected, the smaller is the adjustment of the current expected value $\mu_{i,N}$.
2. The more information we gather, the fewer adjustments to the difference between the already detected and the true expected values we obtain. Thus, one more acquisition step leads us closer to the true value and reduces the variance of the match value detected up to that point. The difference in the variance of one acquisition step is

$$\sigma_{i,N+1}^2 - \sigma_{i,N}^2 = -\frac{\sigma_{i,0}^2}{(N+1)\sigma_{i,0}^2 + \eta_i^2}\sigma_{i,N}^2 < 0. \tag{2.11}$$

   The question we are left with is thus how many information acquisition steps must be performed to make an optimal choice.

References

Akerlof, G. A. (1970). The market for "lemons": Quality uncertainty and the market mechanism. *The Quarterly Journal of Economics, 84*(3), 488–500.

Arrow, K. J., Blackwell, D., & Girshick, M. A. (1949). Bayes and minimax solutions of sequential decision problems. *Econometrica, 17*(3/4), 213.

Artinger, F., Gigerenzer, G., & Jacobs, P. (2022). Satisficing: Integrating two traditions. *Journal of Economic Literature, 60*(2), 598–635.

Bearden, J. N., & Connolly, T. (2008). *On optimal satisficing: How simple policies can achieve excellent results* (pp. 79–97). Springer.

Branco, F., Sun, M., & Villas-Boas, J. M. (2012). Optimal search for product information. *Management Science, 58*(11), 2037–2056.

Caplin, A., & Dean, M. (2015). Revealed preference, rational inattention, and costly information acquisition. *American Economic Review, 105*(7), 2183–2203.

Caplin, A., Dean, M., & Martin, D. (2011). Search and satisficing. *American Economic Review, 101*(7), 2899–2922.

Chetty, R., Looney, A., & Kroft, K. (2009). Salience and taxation: Theory and evidence. *American Economic Review, 99*(4), 1145–1177.

Erdem, T., & Keane, M. P. (1996). Decision-making under uncertainty: Capturing dynamic brand choice processes in turbulent consumer goods markets. *Marketing Science, 15*(1), 1–20.

Friedman, M. (1953). *Essays in positive economics*. A Phoenix book. Business economics. University of Chicago Press.

Gabaix, X., Laibson, D., Moloche, G., & Weinberg, S. (2006). Costly information acquisition: Experimental analysis of a boundedly rational model. *American Economic Review, 96*(4), 1043–1068.

Gigerenzer, G. (2004). Striking a blow for sanity in theories of rationality. In M. Augier (Ed.), *Models of a man: Essays in memory of Herbert A. Simon* (pp. 389–409). MIT Press.

Hayek, F. A. (1945). The use of knowledge in society. *The American Economic Review, 35*(4), 519–530.

Khalil, E. L. (2011). Rational, normative and procedural theories of beliefs: Can they explain internal motivations? *Journal of Economic Issues, 45*(3), 641–664.

Lacetera, N., Pope, D. G., & Sydnor, J. R. (2012). Heuristic thinking and limited attention in the car market. *American Economic Review, 102*(5), 2206–2236.

Lancaster, K. J. (1966). A new approach to consumer theory. *Journal of Political Economy, 74*(2), 132–157.

Reis, R. (2006). Inattentive consumers. *Journal of Monetary Economics, 53*(8), 1761–1800.

Reutskaja, E., Nagel, R., Camerer, C. F., & Rangel, A. (2011). Search dynamics in consumer choice under time pressure: An eye-tracking study. *American Economic Review, 101*(2), 900–926.

Roberts, J. H., & Urban, G. L. (1988). Modeling multiattribute utility, risk, and belief dynamics for new consumer durable brand choice. *Management Science, 34*(2), 167–185.

Rothschild, M. (1974). A two-armed bandit theory of market pricing. *Journal of Economic Theory, 9*(2), 185–202.

Rubinstein, A., & Salant, Y. (2006). A model of choice from lists. *Theoretical Economics, 1*, 3–17.

Selten, R. (1998). Aspiration adaptation theory. *Journal of Mathematical Psychology, 42*(2–3), 191–214.

Simon, H. A. (1955). A behavioral model of rational choice. *The Quarterly Journal of Economics, 69*(1), 99.

Stigler, G. J. (1961). The economics of information. *Journal of Political Economy, 69*, 213 – 225.

Wald, A. (1947). Foundations of a general theory of sequential decision functions. *Econometrica, 15*(4), 279.

Chapter 3
Consumer Choice Under Imperfect Information

Having derived the benchmark of perfect information and introduced a way of gathering information under imperfect information, we can now turn our attention to a standard approach to rational decision-making. That is, we examine how to make a purchase decision when the characteristics of two products under consideration are unknown.

We model information explicitly as a risk-reducing instrument in a risk-averse decision-maker's expected utility evaluation. In our Bayesian Learning procedure, new information contributes to expected utilities through declining variance in the match value that indicates the difference between preferences and a particular good's actual attributes. In the example just discussed in the previous chapter, we have already shown this characteristic of the Bayesian Learning procedure. In the utility function, a risk-reducing characteristic is assessed using a parameter of risk aversion. Others have also included risk aversion parameters in their utility function, e.g., Roberts and Urban (1988). Erdem and Keane (1996) include risk aversion to create brand equity. Crawford and Shum (2005) discuss the role of risk aversion in the context of learning about pharmaceutical drugs. However, that discussion refers to a very specific medical product. The authors find that risk-averse patients are disinclined to switch drugs. Our focus is on information as a general risk-reducing instrument and the motivating role of risk aversion in the information acquisition process.[1] We show that the greater a decision-maker's aversion to risk, the more information they collect to reduce risk. Thus, information may not only bring us closer to knowing the actual properties of the item we are considering, we also reduce the risk of having a wrong perception or idea of its properties.

In a second step – having a rational decision with an optimal stopping of the Bayesian Learning procedure – we compare this result with a heuristic suggestion for decision finding. We find that a heuristic procedure can be a better option

[1] In a completely different context, Reis (2006) uses a macroeconomic model to show that risk-averse consumers update their information more frequently.

T. Gries et al., *The Economics of Ideologies*, Springer Studies in Alternative Economics, https://doi.org/10.1007/978-3-031-93514-5_3

than further information acquisition, because the net effect of further information acquisition reduces indirect utility due to information costs. This is in line with many empirical studies that have found that people choose heuristic rules instead of further information acquisition (Hauser, 2011; Payne et al., 1993). However, as (Gigerenzer & Gaissmaier, 2011) point out, formal models about when and why heuristics are used need to be developed further.

How do we obtain these results? We model information processing by Bayesian updating as described in Chap. 2. Departing from DeGroot (1970), we use a costly Bayesian Learning procedure of revealing information about product attributes, formally in line with Roberts and Urban (1988) and Erdem and Keane (1996). In the empirical work of Erdem and Keane (1996), consumers are uncertain about product quality, but they learn about it both actively through use experience and passively through external advertising signals, while Roberts and Urban (1988) only include word-of-mouth signals. An earlier contribution was provided in the work done by Kihlstrom (1974), who developed a theory about consumer demand for information about product quality. There is a strand of literature that also uses Bayesian updating to acquire information for a technology adoption decision, as examples see Jensen (1982), McCardle (1985), Chatterjee and Eliashberg (1990), and Ulu and Smith (2009). Individuals have a choice between continuing the information acquisition, adopting a particular technology or rejecting it. In a more recent contribution, Zhong (2022) includes flexible choice of information. Branco et al. (2012) consider a sequential single product decision to buy, not buy, or continue learning and develop optimal stopping rules, including optimal pricing strategies. These are examples in which only one product is being considered. In our model, we show that there is a solution to a consumer demand decision about the optimal allocation of product varieties using a standard procedure. Thus, this is not only a decision about buying a product or rejecting it (other than continue searching), but about finding the optimal allocation when learning about several products.

Information acquisition is "costly" in the sense that in our example it reduces leisure time. Decision-makers continue to collect information as long as they expect further information to generate a net benefit. Information acquisition stops when a risk-averse agent's expected marginal utility of the additional information equals the respective marginal information costs. Thus, even if the decision procedure is sequential, consumers behave "as if" they make a rational choice that maximizes expected utility regarding their budget constraints.

However, in real decision-making, heuristic rules play a major role; they are often observed in the empirical and experimental literature in behavioral economics. For example, investors apply the "$1/N$ -heuristic" in asset-allocation decisions (Benartzi & Thaler, 2001). Loomes (1991) also finds evidence for the use of such "diversification heuristics" even if it contradicts rational choice. The reason why heuristics are applied was originally thought to be the trade-off between accuracy and effort (Payne et al., 1993). However, empirical research shows that simple heuristics can yield higher predictive accuracy than statistical methods that use more information, known as the "less-is-more effect" (Gigerenzer & Goldstein, 1996; Wübben & von Wangenheim, 2008). Is a choice induced by a heuristic rule an optimal and rational choice? To answer this question, we include a second scenario under imperfect information. That is, we introduce a social heuristic that takes into account opinions expressed by an individual's social environment. Consumers can either go through a costly Bayesian Learning process or directly use the cost-free heuristic rule to solve their ex ante information problem. Comparing the two procedures, we find conditions under which it is better to choose the heuristic rule. Thus, using the heuristic rule can be a rational choice.

Up to this point, this consumer choice problem has deliberately been left quite generic and can thus serve as a point of departure when it comes to answering the following questions:

- How does an optimal consumer choice that includes optimal information acquisition differ from the benchmark model of perfect information?
- What role does risk aversion play in information gathering?
- Can decisions be based on beliefs, and are they rational decisions?
- Under imperfect information, can a heuristic rule be a substitute for information acquisition as an optimal choice? This question is indeed the most important one of our questions, including for our later discussion of ideologies.

To answer these questions, we develop a decision model and follow three different scenarios. In the first scenario, which is represented by the left-hand path in Fig. 3.1, consumers have perfect information. This was examined in Sect. 2.3. Consumers know the products' attributes characteristics and can determine their true match values with respect to their preferences. They can then make a rational purchase decision by maximizing utility depending on their true match values. The result is an optimal choice of x_i under perfect information. In the second and third scenarios, which are examined in this chapter and represented by the right-

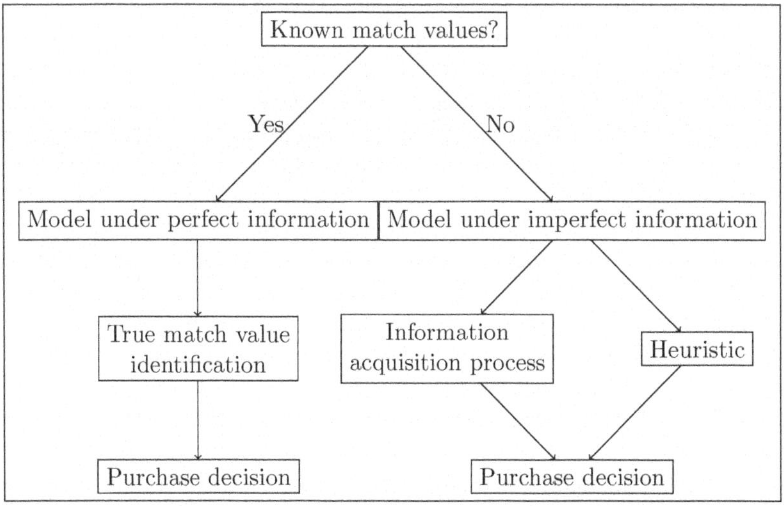

Fig. 3.1 The structure of the decision model

hand path in Fig. 3.1, consumers have imperfect information. On the first left-hand track (in the second scenario), consumers are uncertain about the match values of product's characteristics with their preferences. However, they can learn about the product characteristics and the stochastic match values in a Bayesian manner. They maximize expected utility by collecting information and hence reducing leisure time such that an optimal level of information, as well as an optimal choice of x_i under these imperfect information, is determined. On the right-hand track along path two (third scenario), consumers can apply a heuristic strategy to make a choice of x_i. We develop conditions under which each of these two alternative routes on the right-hand path is chosen. This includes the interesting result that a heuristic can be an optimal subjectively rational choice under the described conditions. Both approaches lead to an optimal purchase decision in which the true match values remain concealed.

3.1 Learning with Information Acquisition

In this section, we answer the first question that was raised in the previous section (How does an optimal consumer choice that includes optimal information acquisition differ from the benchmark model of perfect information?), and we examine the role of risk aversion in information acquisition.

Interpretation of Bayesian Learning and Bayesian Beliefs
The Bayesian Learning method is a way of approaching reality. If we do not know the true value of a variable (in our case the match value), we can learn about that value through each of the steps described in Sect. 2.4. That is, each learning step reveals a little more of the true value, and we need to update the Bayesian Belief (BB) we have held thus far about the true value. As each last step identifies the belief that is closest to reality we can currently obtain from signals, we often refer to this approximation to the true value as "knowledge". Knowledge is the best belief we can systematically derive through learning from the signals that we receive from reality. However, this best belief is not reality, rather it is a belief based on signals received from reality. That is, if the number of learning steps is still small, we do not know much about reality. We may have Bayesian Beliefs, which may also improve with more learning, but these beliefs are still quite inaccurate. This holds for science as well as for personal knowledge. In natural science, we go through exactly the same process. We improve our beliefs about how nature works step by step and with each additional piece of the puzzle we obtain the picture we have of reality improves.

This process is much more difficult in the social sciences, where there are no natural laws to discover. Also, we cannot perform controlled experiments to reduce complexity and focus on individual relationships and causalities, and we also need to understand complex social mechanisms. We can only learn by developing complex theories and seeking empirical evidence for those theories. That is, the uncertainties associated with any Bayesian Belief remain quite high and may contradict other hypotheses without leading to a conclusion. However, even in the social sciences, there have been a number of beliefs that have had to be updated because they were backed by no empirical evidence. Thus, even in the social sciences, we learn more about reality through this process. However, because of the enormous complexity and uncertainty about how the relevant social or economic mechanisms actually work, any approximation to reality is very imperfect. It is a Bayesian Belief, which means it is the best we have, but it can still only grasp reality and its mechanisms to a limited extent. In view of these difficulties, it is obvious that questions of understanding social mechanisms and interpretations not only include Bayesian Beliefs. In addition, there are other belief systems, including their proposals and narratives, that can address the human information problem and are thus interesting heuristics for humans. When people want to solve their information problem in terms of understanding complex social and economic issues as well, belief systems provide a possible answer.

Further, as regards individual knowledge, it becomes even more apparent that the scope of each individual learning process is very limited. While science can slowly progress and continuously improve its approximation to reality, individuals permanently must make decisions and hence need an immediate best possible picture of the relevant facts and a mechanism for making immediate decisions. And, as we will see in the next section, with limited resources and costly information, the individual Bayesian Learning process will also be limited.

Let us now return to our very simple model of a consumer choice to illustrate what we have just discussed more generally.

Utility Maximization

In order to include information costs, we extend our model by adding a time allocation problem. We assume that consumers' working time is institutionally determined. Subtracting their working time from total time gives us a consumer's disposable time $\bar{T}$, which can be used for leisure time t_L and the time for the information acquisition N, such that the time constraint is

$$\bar{T} = t_L + N. \tag{3.1}$$

As in the scenario with perfect information, we assume exponential utility[2] for the two goods and leisure time t_L

$$\mathrm{u} := \mathrm{u}(m_1 x_1, m_2 x_2, t_L) = 1 - \exp(-A(x_1 m_1 + x_2 m_2 + t_L))$$

with $m_1 \sim \mathcal{N}(\mu_1, \sigma_1^2)$ and $m_2 \sim \mathcal{N}(\mu_2, \sigma_2^2)$. Parameter $A > 0$ is the coefficient of risk aversion, and x_i is the quantity of product i. Unlike Roberts and Urban (1988) or

[2] Using an exponential utility function is not unusual for decision-making in the context of stochastic variables and expected utility optimization problems. Roberts and Urban (1988) or Erdem et al. (2005) use exponential utility in the marketing context. Chatterjee and Eliashberg (1990) add a price component for technology adoption that is similar to our modeling of leisure time.

Erdem and Keane (1996), we are not only interested in a discrete purchase decision, but we also want to determine the corresponding quantities of the products. Since m_1 and m_2 are stochastic variables, we now have a modified objective function (compared to Sect. 2.3) when we maximize the expected utility

$$\mathbb{E}[\mathrm{u}] = 1 - \exp\left(-A\left(x_1\mu_1 - \frac{1}{2}Ax_1^2\sigma_1^2 + x_2\mu_2 - \frac{1}{2}Ax_2^2\sigma_2^2 + t_L\right)\right).$$

Further, we can simplify this maximization problem by using the reduced objective function

$$\mathbb{E}[u] = x_1\mu_1 - \frac{1}{2}Ax_1^2\sigma_1^2 + x_2\mu_2 - \frac{1}{2}Ax_2^2\sigma_2^2 + t_L.$$

As we denote the price for each good i by p_i, the budget constraint for a given income y is again

$$y = x_1p_1 + x_2p_2.$$

Note that consumers do not know the true expected values μ_i, yet they know the conditional distribution of the match value given the information set $I_{i,N}$ for each product, $\mathbb{E}\left[m_i|I_{i,N}\right] = \mu_{i,N}$. Therefore, given the joint information set for both products $I_N = I_{1,N} \cup I_{2,N}$, the consumer can determine the current expected utility

$$\mathbb{E}[u|I_N] = x_1\mu_{1,N} - \frac{1}{2}Ax_1^2\sigma_{1,N}^2 + x_2\mu_{2,N} - \frac{1}{2}Ax_2^2\sigma_{2,N}^2 + t_L.$$

Thus, after receiving N signals, a consumer can determine the optimal expected utility $\mathbb{E}^*[u|I_N]$ from the consumption of the optimal product allocation (x_1^N, x_2^N), which is the result of the maximization problem

$$\begin{aligned} \max_{x_1,x_2} \mathbb{E}[u|I_N] &= x_1\mu_{1,N} - \frac{1}{2}Ax_1^2\sigma_{1,N}^2 + x_2\mu_{2,N} - \frac{1}{2}Ax_2^2\sigma_{2,N}^2 + \bar{T} - N \\ \text{s.t. } Y &= x_1p_1 + x_2p_2. \end{aligned} \tag{M}$$

We use $\tilde{u}$ to denote the part of the utility that is generated by the match of consumption goods (not leisure time),

$$\mathbb{E}[\tilde{u}|I_N] := x_1\mu_{1,N} - \frac{1}{2}Ax_1^2\sigma_{1,N}^2 + x_2\mu_{2,N} - \frac{1}{2}Ax_2^2\sigma_{2,N}^2.$$

We refer to this as expected conditional "consumption utility". Note that the expected match utilities $\mu_{i,N}$ can either increase or decrease after updating using an additional information signal (see (2.10)). Therefore, general speaking $\mathbb{E}[\tilde{u}|I_N]$ can either increase or decrease with further information even though this brings consumers closer to the true match values.

A consumer's decision problem ex ante the first purchase is an optimal stopping problem and not a problem of discrete choice from a set of alternatives as in Erdem and Keane (1996). Therefore, at this point, we are closer to the models of technology adoption that depart from McCardle (1985) and Jensen (1982). The functional equation of dynamic programming is

$$V(I_N) = \max\{\mathbb{E}^*[u|I_N], V^a(I_{N+1})\},$$

where $\mathbb{E}^*[u|I_N]$ is the current expected utility of stopping, and the value of continuing, $V^a(I_{N+1})$, is the anticipated value after an additional piece of information.[3] The information acquisition is stopped after N^* steps when the consumer, for the first time, expects no increase in utility through additional information

$$N^* = \min\{N \in \{0, \ldots, \bar{T}\} : V(I_N) = \mathbb{E}^*[u|I_N]\}.$$

In the following section, we show how this stopping problem can be solved sequentially.

3.2 Sequential Information and Optimal Choice

In the previous section, we saw how consumers can learn about the match values of the products that they consider purchasing and formulated their optimal stopping problem. Now we show how to solve this dynamic problem sequentially. We determine the optimal number of steps N^* and illustrate this sequential information acquisition process using a numerical example.

Sequential Choice

In order to show that there is an optimal stopping time, N^*, for the information acquisition process, we need to determine the anticipated value after an additional piece of information $V^a(I_{N+1})$. A consumer cannot know the expected utility after the next step (that would be $E^*[\tilde{u}|I_{N+1}]$) without taking it, which reduces their leisure time. Thus, they must anticipate this value and, after gathering each piece of information, judge whether or not an additional piece of information will increase the expected utility or not.

As noted earlier, even if the consumer gets closer to the true match value with each additional piece of information gathered, new information may decrease the currently expected consumption utility, $\mathbb{E}[\tilde{u}|I_N]$. This could also imply a decrease in $V^a(I_{N+1})$. In this case, information acquisition is stopped early even if subsequent signals indicate high expected match values and thus high expected utility. Therefore, we need to make sure that in our modeling more information indeed

[3] As we have a finite time horizon, we simplify and do not discount the expected value of additional information.

increases expected utility. What is the key benefit of having more information and getting closer to the true value? The answer is a reduction in uncertainty (see (2.11)). For sufficiently risk-averse consumers, more information – by increasing the number of information acquisition steps, N – brings consumers closer to their true expected match value and – most importantly in our modeling – reduces the risk of relying on incorrect assessments. However, as we can see from Eq. (2.11), the more information a consumer has already received, the smaller the reduction in uncertainty when they obtain additional information. Therefore, the magnitude of the increase in utility with further information – via increasing N – decreases with the number of steps (decreasing marginal utility effects from information).

Thus, in our modeling, we assume that the risk aversion parameter $A > 0$ is large enough to meet these requirements. We define the difference between the consumption utilities of two information acquisition steps as

$$\tilde{\Delta}_N := \mathbb{E}^*[\tilde{u}|I_{N+1}] - \mathbb{E}^*[\tilde{u}|I_N].$$

We assume that A is large enough, so that

$$\tilde{\Delta}_N > 0 \text{ and } \tilde{\Delta}_N > \tilde{\Delta}_{N+1} \text{ for all } N \in [0, 1, \ldots, \bar{T}] \tag{A}$$

and for all product allocations (x_1^N, x_2^N). A detailed derivation of this assumption is provided in Appendix A.2. That is, we only consider the set of stochastic dynamic sequences that fulfill this criterion. The generality of our analysis is thus limited in this respect. However, this assumption ensures that additional information always generates an increase in consumption utility. Since the effect of additional information on the variance is unambiguously positive, a sufficiently high-risk aversion implies that additional information will always generate positive marginal consumption utilities. With more information, the variance decreases, and the conditional expected consumption utility function increases for a sufficiently risk-averse individual.

Economically, we focus on the effect that information reduces the risk of making wrong decisions. We do not focus on the effect that information leads us closer to the true match value, as this may be negative (see (2.10)). In this context, the purpose of acquiring information is to reduce risk, so this effect dominates the latter potentially negative effect.

Thus, if we assume that A is sufficiently large – which is ensured by making assumption (A), we can solve the dynamic problem and determine N^*. We use Bayesian Learning for this sequential information acquisition. Consumers start with prior beliefs about the potential matches of their preferences with different products and collect information to update their beliefs. However, this process reduces the time available to generate utility through leisure activities. Therefore, consumers must first decide whether to start the Bayesian Learning process in the first place and, second, when to stop.

Before the Bayesian Learning process can be started, people form a prior belief $\mu_{i,0}$ about the match value m_i for each product i with prior variance $\sigma^2_{i,0}$. In a first step, the consumers have to determine the quantities of the products that give maximum expected utility based on these prior beliefs. That is, given their prior beliefs, they determine the optimal product allocation before information is gathered. This means that they have to solve the prior maximization problem

$$\max_{x_1,x_2} \mathbb{E}[u|I_0] = x_1\mu_{1,0} - \frac{1}{2}Ax_1^2\sigma^2_{1,0} + x_2\mu_{2,0} - \frac{1}{2}Ax_2^2\sigma^2_{2,0} + \bar{T}$$
$$\text{s.t. } y = x_1p_1 + x_2p_2,$$

which results in optimal quantities x_i^0 and optimal expected conditional utility $E^*[u|I_0]$. Note that we do not subtract any time N from utility, as no time has yet been spent collecting information. All disposable time is available as leisure time. Thus, without information acquisition, the product quantities x_i^0 are the optimal choice. Consumers can use the prior expected conditional utility as a reference point for deciding when to start the learning process.

How can they decide? Individuals know that each acquisition step reduces uncertainty, which increases consumption utility due to risk aversion. However, without taking the first acquisition step, they cannot know the extent of this effect and whether it compensates for a reduction in leisure time. So consumers cannot know what signal $m_{i,0}$ they will receive. Thus, they have to anticipate the expected utility $V^a(I_1)$ after taking the first acquisition step to decide whether to start the information acquisition process or not.

Without additional information, the consumers' best guess for the first signal is their prior belief $\mu_{i,0}$, which means they anticipate not getting an update to the expected match value. The second parameter that cannot be known beforehand is the signal variance η_i^2. However, this is needed to determine the reduction in uncertainty. Depending on their subjective perception, consumers can guess $\tilde{\eta}_i^2$ for η_i^2 for each product i. This indicates how precise the decision-maker thinks the information signal is. This subjective anticipation of $\tilde{\eta}_i^2$ indicates another characteristic of a consumer. Without experience or further objective evidence, consumers must use their personal assessment of the usefulness of a gathered piece of information. This assessment not only covers the information itself (if simple or complex information is needed), but also whether they believe they understand the information and can use it to better understand the situation. Thus, as a hypothesis, one could expect educated and confident individuals to be more likely to believe that their own information acquisition has high additional epistemic value, such that $\tilde{\eta}_i^2$ is low. However, $\tilde{\eta}_i^2$ is used to determine the anticipated uncertainty after one acquisition step

$$\sigma^2_{1,ant} := \frac{\sigma^2_{i,0}\tilde{\eta}_i^2}{\sigma^2_{i,0} + \tilde{\eta}_i^2}.$$

To find the anticipated utility after one acquisition step, the maximization problem

$$\max_{x_1,x_2} \mathbb{E}[u|I_{1,ant}] = x_1\mu_{1,0} - \frac{1}{2}Ax_1^2\sigma_{1,ant}^2 + x_2\mu_{2,0} - \frac{1}{2}Ax_2^2\sigma_{2,ant}^2 + \bar{T} - 1$$

$$\text{s.t. } y = x_1p_1 + x_2p_2$$

needs to be solved, which gives optimal quantities x_i^a and maximal anticipated utility $V^a(I_1)$. Then consumers can determine

$$V(I_0) = \max\{\mathbb{E}^*[u|I_0], V^a(I_1)\}.$$

From assumption (A), we know that obtaining additional information always leads to an increase in consumption utility. However, the time that can be spent on leisure activities is reduced, which reduces total utility. Thus, consumers only start the information acquisition process if $V(I_0) = V^a(I_1)$. Otherwise, if $V(I_0) = \mathbb{E}^*[u|I_0]$, they choose the initial optimal quantities x_i^0.

We now continue for a process in which information acquisition has been initiated and a person gathers information. After taking the Nth acquisition step, consumers can determine the optimal expected utility from the current information set $\mathbb{E}^*[u|I_N]$ by solving (M). After each step in this process, consumers have to evaluate whether to continue or stop the information acquisition. Again, they have to anticipate whether further information increases utility or whether their current information set already yields optimal utility. Thus, they have to determine the anticipated utility $V^a(I_{N+1})$. We assume that, based on the experience gained in a first acquisition step, they learn how precise the signal is.[4] Thus, their anticipation of the precision of further signals is equal to the true precision η_i^2. Consequently, the resulting uncertainty for each step $N \geq 2$ can be determined as $\sigma_{i,N}^2 = \frac{\sigma_{i,0}^2\eta_i^2}{N\sigma_{i,0}^2+\eta_i^2}$ (see (2.9)) before conducting the step. Note that consumers still cannot know what the following signal and thus the following match value is. Again, they have to anticipate the signal of taking another step, and their best guess for this signal $m_{i,N}$ is the currently expected match value $\mu_{i,N}$, which means that there is no update.[5] Therefore, consumers have to solve the following maximization problem for anticipated utility in the next $N+1$ period,

$$\max_{x_1,x_2} \mathbb{E}[u|I_{ant}] = x_1\mu_{1,N} - \frac{1}{2}Ax_1^2\sigma_{1,N+1}^2 + x_2\mu_{2,N} - \frac{1}{2}Ax_2^2\sigma_{2,N+1}^2 + \bar{T} - (N+1)$$

$$\text{s.t. } y = x_1p_1 + x_2p_2,$$

[4] This assumption can be made clear using some examples. If a consumer starts collecting information and the signals are quite diffuse, we assume that this observation is correct and η_i^2 is large. If the signals are very clear and consistent, we assume that this observation is correct and η_i^2 is low. This assumption excludes fake news.

[5] This can be seen from Eq. (2.10).

which results in maximum anticipated expected utility $V^a(I_{N+1})$. Consumers can compare this to the current maximum utility $\mathbb{E}^*[u|I_N]$ to determine $V(I_N)$ and make a decision. If $V(I_N) = V^a(I_{N+1})$, the information acquisition continues. The information acquisition ends if $V(I_N) = \mathbb{E}^*[u|I_N]$. At this point, the optimal number of sequential information acquisition steps has been reached.[6] Therefore, we can formulate the following:

Proposition 3.1 *If assumption* (A) *holds, there is an optimal number of information acquisition steps* N^* *and a corresponding optimal product allocation* $(x_1^{N^*}, x_2^{N^*})$ *that result from the sequential information acquisition process.*

Thus, the choice with the incomplete information set I_{N^*} *is efficient and an optimal choice.*

Proof The budget constraint describes a compact set, and $\mathbb{E}[u|I_N]$ is a continuous function in (x_1, x_2). Therefore, we can solve the maximization problem (M) in each step. An explicit solution can be found in Appendix A.1. Further, our assumption (A) for the parameter $A > 0$ ensures that additional information acquisition steps increase consumption utility at a decreasing rate. Thus, the sequential information acquisition process ends when the (anticipated) increase in consumption utility is less than 1, which means that it does not compensate for the reduction in leisure time when one acquisition step is taken. Otherwise, sequential information acquisition stops when the maximum number of steps $N = \bar{T}$ have been taken. ■

If we compare this ex ante optimal choice under imperfect information with the optimal choice decision under perfect information, we identify important differences and implications. First, leisure time is reduced when information acquisition steps are taken, leading to a reduction in utility. Second, and more importantly, the demand structure and hence the related implication for the general allocation are affected. We have seen that under perfect information only one product is chosen. Under imperfect information, the acquisition process may stop when it is optimal to choose positive quantities of both products (see Appendix A.1). Thus, both products are tried, and the optimal quantities are adjusted after experience and continued learning.

Numerical Illustration

In the previous paragraph, we saw that there is an optimal number of steps in the sequential information acquisition process and corresponding optimal product quantities. As we cannot determine a general solution for N^*, we will illustrate

---

[6] The stopping rule corresponds to the brand choice condition of Roberts and Urban (1988) with the addition of the remaining leisure time. This addition is similar to the idea of a "price hurdle" put forward by Chatterjee and Eliashberg (1990) in relation to technology adoption. Consumers choose the product allocation that generates the highest utility through a high match and/or small uncertainty. As long as it is anticipated that this part of the benefit will increase by an amount that offsets the loss of benefit due to the reduction in leisure time, the collection of information will continue.

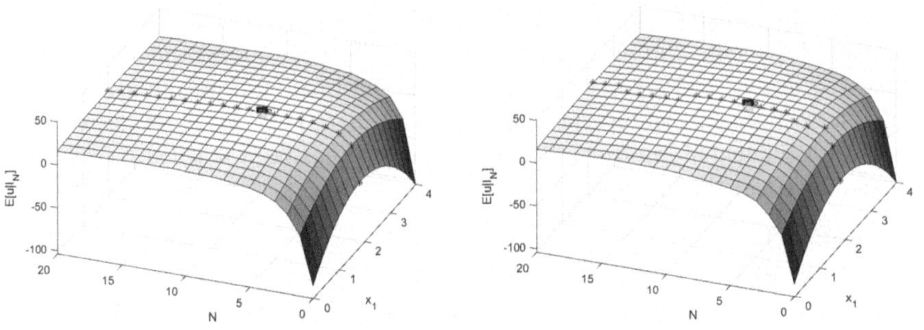

(a) (b)

Fig. 3.2 Two outcomes for $\mathbb{E}[u|I_N]$ with $\mu_{1,0} = 5, \mu_{2,0} = 4.7, \sigma^2_{1,0} = 0.9, \sigma^2_{2,0} = 0.8, \eta_1^2 = 1, \eta_2^2 = 1, \mu_A = 6, \mu_B = 6, A = 20, T = 20, p_1 = p_2 = 3, Y = 12$ and $\tilde{\eta}_1 = \tilde{\eta}_2 = 0.1$

the acquisition problem with some numerical examples. These examples show two different scenarios. In the first scenario, the two products under consideration have the same true expected match value. In the second scenario, one product has a greater true match than the other. For both scenarios, suppose that a consumer considers two products that – without any further information – seem very similar. Therefore, the consumer's prior beliefs are quite close together, namely $\mu_{1,0} = 5$ and $\mu_{2,0} = 4.7$ with prior variances $\sigma_{1,0} = 0.9$ and $\sigma_{2,0} = 0.8$. The budget is $y = 12$, and the prices for the two products are $p_1 = 3$ and $p_2 = 3$.[7]

We start with the first scenario and assume that both products under consideration have the same true expected match value. Thus, the information acquisition process should reveal that a balanced product allocation, $x_1 = x_2$, is the optimal choice. However, we will see that the result depends on the specific stochastic signals the consumer receives. We illustrate the decision path for two different sequences of signals in Fig. 3.2, where we see the expected conditional utility $\mathbb{E}[u|I_N]$ depending on the quantity x_1 and acquisition steps N. As we can only draw three dimensions, we rearrange the budget constraint, $x_2 = \frac{y - x_1 p_1}{p_2}$, and plug it into the utility function so that we can reduce our analysis to x_1 and N and draw the surface of the conditional expected utility. The risk aversion parameter is chosen so that it fulfills assumption (A). For every time step $N = 0, 1, \ldots, \bar{T}$, the maximization problem for $\mathbb{E}[u|I_N]$ is solved to find the optimal choice of x_1. In Fig. 3.2, the corresponding maximal utility in each step is indicated by an asterisk. The optimal result of one path is depicted as a black square "S". It illustrates the optimal number of steps N^*, the optimal quantity x_1^*, and the optimal expected conditional utility $\mathbb{E}^*[u|I_N]$ from the sequential information acquisition process.

[7] We choose the same prices for both products as we want to illustrate the effects of the match that ought not to be influenced by price effects.

In the first scenario, both true expected match values are equal to 6. Figure 3.2a depicts the result for one stochastic sequence of signals, and Fig. 3.2b depicts the result of another sequence, while all parameters remain equal. In case Fig. 3.2a, the optimal prior allocation is $x_1^0 = x_2^0 = 2$, and this does not change in the subsequent steps, which means that the signals are very similar. The information acquisition process is continued as long as the anticipated utility is positive although the optimal allocation is not adjusted. The optimal number of steps is $N^* = 8$ with $\mathbb{E}^*[u|I_{N^*}] = 26.2673$. In case 3.2b, the signals differ more, which leads to different optimal allocations in the different steps. The process stops after $N^* = 8$ steps with $x_1^{N^*} = 2.2$, $x_2^{N^*} = 1.8$ and $\mathbb{E}^*[u|I_{N^*}] = 25.5022$. Thus, the results differ slightly depending on the stochastic sequence of signals.

In the second scenario, the true match value of product 2 is $\mu_2 = 4$ not 6. All the other parameters remain unchanged. In Fig. 3.3, we see two decision paths on the conditional expected utility surface for different sequences of signals. This time, additional information ought to reveal that product 1 is the better choice, as it has the highest true expected match value. This can be observed in both cases Fig. 3.3a, b in Fig. 3.3. In case Fig. 3.3a, however, the first signals do not suggest as clear a difference in the match values as the signals do in case Fig. 3.3b. Therefore, the decision path in case Fig. 3.3a moves more quickly toward an optimal choice where $x_1^{N^*}$ is close to 4 and $x_2^{N^*}$ is close to 0 than the path in case Fig. 3.3b does. However, sequential information acquisition stops at an optimal number of steps $N^* = 8$. In case Fig. 3.3a, we have $x_1^{N^*} = 2.8$, $x_2^{N^*} = 1.2$ with $\mathbb{E}^*[u|I_{N^*}] = 25.1003$, and in case Fig. 3.3b, we have $x_1^{N^*} = 2.6$, $x_2^{N^*} = 1.4$ with $\mathbb{E}^*[u|I_{N^*}] = 24.9715$. Thus, acquisition ends before the consumer knows that product 1 is the better choice. However, acquiring further information reduces leisure time and utility. Thus, the process ends when the consumer does not anticipate an increase in utility after taking an additional step and chooses both products ex ante. Ex post they continue learning and will eventually find that product 1 is the optimal choice.

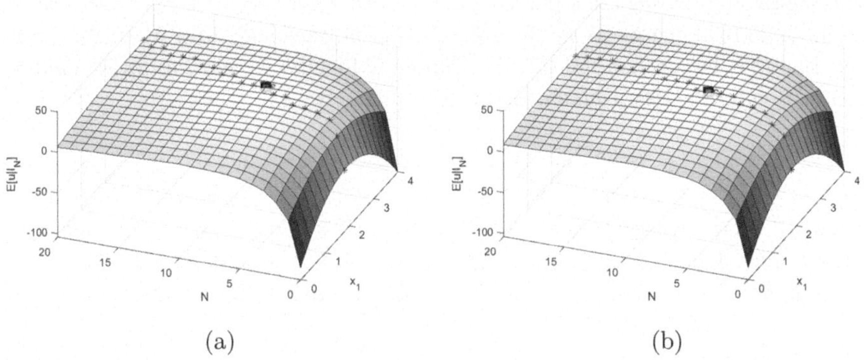

Fig. 3.3 Two outcomes for $\mathbb{E}[u|I_N]$ with $\mu_{1,0} = 5$, $\mu_{2,0} = 4.7$, $\sigma_{1,0}^2 = 0.9$, $\sigma_{2,0}^2 = 0.8$, $\eta_1^2 = 1$, $\eta_2^2 = 1$, $\mu_A = 6$, $\mu_B = 4$, $A = 20$, $T = 20$, $p_1 = p_2 = 3$, $Y = 12$ and $\tilde{\eta}_1 = \tilde{\eta}_2 = 0.1$

Comparative Statics

To find out what the determinants of the decision are, we analyze the behavior of the solution obtained for Proposition 3.1 with respect to some parameters of interest, and we obtain intuitive results. First, we are able to show the impact of risk aversion on the information acquisition process.

Proposition 3.2 *Let N^* be the solution to the dynamic maximization problem and let assumption* (A) *hold. If the risk aversion parameter A is increased, the number of optimal information acquisition steps N^* is at least as high as before. Thus, if A is increased, the number N^* will increase or remain unchanged.*

Therefore, the more risk averse a decision-maker is, the more information is collected and the choice can be made with expected conditional match values that are closer to the true match values. A formal proof of Proposition 3.2 can be found in Appendix A.3. Risk-averse consumers need more time to make a decision, and it is made under less uncertainty. That is, a highly risk-averse decision-maker reduces uncertainty by using the instrument of optimal information gathering.

Additionally, we look at the effect of signal precision. Changes in the quality of the information signal η_i are not unambiguous. Therefore, we can only derive sufficient conditions to show the impact of an increase in η_i for one product i on the information acquisition steps N^*. These conditions are not necessary. Thus, we have to make some further assumptions. First, we can assume that for each information acquisition step N the signal lies within a finite range of the current expected value. Thus, we assume[8]

$$|\mu_{i,N} - m_{i,N}| \leq 3\sigma_{i,N} \tag{3.2}$$

for every information acquisition step N. Second, we assume

$$2\sigma_{i,0}^4 \geq \eta_i^4. \tag{3.3}$$

This assumption ensures that the reduction in uncertainty between two search steps (as in (2.11)) increases as η_i increases.[9] This is especially true when the prior uncertainty is larger than the signal uncertainty. Finally, we need to make another assumption for the risk aversion parameter A, namely

$$6(x_i^{N^*} - x_i^a) < A\sigma_{i,0}((x_i^{N^*})^2 - (x_i^a)^2), \tag{3.4}$$

where $x_i^{N^*}$ is the optimal quantity of product i after N^* information steps and x_i^a is the anticipated quantity of product i after an additional information step. Note that the sign of $(x_i^{N^*} - x_i^a)$ and $((x_i^{N^*})^2 - (x_i^a)^2)$, respectively, can be either positive or

[8] This assumption is appropriate, since for normal distributions, 99.73% of the observations fall within this interval.

[9] Thus, this ensures that the derivative $\frac{\partial\sigma_{i,N}^2}{\partial\eta_i} - \frac{\partial\sigma_{i,N+1}^2}{\partial\eta_i}$ is positive.

negative. Therefore, at this point, we need to both assume that A is large enough so that (3.4) holds and, if necessary, that $\sigma_{i,0}$ is small enough.

We obtain then the following insight:

Proposition 3.3 *Let $N^* \geq 1$ be the solution to the dynamic maximization problem and let assumption* (A) *hold. Further, let the assumptions* (3.2), (3.3), *and* (3.4) *hold. If the signal variance η_i is increased for at least one product i, the number of optimal information acquisition steps N^* is at least as high as before.*

Thus, if η_i is increased, the number N^* is increased or remains unchanged.

A proof of Proposition 3.3 is quite extensive and thus is given in Appendix A.4. When the signals are less precise, risk-averse consumers cannot collect less information. They need at least as much, or even more, information to reduce their uncertainty about the match value. The optimal choice may be made with more information.[10]

Note that this is not true for $N = 0$. A larger anticipated signal variance $\tilde{\eta}_i$ prevents consumers from starting the information acquisition process in the first place. The proof is also provided in Appendix A.4. In this case, an increase in the signal variance $\tilde{\eta}_i$ does not increase the number of the information acquisition steps but prevents the process from being started in the first place.

Implications for the Human Information Problem

We have learnt that the acquisition of costly information leads to an optimal choice. Since Bayesian Learning is a process that approximates to reality, it is a good solution to the human information problem, but it remains an imperfect approximation to reality. Even if a consumer has optimally revealed some properties of the goods they are interested in, the set of information acquired remains limited. That is, there is a Bayesian Belief about the characteristics of the goods. This belief determines the belief about the match value and leads to a purchase decision. The choice is *subjectively rational* because the consumer cannot do better under the given conditions. In other words, the subjectively rational choice is based on a belief. It is a Bayesian Belief – based on information acquisition – and not just any belief, but it a remains a belief. So, if we relax the assumption of imperfect information, decisions are based on beliefs that can be close to or far from the actual properties of the goods in question. Beliefs are a natural part of human existence, even in rational decision-making. This is true even if we consider the simplest type of a decision: a consumer choice. In terms of the topic of this book, however, we get a first idea of why it is so interesting to look at beliefs, or even belief systems. In the next section, we go one step further and discuss another type of belief: heuristics.

---

[10] This is in line with the findings of Lippman and McCardle (1987), who show that if signals are more precise than the prior belief, then increasing the signals' precision (smaller η_i^2) leads to a decrease in information acquisition time (N^*). Their condition is ensured here by assumption (3.3). However, we need to make further assumptions for our result because the product quantities determine the expected utility.

3.3 A Heuristic Approach and Optimal Choice

In this section, we want to answer the third and most important question of this chapter: Can a heuristic rule substitute information acquisition as an optimal choice? An important strand of literature in behavioral economics and psychology reveals that most consumers do not optimize the utility function to make a decision; instead, they apply simpler rules, known as heuristics (Benartzi & Thaler, 2001; Hauser, 2011; Payne et al., 1993). In this section, we introduce a social heuristic approach to reaching a purchase decision. However, other heuristics that determine a product allocation are possible as well. Even if beliefs and heuristics often are associated with irrational activities, our aim here is to show when the use of heuristics is subjectively rational. In the optimal decision problem set out in Sect. 3.2, consumers have to spend time gathering information to improve their knowledge about goods. As a result, they reduce uncertainty by completing the optimal number of information acquisition steps necessary to maximize their expected utility under their income constraints. By contrast, the heuristic approach is another potentially plausible way to arrive at a decision. Consumers can decide which path to choose. The question is whether they behave optimally and hence subjectively rationally under the respective conditions or whether they behave irrationally. Thus, we compare the two scenarios and analyze when a consumer prefers the heuristic approach and when they choose information acquisition.

A decision based on heuristic reasoning is a decision in which plausible considerations "serve as an aid to learning, discovery, or problem solving by experimental and especially trial-and-error methods".[11] While there are many heuristics that could be applied to the above decision problem of choosing one variation of a particular good, we suggest a simple social heuristic approach based on opinions offered by the individual's social environment. For example, family and friends can share their experiences and give advice. One of the simplest forms of social heuristics is the imitate-the-majority heuristic (Boyd & Richerson, 2005), which means that a person follows the behavior of the majority; another is the imitate-the-successful heuristic, where the behavior of the most successful person is imitated. Pachur et al. (2005) introduce the social-circle heuristic, which is used to choose the better of two alternatives by assessing the opinions of an individual's social contacts ordered by distance (themselves, family, friends, acquaintances). The search is stopped when the majority in the circle shares the same opinion; otherwise, the next circle is considered. This can lead to the early termination of the process, meaning that peripheral opinions are neglected. For the sake of simplicity, in our model, we suggest that consumers have a group of social contacts that can be asked to share opinions about the products under consideration. We assume this can be done at no cost. Each individual can give their personal assessment, based on their beliefs or experiences, about the expected value with a degree of uncertainty. However,

[11] Merriam-Webster.com Dictionary, Merriam-Webster, https://www.merriam-webster.com/dictionary/heuristic. Retrieved 5 May 2022.

people do not trust each family member, friend, or colleague equally. Their trust may depend on the product category, the relationship, or the experience the consumer thinks the other person has already had with it. Thus, the consumer assigns weight to each person's opinions.

We use $\mu_{i,p}$ to denote the expected match value and $\sigma_{i,p}^2$ to denote the uncertainty about product i for person p. Further, we use $w_{i,p}$ to denote the weight the consumer attaches to person p' opinion about product i. After interviewing the social environment, the expected match value is given by the weighted sum of opinions

$$\mu_{i,H} = \frac{1}{|P|} \sum_{p \in P} w_{i,p} \mu_{i,p},$$

and the uncertainty is

$$\sigma_{i,H}^2 = \frac{1}{|P|} \sum_{p \in P} w_{i,p} \sigma_{i,p}^2,$$

respectively. The denominator $|P|$ represents the number of people asked for their opinion.

At this point, consumers have to decide whether to follow the heuristic of being guided by trustworthy individuals or whether to start collecting information themselves as described in the above. Thus, they need to judge which procedure yields better results. First, they can compare the expected utility based on their own prior ad hoc beliefs described by the pairs $(\mu_{i,0}, \sigma_{i,0}^2)$ and the expected utility of the heuristic described by the pairs $(\mu_{i,H}, \sigma_{i,H}^2)$. The two outcomes can be determined and compared after finding the optimal quantities of the products in each case.

Thus, the prior maximization problem needs to be solved first, which results in optimal quantities x_i^0 for their own prior beliefs and initial expected utility $\mathbb{E}^*[u|I_0]$ (see sequential information acquisition in Sect. 3.2). This result is the benchmark derived from an ad hoc belief. If consumers are rational, $(\mu_{i,0}, \sigma_{i,0}^2)$ is only the point of departure for their optimal information acquisition procedure as described in the previous section. However, there is another alternative, and that is a heuristic approach. The heuristic described in the above leads to an expected match value and an assessment of uncertainty given by pairs $(\mu_{i,H}, \sigma_{i,H}^2)$. Both are expected values, as they are the result of trusted answers from talking to others and are weighted in the best possible way. So there is no reason not to maximize the expected utility based on the findings of the heuristic rule and determine the optimal values of x_i. Thus, the maximization problem

$$\max_{x_1,x_2} \mathbb{E}[u|I_H] = x_1\mu_{1,H} - \frac{1}{2}Ax_1^2\sigma_{1,H}^2 + x_2\mu_{2,H} - \frac{1}{2}Ax_2^2\sigma_{2,H}^2 + \bar{T}$$

$$\text{s.t. } y = x_1 p_1 + x_2 p_2$$

needs to be solved, which has solutions x_i^H and yields optimal expected utility $\mathbb{E}^*[u|I_H]$. These optimal quantities are chosen if the heuristic strategy is followed. Note that we have $t_L = \bar{T}$ here, as we assume that the heuristic approach does not reduce leisure time.[12] Whether the heuristic strategy is indeed followed depends on the outcome of comparing the resulting expected utilities.

At this point, consumers have to judge whether the heuristic is the best approach to follow or whether they should begin their own information acquisition process. We now have $V^a(I_1) = \mathbb{E}^*[u|I_H]$ and

$$V(I_0) = \max\{\mathbb{E}^*[u|I_0], \mathbb{E}^*[u|I_H]\}.$$

This indicates how the individual proceeds. First, if the expected utility of the heuristic is lower than the expected prior utility, $V(I_0) = \mathbb{E}^*[u|I_0]$, consumers do not choose to apply the heuristic and begin their information acquisition process. They expect to obtain an even higher expected utility from the information acquisition due to our assumption (A) of an increasing utility from information. Therefore, they accept they will have to invest time to obtain a better result.
Second, if the expected utility of the heuristic is greater than the expected prior utility, $V(I_0) = \mathbb{E}^*[u|I_H]$, consumers have to decide whether to simply follow the heuristic or whether to apply the information acquisition process, which may beat the heuristic promise. To come to a decision, consumers can use the decision rules as described in Sect. 3.2 (sequential information acquisition). They can determine the anticipated utility of a first acquisition step, $V^a(I_1)$. For this first step, we have to slightly adjust the dynamic programming functional equation,

$$V^H(I_0) = \max\{\mathbb{E}^*[u|I_H], V^a(I_1)\}.$$

Comparing the utilities of the heuristic approach and information acquisition, we obtain two different cases. First, if $V^H(I_0) = V^a(I_1)$, the expected utility from the heuristic is not high enough. People opt to collect more information. The reduction in uncertainty on account of gathering new information not only compensates for the reduction in leisure time, the increase in net utility is big enough to overcompensate for the original advantage of applying the heuristic.

The second case – that of a high expected heuristic utility ($V(I_0) = \mathbb{E}^*[u|I_H]$) is $V^H(I_0) = \mathbb{E}^*[u|I_H]$), which means that the anticipated utility of the first step does not exceed the expected utility of the heuristic. In this case, it is subjectively rational to follow the heuristic, as this yields the highest expected utility. Thus, the consumer's purchase decisions are the heuristic quantities x_i^H.

[12] This assumption is based on the idea that consumers regularly interact with their social environment so that they do not have to reduce their leisure time to get other people's opinions. It is even more obvious for another heuristic like the "$1/N$"-rule.

Implications for the Human Information Problem

In Sect. 3.2, we deduced that consumers base their choices on a Bayesian Belief about the characteristics of the goods in question. In the absence of perfect information, the human information problem is solved by using the Bayesian Belief instead. This choice is subjectively rational because, under the given conditions, the consumer cannot do any better, even if the choice is based on a belief. While Bayesian Beliefs have the potential to approximate to reality and can be viewed as the best we can believe given the signals we receive from reality, it is not the only way to solve the information problem. In particular, when information costs are high, only a small number of information acquisition steps can be performed. Thus, the acquired information set remains small, and other ways of solving the information problem need to be found. In this case, heuristics are that other way.

Furthermore, as we move from our simple example to more complex evaluations and decisions, it becomes clear that individuals are unlikely to be able to gather enough information to base their choices on a Bayesian Learning procedure. Advice from heuristic rules is likely to be the subjectively rational choice.

3.4 Comparison and Implications

In the previous sections, we introduced the optimal choice of differentiated goods under perfect information, imperfect information with Bayesian Learning, and heuristic rules. As we have already discussed, in each situation, a consumer's decision is the best under the given circumstances. Nevertheless, the allocation structure and resulting utilities under these various approaches differ. In this section, we study these differences and discuss the implications for the role of belief systems.

Comparison of Choices in Different Information Scenarios

The differences in the allocation structure and resulting utilities under the various approaches are illustrated in Table 3.1.

We start with the optimal choice of only one product i with quantity $\bar{x}_i^*$ which implies utility $\bar{\mathrm{u}}_i$ under perfect information (see (2.5)) as our benchmark (row 1, chosen product under perfect information). This is different in a world of imperfect information (row 2). In the case of information acquisition, it is more likely that a consumer will decide to purchase positive quantities of both products $x_i^{N^*}$ and $x_j^{N^*}$. As information acquisition reduces leisure time and utility is also reduced by uncertainty, $\mathbb{E}^*[\mathrm{u}|I_{N^*}]$ is lower than the benchmark utility $\bar{\mathrm{u}}_i$. Even if the benchmark product i is chosen, the quantity $x_i^{N^*}$ and the expected utility $\mathbb{E}^*[\mathrm{u}^i|I_{N^*}]$ are lower than the benchmark for the same reason. However, it is also possible that the other product j is chosen. In this case, consumers will never know the true expected match value of the benchmark product i as they do not continue to learn. The wrong product j is permanently chosen, which causes utility losses. Heuristic reasoning leads to similar results (see row 3). It is also likely that consumers will try both products. However, following the heuristic strategy does not reduce

Table 3.1 Comparison of optimal quantities and utilities in the different cases of the three scenarios

		Quantity	Utility
Perfect information		$\bar{x}_i^*$ benchmark product i	$\bar{U}_i$ benchmark utility
Imperfect information	Information acquisition	$x_i^{N^*}$ and $x_j^{N^*}$	$\mathbb{E}^*[U\|I_{N^*}] \leq \bar{U}_i$
		$x_i^{N^*}$	$\mathbb{E}^*[U^i\|I_{N^*}] \leq \bar{U}_i$
		$x_j^{N^*}$ wrong product	$\mathbb{E}^*[U^j\|I_{N^*}] < \bar{U}_i$
	Heuristic	x_i^H and x_j^H	$\mathbb{E}^*[U\|I_H]$ can be greater or lower than $\bar{U}_i$
		$\bar{x}_i^*$	$\mathbb{E}^*[U^i\|I_H]$
		x_j^H	$\mathbb{E}^*[U^j\|I_H]$

leisure time as assumed above. The expected utility $\mathbb{E}^*[\mathrm{u}|I_H]$ can be higher or lower than the benchmark utility $\bar{\mathrm{u}}_i$ depending on what the consumer perceives in their social circle. This means that the signals from the social environment can cause a deception that leads to an overoptimistic or underoptimistic perception of reality (perfect information). Analogously to the information acquisition process, the heuristic approach can favor one product. It can favor the benchmark product, which is chosen at benchmark quantity $\bar{x}_i^*$ and implies expected utility $\mathbb{E}^*[\mathrm{u}^i|I_H]$. This expected utility can also be higher or lower than the benchmark depending on the social environment. Again, the signals from the social environment can cause a deception that leads to an overoptimistic or underoptimistic perception of reality. Thus, heuristic allocation can lead to the benchmark product in the purchase decision. Consequently, heuristics can be a good strategy. However, heuristics can also favor the wrong product j, which yields consumption at quantity x_j^H and expected utility $\mathbb{E}^*[\mathrm{u}^j|I_H]$ which can also be higher or lower than the benchmark – again due to a deception.

Unlike standard optimal choice models, our model shows that allocation distortion is possible under imperfect information and can even occur permanently. Thus, models under perfect information can only be regarded as a sufficient approximation for consumption choice when consumers continue learning about products' attributes and characteristics. Whenever learning about a product is stopped, allocation under imperfect information can differ from allocation under perfect information.

Implications for the Role of Beliefs and Understanding Ideologies

In this section, we focus on the information problem in household decisions. Eliminating the information problem in standard economic theory was a simplifying step in the development of rational choice theory and for a better understanding of decision-making. However, ignoring the information problem omits an important element of real-world decision-making. We usually do not have a clear or even true view of the issues we are deciding about. So we need to deal with this state of relative ignorance in decision theory. Taking the simplest example, we considered a standard economic decision, a consumer's choice between product variations. For an uninformed consumer, acquiring information in an optimal Bayesian Learning process or applying heuristic decision rules can be strategies for solving the information problem when making a choice ex ante.

Why and how does this relate to our topic of belief systems and ideologies? The above findings relating to a consumer problem have implications for our more general topic of belief systems and ideologies. It also leads us back to the more general questions and objectives we stated at the beginning of this chapter. (1) When we compare optimal decisions under perfect information with optimal decisions under a costly information acquisition process, we see clear differences in the allocative structure as well. Thus, not considering the information problem is anything but a trivial simplification. (2) We were able to work out that in the Bayesian Learning process information can primarily have the function of reducing risk for risk-averse individuals. We specifically emphasized this function in our analyses and were thus able to derive many of the results based on this assumption. (3) We have shown in the most simple way using a rational consumer that beliefs matter for his or her choices. A choice is *subjectively rational* because a consumer cannot do better under the given conditions. Very often, beliefs are associated with irrational activities. Here we learn that the acquisition of costly information leads to an optimal choice. Hence, even if information were acquired and optimally revealed some properties of reality (the good), the set of information acquired remains limited and thus remains an imperfect approximation to reality. That is, even if there is a Bayesian Belief about reality based on information acquisition, a Bayesian Belief remains a belief. So, if we relax the assumption of perfect information, decisions are based on beliefs that can be close to or far away from actual reality. Beliefs are a natural part of human existence, even in rational decision-making.

(4) As an alternative to the costly acquisition of real information, it can also be subjectively rational to use heuristics if they promise a certain prospect of success. Heuristics are another way of handling the information problem. They are a cost-effective substitute for real information gathering, which can be very expensive without generating corresponding benefits. Therefore, there is also an optimal and subjectively rational use of heuristics. If we look at the topic of this book – ideologies – we can already argue that belief systems and ideologies can have a similar function with respect to the information problem as heuristics do. The definition of an ideology in Chap. 1 includes the following: "the belief system/ideology provides individuals permanent interpretations, evaluations, ... and proposes strategies and actions ... to achieve goals". Thus, in the absence of information, an ideology and its narratives can function as a kind of heuristic advice for decision-making. When we move away from simple choices – such as consumer choices – and consider complex political or economic issues, it becomes clear that an individual is unable to rely on Bayesian Learning procedures and instead is guided by those beliefs in which they have confidence. Ideologies and their narratives can fulfill precisely this function of a heuristic

in the case of incomplete information. Ideologies, being a set of narratives, are introduced as a rational substitute for information. Thus, we argue that ideologies simply reflect and are an answer to the human information problem. We will come back to transferring this discussion to ideologies in Sect. 6.2.

References

Benartzi, S., & Thaler, R. H. (2001). Naive diversification strategies in defined contribution saving plans. *American Economic Review, 91*(1), 79–98.

Boyd, R., & Richerson, P. (2005). *The origin and evolution of cultures*. Evolution and Cognition. Oxford University Press.

Branco, F., Sun, M., & Villas-Boas, J. M. (2012). Optimal search for product information. *Management Science, 58*(11), 2037–2056.

Chatterjee, R. A., & Eliashberg, J. (1990). The innovation diffusion process in a heterogeneous population: A micromodeling approach. *Management Science, 36*(9), 1057–1079.

Crawford, G. S., & Shum, M. (2005). Uncertainty and learning in pharmaceutical demand. *Econometrica, 73*(4), 1137–1173.

DeGroot, M. H. (1970). *Optimal statistical decisions*. McGraw-Hill.

Erdem, T., Keane, M., Öncü, T., & Strebel, J. (2005). Learning about computers: An analysis of information search and technology choice. *Quantitative Marketing and Economics, 3*, 207–247.

Erdem, T., & Keane, M. P. (1996). Decision-making under uncertainty: Capturing dynamic brand choice processes in turbulent consumer goods markets. *Marketing Science, 15*(1), 1–20.

Gigerenzer, G., & Gaissmaier, W. (2011). Heuristic decision making. *Annual Review of Psychology, 62*(1), 451–482.

Gigerenzer, G., & Goldstein, D. G. (1996). Reasoning the fast and frugal way: Models of bounded rationality. *Psychological Review, 103*(4), 650–669.

Hauser, J. (2011). A marketing science perspective on recognition-based heuristics (and the fast-and-frugal paradigm). *Judgment and Decision Making, 6*, 396–408.

Jensen, R. (1982). Adoption and diffusion of an innovation of uncertain profitability. *Journal of Economic Theory, 27*(1), 182–193.

Kihlstrom, R. (1974). A Bayesian model of demand for information about product quality. *International Economic Review, 15*(1), 99.

Lippman, S. A., & McCardle, K. F. (1987). Does cheaper, faster, or better imply sooner in the timing of innovation decisions? *Management Science, 33*(8), 1058–1064.

Loomes, G. (1991). Evidence of a new violation of the independence axiom. *Journal of Risk and Uncertainty, 4*(1), 91–108.

McCardle, K. F. (1985). Information acquisition and the adoption of new technology. *Management Science, 31*(11), 1372–1389.

Pachur, T., Rieskamp, J., & Hertwig, R. (2005). The social circle heuristic: Fast and frugal decisions based on small samples. In K. Forbus, D. Gentner & T. Regier (Eds.), *Pro-ceedings of the 26th Annual Conference of the Cognitive Science Society* (pp. 1077–1082). Erlbaum.

Payne, J. W., Bettman, J. R., & Johnson, E. J. (1993). *The adaptive decision maker*. Cambridge University Press.

Reis, R. (2006). Inattentive consumers. *Journal of Monetary Economics, 53*(8), 1761–1800.

Roberts, J. H., & Urban, G. L. (1988). Modeling multiattribute utility, risk, and belief dynamics for new consumer durable brand choice. *Management Science, 34*(2), 167–185.

Ulu, C., & Smith, J. E. (2009). Uncertainty, information acquisition, and technology adoption. *Operations Research, 57*(3), 740–752.

Wübben, M., & von Wangenheim, F. (2008). Instant customer base analysis: Managerial heuristics often “get it right”. *Journal of Marketing, 72*(3), 82–93.

Zhong, W. (2022). Optimal dynamic information acquisition. *Econometrica, 90*(4), 1537–1582.

Chapter 4
Needs and Preferences: An Extended Concept

This chapter focuses on individuals' needs and preferences.[1] Its main claim is that the preference system in standard economic modeling does not sufficiently capture the full spectrum of universal needs and preferences of individuals. There is no doubt that people have physical needs and demands. Humans need to eat and drink, and – even though additional consumption is not fundamentally necessary for survival – they have infinite wishes for goods they would like to consume. People have a demand for all kinds of goods and services. The question of how to best satisfy this demand is the key question of economics. In standard consumer theory, economists talk about preferences for different goods and the wish to consume those goods. While in the early stages of the development of neoclassical theory, these goods were meant to be physical consumption goods like apples, bananas, and cars, later on – in particular in contributions by Becker and others – the standard model was extended to include time allocation and more abstract wishes such as leisure time, health, and safety.[2] Even though some of these models may have been oversold, they cannot be fully ignored. One interesting implication that arose from empirical tests of such models was that the assumption that rationality matters. The idea that behavior and decision can be traced back to rational choices is undeniable. People make choices about abstract wishes and needs, and they make choices under the constraints of their resources and subjective estimations of enquiring about decision-related information and its costs, as well as the cost of fulfilling their wishes. Even though economists evaluating everything in terms of money prices

[1] This chapter is also related to Gries and Müller (2020) and Müller and Gries (2024).

[2] For the start of these discussions, see seminal papers on time allocation and leisure in Becker (1965), on health in Grossman (1972) and Fuchs (1982), on education in Becker (1964) and Freeman (1976), and on safety in Hirshleifer (1983). Further, for noneconomists (and also some economists), even curious issues like the economics of marriage and the choice of spouse, e.g., Becker (1973), Becker (1974), Lundberg and Pollak (1996), Willis (1999), or recently e.g., Arcidiacono et al. (2016) were introduced.

T. Gries et al., *The Economics of Ideologies*, Springer Studies in Alternative Economics, https://doi.org/10.1007/978-3-031-93514-5_4

sometimes leads to a feeling of unease, there is no doubt that intangible goods like health and education are elements of our system of wishes and demands. The important thing here is that intangible goods are well known in economic theory, but there is more to be considered.

Society today is facing a multitude of demanding challenges that require comprehensive transformation, a shift in thinking, and the learning of sustainable resilience. However, this requirement for transformation is not limited to the economy, political system, and society as a whole. The demands on the individual to adapt to the current upheavals and transformation processes and to endure uncertainty, ambiguity, unpredictability, and a possible loss of control have also increased to the same extent.

In contemporary discourse, there is a growing acknowledgment of the challenges presented by such environments, which are characterized as volatile, uncertain, complex, and ambiguous (VUCA). Scholarly as well as professional interest has increasingly focused on the impact of these VUCA conditions on cognitive processes, emotions, and decision-making strategies. Such environments are marked by rapid and often unforeseen changes, complex interdependencies, and the frequent emergence of ambiguous information. Given that our current environment is characterized by VUCA and due to the interconnected nature of modern life, predictability and consistency have markedly decreased. Consequently, VUCA environments have heightened people's need to simplify complexities, forecast outcomes more accurately, minimize ambiguous information, and seek greater certainty and consistency in their lives. People have always sought answers to life's significant questions in order to understand the purpose of their existence, identify their place in society, and make autonomous decisions aligned with their aspirations and preferences.

Next to consumer needs, we identify four clusters of psychological needs in Fig. 4.1. (1) needs related to existential conditions like threats; (2) needs rooted

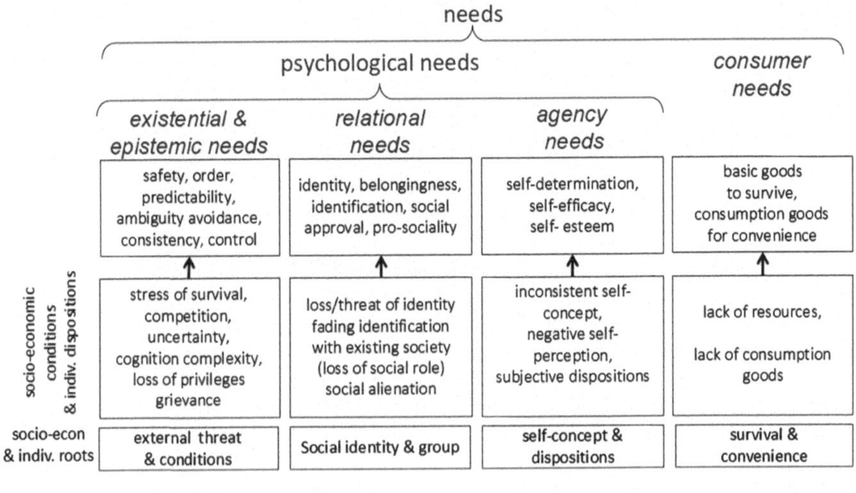

Fig. 4.1 Clusters of human needs

in epistemic wishes; (3) needs rooted in humans as social beings and the need to relate to other humans; (4) needs rooted in individuals' need for self-determination (agency needs), and (5) needs and preferences with respect to consumption. Each of these needs in its cluster is influenced by internal factors, like an individual's dispositions, and external factors, including economic, social, political, and environmental conditions. In the next sections, we will discuss these needs in more detail.

4.1 Existential and Epistemic Needs

Existential and epistemic human needs are needs that refer to a safety-seeking, threat-avoiding mechanism. These needs motivate people not only to secure their own existence and deal with uncertain, ambiguous, and threatening situations but also to organize and control their environments and to seek an understanding of the universe and their personal existence. To adapt to dynamic and constantly changing environments, individuals have to manage uncertainties and make decisions, requiring them to have new experiences, process large amounts of information, and develop new cognitive and behavioral skills. While these existential and epistemic needs are fundamental in nature, that is, they can be applied to every human being across various cultures and environments, the manifestation of each need varies across individuals. This means that not every individual has the same need intensity. This variation may be influenced by a mix of genetic, environmental, social, and personal factors. In our discussion, we focus on the universal aspects of these needs – the need for safety, order, control, ambiguity/uncertainty avoidance, consistency, and predictability – without delving more deeply into individual differences.

The Existential Need for Safety/Existential Security

Individuals often seek to mitigate threatening and uncertain situations in order to feel safe and secure. As highlighted by Maslow (1943), one primary motivation that is rooted deeply in biology and goes beyond mere physiological needs is the maintenance of existential safety. The need for safety can be understood as the human motivation to feel protected from environmental threats and to have sufficient material resources to ensure basic survival. Existential safety needs essentially reflect the human desire to stay alive – that is, having enough resources to ensure survival – and to avoid situations that evoke thoughts of one's own mortality or existential anxiety (Evans et al., 2005). Fulfillment of this need is heavily influenced by environmental conditions and external events such as climate change, pollution, diminishing water supplies, economic shocks, terrorist attacks, wars, and natural disasters, all of which can significantly impact safety (Kasser, 2009). However, beyond physical and material safety, there is also a need for subjectively perceived feelings of safety. Unlike tangible physical safety, feelings of existential insecurity can emerge even in the absence of actual danger. Consequently, psychologists distinguish between the physical need for safety and the psychological need for safety (Deci & Ryan, 2000). Psychological safety pertains to an individual's sense of security and confidence in their ability to handle threats and changes (Newman et al., 2017). Clinical research indicates that mental disorders such as anxiety, phobia, and depression are often associated with unmet psychological safety needs or the subjective perception of an inability to manage threats and change (Zheng et al., 2016; Weinstein & Stone, 2018).

Experiments with nonhuman organisms show that they process threatening information more quickly than rewarding information, which may be attributed to an evolutionary survival strategy. In essence, when safety needs are unmet, heightened feelings of threat and anxiety trigger either approach or avoidance behaviors. Appraisal theory supports this finding by indicating that emotions associated with harm or threat are activated more swiftly and automatically than those associated with blame or anger. When something uncontrollable or unexpected happens, an individual will first perceive it as a threat (fear/uncertainty) and next evaluate its hedonic value (sad/happy). This implies that the need for safety is an evolutionary adaptation mechanism that helps individuals cope with unexpected events and an uncertain environment (Zheng et al., 2016).

One well-supported hypothesis posits that when survival and sustenance are at risk individuals seek the means or material resources to ensure their safety and security. Kasser (2009) illustrates this by comparing modern economic security to ancestral practices: "Having a steady job and money in a savings account makes people feel more secure and thus fulfills the same needs that drove our ancestors to store dried meat for another long winter" (p. 29). This concept is reinforced by experimental studies that suggest that consumption and financial stability cater to both the physical and psychological need for safety. Research has shown that a higher income is associated with a greater capacity to secure one's own existence and to more effectively manage and control one's circumstances (Diener & Biswas-Diener, 2002; Howell & Hill, 2009). Moreover, individuals of lower socioeconomic status are often seen as having weaker internal systems for coping with threats due to their limited access to the necessary resources (Cummins, 1998). Empirical evidence supports this, demonstrating that increased income and reduced personal debt enhance feelings of physical safety and psychological existential security, which in turn increase overall subjective well-being (Howell et al., 2013).

However, beyond physical goods, nonmaterialistic means such as social ties, being able to make decisions, and a cognitively consistent environment can also serve the human need for safety (De Donder et al., 2012). Terror management theory (TMT) suggests that individuals are driven to create a secure and lasting environment to manage their mortality-related anxieties. This is achieved through a dual-component anxiety buffer that includes "(a) a cultural worldview – a humanly constructed symbolic conception of reality that imparts order, permanence, and stability, provides standards for achieving personal value, and offers hope for transcending death, either literally or symbolically, for those who adhere to these value standards; and (b) self-esteem, which is derived from the belief that one is meeting the value standards of one's cultural worldview" (Pyszczynski et al., 1997, p. 2). A real-life example of such an anxiety buffer is gun culture in the

United States. Guns are deeply embedded in U.S. cultural identity and are linked to personal freedom. Whether they are used for protection, hunting, or shooting sports, gun ownership allows individuals to defend themselves and control their environment, fostering a sense of personal security and existential safety (Lott, 2002). According to the PEW Research Center, two thirds of gun owners surveyed cite protection as their primary reason for owning a gun. The survey also indicates that particularly white, male, Republican-leaning adults in rural areas (often with lower levels of education) are more likely to own guns. Further, 91 percent of Republican gun owners view owning a gun as essential to their freedom and safety (Pew Research Center, 2017). The cultural theory of risk suggests that perceptions of threats are shaped by one's "cultural way of life". People in competitive, individualistic environments often believe they must protect themselves without relying on collective support or government assistance (Kahan, 2012; Celinska, 2007). Thus, gun ownership becomes a practical expression of self-reliance, meeting the psychological need for safety and "existential security".

The Existential Need for Control

Alongside the basic human need to feel safe and secure, the need for control is another crucial internal driver within the safety-seeking mechanism. Modern cognitive psychology suggests that individuals actively seek to understand their social environment and their role within it. They seek explanations for unexpected events and to understand how the social system works and their place in it. Believing that one can fully understand, influence, and manage a situation has profound implications for one's mental and physical health. Consequently, a perceived sense of control – regardless of its actual extent – significantly influences an individual's mental and physical well-being and assists in managing existential anxieties (Kluegel & Smith, 1986).

Individuals exert control over their environment by making decisions that reflect their preferences and affirm their agency. Having choices, even minor ones, strengthens one's perception of control and self-determination (Leotti et al., 2010). The more control a person feels they have over a situation, the less threatening they find that situation and the surrounding environment. Empirical studies show that humans and animals prefer choice over nonchoice, even if the choice option does not imply any improvement in the expected outcome. Economically, this preference for choice might seem irrational, but the potential to exercise control is intrinsically rewarding, leading to improved physical and psychological health (Steptoe & Appels, 1989), as well as increased confidence and self-efficacy. According to Leotti et al. (2010), "The benefits of perceived control can exist even in the absence of true control over aversive events, or if the individual has an opportunity to exert control but never actually exercises that option" (p. 459). Studies involving nursing home residents demonstrate that those given control over external factors, such as meal types and timing, or entertainment options, or who practiced internal self-control techniques, generally lived longer than those in the control group (Rodin & Langer, 1977; Pagnini et al., 2016). Similar findings in studies of cancer patients indicate that low perceived control and feelings of desperation about one's health can increase the likelihood of relapse and death (Shapiro Jr. et al., 1996).

The implication of the above is that a perceived lack of control tends to increase feelings of helplessness and self-uncertainty, which appear to predict reduced somatic and psychological functioning (Gebhardt & Brosschot, 2002). Studies involving both humans and animals have shown that when control is absent there is an increase in cortisol release, suppression of the immune system, and development of maladaptive behaviors. Experimental research indicates that removing the ability to exert control heightens anxiety, reinforces negative perceptions of the environment, and intensifies efforts to regain control (Leotti et al., 2010). These adverse effects are consistent across age groups, from four-month-old infants to seniors (Sullivan & Lewis, 2003). Therefore, the desire for control is considered a fundamental intrinsic motivation and one of the most vital human needs. The capacity to achieve and sustain a sense of control is crucial for evolutionary survival (Bandura, 1994; Ryan & Deci, 2006).

As a result, the threat of losing control increases levels of distress, which in turn prompt efforts to regain control. These efforts can manifest as conformity, aggression, violence, and changes in attitudes; if unsuccessful, they can lead to feelings of helplessness and withdrawal (Friedland et al., 1992). But cognitive strategies like self-blame or denial can also create a sense of control. Research indicates that individuals with lower incomes often attribute negative outcomes to their own shortcomings rather than to external factors. This approach helps them maintain a sense of personal control. Conversely, attributing negative outcomes to external, uncontrollable factors such as discrimination suggests that one does not have the ability to alter or influence one's environment and future results. Attributing outcomes to oneself, however, implies that one has the potential to influence future situations (Kluegel & Smith, 1986).

Being able to make choices and potentially influence future outcomes – even if those choices are illusory – impacts individuals' affective and cognitive processing. According to Leotti et al. (2010), "Although the affective experience of choice itself has not been examined directly, there is converging evidence that implicates a corticostriatal network as the neural substrate for perceiving control. The prefrontal cortex (PFC) and striatum are highly interconnected and have been consistently implicated in affective and motivational processes. Certain regions within this corticostriatal network explicitly code for actions that are most adaptive in a given context" (p. 460). This indicates that both animals and humans prefer to actively make choices rather than passively observe their interactions with the environment. The opportunity to make decisions engages the neural pathways associated with reward and cognitive processing. Neurocognitive studies have found that rewards resulting from choices activate the striatum more than identical rewards received passively (no-choice option). Participants reported higher perception of control over monetary outcomes when the choice option was available, which indicates that choice itself is inherently rewarding (Tricomi et al., 2004). Additionally, studies suggest that in stressful and threatening situations, perceived control can mitigate and regulate negative emotions. In these cases, even the mere perception of control, irrespective of actual control, can moderate negative emotional responses in threatening scenarios (Amat et al., 2005; Leotti et al., 2010; Leotti & Delgado, 2011). These findings demonstrate that the subjective perception of control – whether real or unreal – significantly influences the regulation of behavior, emotion, and physiology. Believing that one has control and the ability to affect future outcomes can provide palliative and rewarding effects, while a lack of control can lead to compensatory or maladaptive behaviors.

The Epistemic Need for Ambiguity Avoidance

Let us consider a scenario where a patient has to choose between two treatment options: Treatment A and Treatment B. Treatment A is a well-established method with extensive usage history, providing reliable data on the likelihood of various outcomes. Treatment B, on the other hand, is a newer method that has been little used, resulting in ambiguous information about its probable outcomes. While the success rate of Treatment A can be assessed based on historical frequencies or past events, Treatment B's effectiveness is not well-documented, leading to significant informational gaps. This scenario presents two distinct types of uncertainty: risk, or expected uncertainty, and ambiguity, or unexpected uncertainty. Risk involves situations where the probabilities are known or can be estimated from past data, as is the case with Treatment A. Ambiguity occurs when there is insufficient knowledge about potential outcomes, as is the case with Treatment B. This type of uncertainty can be mitigated by gathering more data, such as by increasing the number of observations or extending the period of study.

Ambiguity often intensifies when conditions shift to a novel state, where historical data are limited or nonexistent (O'reilly, 2013). Research across various fields indicates that people generally prefer betting on outcomes with known risks over those with ambiguous probabilities (Hsu et al., 2005), reflecting a common aversion to ambiguity. This behavior aligns with our example, in which most individuals would likely opt for Treatment A rather than Treatment B (Curley et al., 1986). Ambiguity can thus be defined as an unknown probability, that is, a decision-maker is aware of possible future events that may occur but does not have the appropriate information to make subjective estimates (Weber & Tan, 2012).

This leads to the question of why individuals strive to minimize or avoid ambiguous situations. Psychological research suggests that people often perceive ambiguous situations as threatening (Campbell & Tesser, 1983; Majid & Pragasam, 1997). Ambiguity involves complexity, novelty, and unpredictability, which induces certain cognitive, emotional, and behavioral reactions that enable individuals to cope with the unknown. Potential cognitive reactions may include the tendency to assess an ambiguous situation rigidly in black or white; emotionally, individuals may respond with discomfort, anger, or anxiety; and a typical behavioral reaction is avoidance or withdrawal (Grenier et al., 2005). The inclination to avoid completely unknown options viewed as potentially threatening is considered nearly as crucial as the instinct for survival itself. Neurocognitive research shows that in situations of uncertainty the brain becomes alert to the absence of necessary information. Decisions made with incomplete data are fraught with unknown and potentially hazardous consequences. In response to this, the amygdala processes the ambiguity by generating "fear signals" that prompt individuals to adapt and respond to threatening environmental stimuli (Payzan-LeNestour & Bossaerts, 2012).

The concept of intolerance of ambiguity, or the human need to avoid ambiguous situations, originated with Frenkel-Brunswik (1949), who described it as "a tendency to resort to black-white solutions, to arrive at premature closure as to evaluative aspects, often at the neglect of reality" (p. 115). While most scholars view intolerance of ambiguity as part of a set of subjective traits, some theories also consider external factors. These include the influence of vast amounts of information, time pressure, and uncertain situations, which can heighten perceptions of threat, leading to increased uncertainty and anxiety, a rejection of the unknown, and a preference for sticking to preconceived notions (Lauriola et al., 2016). Recent studies on ambiguity avoidance have revised this concept by focusing more on how people process information and make cognitive judgments. This redefinition emphasizes the desire for clear answers, the avoidance of uncertainty and confusion, and the tendency to use simpler cognitive structures for information processing, collectively described as the need for cognitive closure (Webster & Kruglanski, 1994).

As a dispositional trait, the need for cognitive closure expresses itself in the desire for predictability, order, and a stable cognitive framework. The process of processing vast amounts of information is viewed as costly (time-consuming) and effortful, potentially leading to uncertainty, confusion, and indecision (Webster & Kruglanski, 1997). However, the discussion presented in the above suggests that the inclination toward ambiguity avoidance can vary according to the specific situation. Various psychological experiments have shown that time pressure heightens people's reliance on preconceived notions and stereotype-based judgments and encourages them to base their decisions on initial impressions (Kruglanski & Freund, 1983; Sanbonmatsu & Fazio, 1990; Webster, 1993). This indicates that individuals with a great need for ambiguity avoidance are likely to make quicker judgments when processing information is challenging and demanding. Additionally, reliance on stereotypes can also occur when information is inconsistent, which might even lead to the source of information being dismissed.

While there are numerous instances in economic experiments of individuals seeking or even paying for irrelevant information (Powdthavee & Riyanto, 2015), there is also evidence to suggest that people often prefer to avoid receiving information (Golman et al., 2017). Research in both laboratory and field settings indicates that investors, for instance, tend not to check their financial portfolios when stock markets are down (Sicherman et al., 2016) and individuals with higher health risks may decline to have medical tests even if the information could enhance their decision-making (Golman et al., 2017). Although avoiding information can hinder the making of informed decisions and obtaining of valuable feedback, it can also yield positive effects in terms of utility.

Economic models of belief-based utility suggest that individuals not only derive utility from their actual circumstances but also from the information they receive about those circumstances (e.g.,Kőszegi, 2010; Caplin & Leahy, 2001;

Loewenstein & Molnar, 2018). Therefore, information avoidance can occur if individuals maintain favorable beliefs about their reality that they prefer not to challenge (Golman and Loewenstein, 2018). According to Golman et al. (2017), "A number of studies in both psychology and economics find that people weigh and interpret evidence in ways that support their desired beliefs, and they tend to dismiss the quality of evidence that contradicts their current or desired beliefs" (p. 101). Consequently, individuals often choose to reject information that could induce feelings of ambiguity, anxiety, uncertainty, or suggest a high likelihood of negative future outcomes. For instance, learning about one's poor health may increase the potential benefits of receiving medical treatment at a later stage, but it can also cause disutility by creating uncertainty about one's lifestyle and personal identity.

The Epistemic Need for Consistency

Research on cognitive consistency first appeared in the psychological literature in the 1950s and was initially described using various terms such as "balance", "dissonance", "symmetry", and "congruency". These concepts shared the underlying idea that "the person tends to behave in ways that minimize the internal inconsistency among his interpersonal relations, among his intrapersonal cognitions, or among his beliefs, feelings, and actions" (McGuire, 1966, p. 1). One of the seminal theories in this field is Festinger (1957) theory of cognitive dissonance, which argues that cognitive inconsistencies create a state of arousal (dissonance) that compels an individual to reduce these contradictions and restore harmony or consonance (Gawronski, 2012). Inconsistencies may occur when an individual holds multiple related but contradictory pieces of knowledge (ideas, beliefs, values), leading to a cognitive conflict between established beliefs and new information or evidence. This conflict can produce feelings of uncertainty, anxiety, self-doubt, and confusion. To alleviate these negative emotions and resolve contradictions between personal perceptions and new evidence, individuals often adjust their cognitions (McGuire, 1966). The need for consistency is considered as fundamental as the need for survival and water because it identifies potential "errors" in one's belief system that might necessitate reassessment. These "errors", or inconsistencies, require a reassessment of one's beliefs, since cognitive inconsistency may disrupt context-appropriate behavior and lead to inadequate courses of action. Thus, the state of arousal that is triggered by inconsistencies serves as a signal that one's current belief system has to be revised in order to deal with the environment (Gawronski, 2012).

However, there is an extensive body of research that suggests that the primary motive is not necessarily to restore consistency but rather to address the negative emotional outcomes that arise from these inconsistencies (Kruglanski & Shteynberg, 2012). Newly acquired information may be perceived as threatening when it contradicts existing beliefs and attitudes. Therefore, individuals might tolerate inconsistencies because resolving them could require significant cognitive effort or even a change in attitude (Kluegel & Smith, 1986). Empirical studies have found that people often rely on stereotypes or heuristics rather than fully engaging with all the relevant information to achieve consistency in their beliefs and opinions (Degner & Wentura, 2010). In seeking efficient and quick solutions to discrepancies, or using categorization methods, individuals manage inconsistencies without necessarily challenging their prevailing beliefs and attitudes. Instead of addressing the cognitive arousal caused by these inconsistencies, people may choose to dismiss it, relying on preconceived explanations to justify their views. Additionally, individuals might discard information that causes cognitive inconsistencies by ignoring or discrediting the source of the information.

Empirical research demonstrates that individuals generally prefer information that aligns with their existing attitudes, beliefs, and actions rather than information that contradicts them (Schulz-Hardt et al., 2000; Jonas et al., 2001). For instance, consider a habitual smoker who learns that smoking is detrimental to health. Theoretically, this smoker might try to reduce the dissonance by altering their behavior to align with the new information by either quitting or reducing the amount they smoke. However, in reality, people often employ alternative strategies to mitigate cognitive dissonance. This might include a smoker dismissing the information about smoking being harmful or seeking out supportive facts or opinions to justify their behavior (Festinger, 1957).

Finding alternatives in order to eliminate contradictions and reach cognitive consistency is part of the self-affirming and image-maintaining approach. The goal of the rationalization and justification process is to maintain overall self-integrity. Faced with a threat to one's self, the subject can also accept the threat without countering it by instead emphasizing some other important aspects of their self. A habitual smoker, for example, having realized that each type of rationalization for their smoking is socially disqualified still copes with the cognitive arousal and self-threat by emphasizing other personal traits, for example, a strong work ethic, to sustain their sense of self-worth. Personality research postulates that individuals with high self-esteem and a positive self-image feel less threatened by dissonant information and thus feel less pressure to rationalize the self-implications of this perceived threat (Steele et al., 1993).

However, external factors, such as violent assaults, conflicts, natural disasters, or terrorist attacks, all of which threaten individuals' physical and psychological existence, tend to "shatter" fundamental assumptions about oneself and a consistent and reliable environment (Janoff-Bulam, 1992). The self is perceived as helpless and fragile, the environment as dangerous and life-threatening. Such a cognitive disturbance or "disconnection" from oneself and the environment gives rise to anxiety and can lead to serious mental disorders (Edmondson et al., 2011). After such threatening events, individuals tend to engage in strategies to decrease their accrued negative feelings and resolve the inconsistencies between their own perception and acquired evidence (Janoff-Bulam, 1992). Having consistent beliefs, views, or assumptions about oneself and the environment helps individuals to better cope with threatening situations, to interact with and adapt to the external environment, and to make fast and (self-)consistent decisions. Individuals need a stable and reliable conceptual system to deal with the complex world and thus strive to maintain cognitive consistency.

The Epistemic Need for Predictability

Early theories of the need for predictability were introduced in the psychological literature during the 1950s (Pervin, 1963). Predictability refers to understanding the conditions under which certain events will occur and the characteristics of those events. To gain this understanding, individuals actively gather information. Experimental research has demonstrated that both animals and humans prefer having information about the onset of aversive stimuli, even if the information itself does not alter the outcome. The ability to anticipate potential events alleviates stress by enabling both humans and nonhumans to foresee important aspects of a situation, thereby enhancing their capacity to adapt to the circumstances (see Miller, 1979 for a review).

Further studies have indicated that the ability to self-administer and predict electric shocks – as opposed to having shocks administered unpredictably by an experimenter – diminishes stress and results in lower physiological arousal, as measured by galvanic skin response. Being able to anticipate shocks allows individuals to respond based on the significance of the stimuli. Conversely, the inability to predict shocks increases the perceived significance of all stimuli. Therefore, having predictable information about events can significantly support individuals in appropriately responding to and managing stressful situations, reducing feelings of helplessness, cognitive strain, and confusion (Staub et al., 1971).

Social and personality psychologists suggest that individuals with a high need for predictability are more likely to adhere to social norms and rules, which provide a structured framework for behavior and social interactions (Kiesler, 1973). Those who deviate from established norms or do not conform to predefined social roles are often seen as threatening and are likely to be ostracized by those who value predictability. An empirical study conducted with community samples from the United Kingdom and Belgium (Makwana et al., 2018) found that individuals with a pronounced need for predictability, order, and cognitive closure are more likely to reject those who diverge from conventional social behaviors and roles, such as gender norms. Particularly, those who are obedient tend to strictly follow social rules, respect authority, and support traditional gender roles and social hierarchies. A social environment characterized by predictable and clearly defined roles offers a sense of certainty and order, shaping how individuals process incoming stimuli and perceive others. The findings from the study indicate that individuals who favor such structured social environments tend to dismiss those viewed as violating societal norms and gender expectations. This rejection stems from their reliance on cognitively consistent and predictable social frameworks (Makwana et al., 2018). This means that subjects' belief in a predictable environment increases their sense of order, safety, and control and provides guidance on how to perceive their social environment. Information, behavior, or norms that tend to violate their sense of order and predictability are thus perceived as a threat and become subject to disaffirmation.

A neurocognitive study utilizing functional magnetic resonance imaging (fMRI) demonstrated that predictability can activate the human brain's reward system. In the experimental design, participants were given small amounts of water and juice orally in either a predictable or unpredictable sequence. In the predictable sequence, the order of juice and water alternated at a consistent ten-second interval, whereas in the unpredictable sequence both the order and the timing of the stimuli were randomized. Post-scanning, subjects were asked to express their preferences for either water or juice. The findings revealed that activity within the reward system was more strongly correlated with the predictability of the sequence of these pleasurable stimuli than with the participants' expressed preferences. The brain's response to the preferred beverage showed minimal differential activity compared to the nonpreferred beverage, indicating that the main effect of predictability was more significant than that of stated preference (Berns et al., 2001). Another study provides evidence that individuals search for predictability in the shape of rules that govern decision-making even in the presence of randomness (Paulus et al., 2001). A common claim in neuroscience is that the brain actively predicts upcoming stimuli in order to code information efficiently. The predictability of sensory input alters the processing of upcoming stimuli and is efficient "in the sense that the brain does not need to maintain multiple versions of the same information at different levels of processing hierarchy" (De-Wit et al., 2010, p. 8702). Consequently, predictable stimuli require less neural activation to be transferred from lower to higher cortices and thus influence the representation of the subjective experience of the stimuli.

A study by Carlsson et al. (2006) discovered that identical pain stimuli are perceived as more painful when unpredictable compared to when they are predictable. Unpredictable pain stimuli lead to heightened ratings of anxiety and uncertainty, while predictability allows subjects to formulate responses to external aversive events. Anticipating pain reduces its perceived threat and facilitates appropriate preemptive behaviors (adaptation). Essentially, predicting incoming pain creates a subjective certainty about the imminent occurrence of a negative event, enabling the organism to "prepare" and adjust. The activation of fear responses mobilizes the organism to take action (fight, flight, or freeze) or, if infeasible, to minimize the impact of the stimuli through mechanisms such as cognitive distraction (Ploghaus et al., 2003).

These insights suggest that predictability enables individuals to "effectively" process incoming information and mentally adapt to circumstances, even if they cannot be avoided. It fosters subjective certainty and a perception of control over the situation. The ability to anticipate future events or incoming information reduces the perception of threat and stress by allowing individuals to foresee crucial aspects of a situation. This, in turn, provides existential safety, as individuals "know" when the next negative stimuli will occur, thereby reducing cognitive overload from constantly evaluating incoming stimuli.

The Epistemic Need for Order

Cognitive psychologists assume that individuals strive to order everyday stimuli, information, and experiences into coherent units in order to establish meaning and consistence in their lives (Baumeister, 1991, 2005). From an evolutionary perspective, this would imply that structuring incoming stimuli into coherent units helps to avoid danger and makes the world more manageable. This enables individuals to determine which stimuli in the environment are pleasurable (and thus species-promoting) and which are troublesome.

Organizing the environment into coherent meaning reduces uncertainty and self-doubt and generates a sense of control. This, in turn, helps to reduce the feeling of living in a random universe, which is essential for avoiding feelings of helplessness and uncontrollability (Thompson et al., 2001). However, the psychological literature also assumes that individuals differ in terms of their need for order and structure. An individual with a great need for structure and order prefers a structural categorization of the social environment, clarity in most situations, and reduced ambiguity (Neuberg & Newsom, 1993). To them, an ordered environment is a place where they can make consistent decisions and act confidently. Accordingly, such individuals dislike unpredictable environments or other individuals who do not conform to the predefined social order or who even disturb or threaten established settings. They are thus rejected in an effort to protect the certainty and stability provided by the established order (e.g., Brandt & Reyna, 2010).

Personality studies using the personal need for structure (PNS) scale have shown that individuals who have a great need for structure tend to apply stereotypes and rely on social categories to make judgments and decisions. Furthermore, they are more likely to apply predefined attitudes and beliefs to new situations, to rely on stereotypical notions to evaluate other people, and to have simpler ways of organizing social information (Moskowitz, 1993; Schaller et al., 1995). Behaviorally, such individuals establish daily routines and rely on predefined roles and schemata, or even prefer hierarchical structures, that reduce the amount of information they have to process on a daily basis. Such a cognitive order enables individuals to draw inferences about new events and thus to understand the world without expending a lot of cognitive resources (Neuberg & Newsom, 1993). These individual differences in the need for order show that individuals strive to understand their social environment and find coping mechanisms so they can deal with complexity and indeterminacy.

A very prominent and often-cited example in this regard is that individuals form beliefs about the society and environment they live in because it provides guidance on how to perceive and evaluate information, people, events, and experiences. In the United States, for example, individuals generally believe that one gets what one deserves (Lerner, 1980). When this "cognitive order" is violated, individuals tend to assimilate the event to restore cognitive consistency (e.g., blaming victims for their own misfortune). The deservingness principle has been examined in various studies, which show that the subjective manifestation of the need for order has an impact on how individuals react to penalties that are imposed if someone commits an offense (Feather, 2006). The study shows that individuals' need for order and an offender's perceived responsibility ultimately determine the degree to which the offense is perceived as serious (Feather, 1996). Hence, individuals with a greater need for order may assess a crime or offense more strictly because they perceive it as a violation of legitimate authority such as the rule of law or social order (Rozin et al., 1999).

However, according to Van den Bos and Maas (2009), "when people are confronted with others (such as innocent victims) who get something they do not deserve, people's principles of deservingness are violated. As a result, people need to restore their belief that the world is a just place in which good things happen to good people and bad things to bad people. Especially when the events that have happened cannot be changed, people often tend to come to the conclusion that victims somehow deserved their ill fates and are to be blamed for what happened to them" (p. 1567). Some psychological researchers claim that when individuals are confronted with such ambivalence or cognitive inconsistency the need for order becomes affirming (Van Harreveld et al., 2014). This need can be served, for instance, by social hierarchies that reflect a form of social structure and interpersonal organization. Empirical studies show that after external shocks, such as economic crises or terrorist attacks, individuals tend to adhere more strongly to hierarchy-promoting social structures because they provide order, certainty, and consistency in their lives (Friesen et al., 2014). Giving the world a simplified and manageable form reduces threats and generates the illusion of a controllable environment.

Further empirical studies provide evidence that individuals with a strong need for order/structure are more likely to organize information in simpler ways and to apply previously formed social categories (e.g., stereotypes) to new and ambiguous situations (Neuberg & Newsom, 1993). Relying on such predefined social categories generates a clear, predictable, and unambiguous environment and provides guidance on how to process information and make decisions. Especially in traditional and hierarchical social settings, prescribed rules, norms, roles, and beliefs present a strict order that provides information about who should be doing what, about interpersonal patterns, and about one's role in the social system. This means that hierarchies appear to provide a cognitive sense of order and structure, especially for low-status individuals, who appear to have a low sense of personal control (Friesen et al., 2014). Order is generated by restrictions, obligations, prescribed roles, norms, and rules that dictate what kind of behaviors are permitted or prohibited. This social order implies certain expectations and actions that guide appropriate social behavior (Cummins, 2000). One neurocognitive study found that hierarchically induced order tends to reduce uncertainty and stressful responses to threat, providing instead predictable and reliable guidance on how to process information and act in a given setting (Timmer et al., 2011).

All these findings imply that an established cognitive or social order helps individuals to restore structure and meaning in their lives. It provides guidance on how to behave and evaluate information and on how to perceive oneself and others (cognitively ordered categories). Moreover, it reduces uncertainty and increases one's sense of personal control and (ordered) existence, especially for those who feel socially low-ranked, but not only for them.

4.2 Relational Needs

Beyond existential and epistemic needs, human beings possess fundamental needs related to relationships, identity, and the social self. Identity and group belonging are crucial for understanding how individuals make decisions, interact with others, and perceive themselves within a social context. Identity economics, a relatively new field within economics, provides a framework for analyzing subjective decision-making where an individual's identity serves as the primary motivation for choice (Akerlof & Kranton, 2010).

Identity, which encompasses one's self-conception and aspirational self, shapes everyday decisions and defines social categories. These identities influence decisions because different norms governing behavior are associated with different social categories. For instance, a woman may view herself as a mother at home but as a professional at work, with these distinct social categories influencing her self-perception at any given time. Each social category carries specific norms and ideals that, in turn, affect her preferences and decision-making. "Identity utility" refers to the gain or loss experienced when subjective actions either conform to or deviate from these norms. This utility changes not only based on personal choices but also because of the choices made by others. Thus, identity economics posits that individuals have personal tastes in their utility functions, while social norms, internalized through social interactions, also play a significant role (Akerlof & Kranton, 2010). Consequently, subjective motivations, attitudes, beliefs, and behaviors are largely shaped by the nature of one's social interactions (Cilliers, 2010).

Subjective decision-making is not only influenced by individual preferences but also by internalized social norms and values. These social norms provide a sense of belonging and guide individuals on how to behave within the social strata (Akerlof & Kranton, 2010).

Social bonds and attachments to others play a significant role for identity formation. Belonging to and identifying with a group provide certainty, stability, order, and orientation in life. They shape how individuals perceive themselves and their social environment and generate a sense of acceptance and self-significance. The absence of emotional and interactive relationships, whether during early childhood, adolescence, or adulthood, can have devastating consequences for one's development, health, and mental well-being. Social relationships are crucial in helping individuals overcome threatening situations, external stressors, and personal failures.

Individuals define themselves through group membership, with the norms and values of that group influencing their behavior, decision-making, thought processes, and information processing. Social identification underpins various forms of social interaction, including empathy, reciprocity, trust, and mutual commitment. Belonging to a social group is fundamental for self-formation, assimilation, differentiation, orientation, and stability. Social approval shapes and reinforces individuals' self-image, self-assurance, and self-esteem. A stable identity is vital for managing and combating threatening situations, being self-aware and self-reflective, making consistent choices, and maintaining cohesion in the face of change. These insights suggest that human beings have fundamental relational needs for identification, social belonging, and social approval that are essential for forming stable, positive, and coherent identities. Social groups serve individuals' relational needs by providing sources of identification, belonging, and approval. Accordingly, individuals define and perceive themselves in terms of group membership, and they form social categories and strive for in-group positivity – a positive (and potentially biased) evaluation of one's own group that reflects on oneself.

While relational needs are universal across all human beings and cultures, the manifestation of these needs varies among individuals. The following discussion addresses the universality and significance of the relational need for identification, belonging, and social approval.

The Relational Need for Identification

Individuals strive to develop both personal and social identities by defining and evaluating themselves in group terms. This process involves associating oneself with others and adopting their characteristics or attitudes: An infant identifies with parents; an adolescent gradually adopts the views and traits of their peer group; and an adult may identify with a particular profession or political party. Such identification and affiliation significantly influence how individuals perceive themselves and their environment, as well as how they interact with others. Generally, individuals aim to portray their own in-group in a positive and distinct manner, engaging in intergroup comparisons to differentiate their in-group from out-groups. A positive conception of one's group enhances self-esteem (Koomen & Van Der Pligt, 2015). Moreover, identifying with a group, along with its shared norms, values, worldviews, attitudes, and symbols, fosters feelings of certainty and stability. This sense of stability and certainty, in turn, provides orientation and confidence when it comes to behavior, evaluations, and expectations of the social environment.

Conversely, uncertainty about oneself, attitudes, behavior, values, and perceptions diminishes the sense of a stable and controlled environment (Fiske & Taylor, 1991). Uncertainty-reduction theories suggest that individuals seek to identify with well-defined, consistent, and stable groups to gain orientation and certainty in their lives. Empirical studies support this view, showing that individuals with strong self-doubts and self-uncertainty tend to identify more strongly with their in-group and value it more highly than those with a certain self-concept. In other words, individuals are more likely to identify strongly with a social category if they feel uncertain about aspects relevant to their self-definition (Hogg, 2000).

From an evolutionary perspective, identifying with a group and adhering to its norms, values, and rules are essential for securing individual survival, reducing intragroup conflict, and establishing cooperation and mutual reciprocity. Within a group, individuals learn to trust, interact, and evaluate themselves and their environment, with social identifiers providing a stable foundation for these processes. Trust fosters cooperation and enhances social behavior. Consequently, heightened social identification motivates individuals to contribute to the public good, thereby sustaining social welfare. Empirical studies have demonstrated that social identification positively impacts group members' contributions to the common good, with increased identification even mitigating selfish behavior. This suggests that "increasing the group salience encourages people who are normally only focused on their personal outcomes to make efforts in obtaining good outcomes for the group even when it runs against their direct self-interest" (De Cremer and Van Vugt, 1999, p. 887).

These theories and empirical findings, which have only been outlined here, demonstrate that the human need for identification is universal and transcultural – every individual, regardless of cultural background or external environment, has an inherent need to identify with social others. Identification enables individuals to develop their own identity, perceive and define themselves, and understand their social environment. It enhances subjective well-being and acts as a buffer against threatening and discriminatory events. Identification processes have significant intra- and intergroup implications. One's in-group serves as a crucial reference point in daily life, guiding self-evaluation, behavior, and information processing. Identifying with a particular group, whether defined by nationality, ethnicity, gender, or religion, shapes how individuals define themselves and their surroundings, interpret circumstances and events, and make decisions and form preferences. However, emphasizing the value of one's own group can also lead to in-group bias and the accentuation of intergroup differences, fostering "us-versus-them" attitudes.

In the following discussion, we examine how belonging to a social group – not just identifying with it – can have palliative effects, and why belongingness is a fundamental human need.

The Relational Need for Belongingness

Identifying as a member of a particular social group, recognizing intragroup similarities, and reassuring oneself of a shared identity and shared characteristics are foundational for group belongingness (Ashmore et al., 2004). Belonging to a social group and forming attachments and social bonds are innate human tendencies crucial for survival. The need to belong is the fundamental human desire to form close relationships and stable, reliable attachments (Baumeister & Leary, 1995). This need encompasses two important criteria: continuity and mutual interactions. Individuals strive for nonnegative, long-lasting interactions filled with mutual concern and empathy (Baumeister, 2012). According to Lambert et al. (2013), "[c]lose relationships offer a symbolic promise of lastingness and continuity that provide individuals with a sense of symbolic immortality. They allow people to feel part of a larger symbolic entity (e.g., couple or group) that transcends the limitations of their own body and expands the capacities and boundaries of their own self" (p. 1419). Group belongingness reduces self-uncertainty, provides stability, and enhances positive self-esteem. A social group offers a platform for sharing, communication, and affection, aiding individuals in forming a social identity and pursuing collective goals (Haslam et al., 2008).

From a biological and evolutionary perspective, humans build groups and communities to sustain their existence. Mutual cooperation, cohesion, and the exchange of goods, services, and knowledge were, and still are, essential for survival. Early hominids depended on secure bonds and information exchange to adapt to changing environments. This indicates that all humans are predisposed to form attachments and experience mental distress when social relationships dissolve. Forming and maintaining social relationships increase life satisfaction, happiness, and mental health (Carvallo & Gabriel, 2006).

Belongingness is also crucial for a sense of meaningful existence. Four studies indicate that being part of a group and having a strong sense of belonging enhance meaning in life and promote psychological health (Lambert et al., 2013). Failure to form close relationships can lead to feelings of isolation, alienation, and a lack of meaning in life. The absence of positive and stable interpersonal relationships often results in adverse emotions such as anxiety, depression, and mental distress. Isolation or exclusion from a group or society can have devastating effects on one's physical and mental well-being. Extensive research has shown that negative feelings of non-belonging can lead to antisocial behavior, crime, and violence (Sampson & Laub, 1993); substance abuse (Williams, 2007; Hales et al., 2015); poor academic performance; and a sense of lost control (Williams et al., 2000). Researchers suggest that individuals' self-esteem is closely tied to their sense of belonging (Baumeister, 2012). Strong self-esteem develops from social interactions and feelings of belonging and identification. These social experiences shape cognitive awareness of the self in relation to others. Continuous and stable relationships provide individuals with a social lens through which they perceive the world, determine how to behave, and evaluate information.

As a result, people with high levels of social belongingness tend to be more confident in their evaluations and perceptions. These "backup" resources increase their self-esteem and interpersonal trust, enabling them to manage negative emotions and experiences more effectively (Lee & Robbins, 1998).

However, research also indicates that it is not merely social contact that is crucial but rather the presence of stable, continuous, and positive relationships that provide a buffer against stress and loneliness. Continuity, reliability, affection, and stability are essential to fulfilling the need for belongingness. Interaction, mutuality, and interdependence are hallmarks of close, affectionate relationships that provide a social compass (Baumeister & Leary, 1995). Such stable and reliable relationships foster the formation of social trust, a significant condition for a harmonious society. Economic studies support this notion, showing that a sense of group belongingness, solidarity, and cohesion influences individuals' willingness to adhere to social norms and contribute to social welfare. Feelings of belonging to a particular group or nation shape how individuals make choices, perceive their environment, and decide how to consume and invest (Sen, 2017). Acceptance and approval by friends, colleagues, or society motivate individuals to sustain these positive conditions. People work, consume, and obey social norms in order to be liked and approved by others, thereby maintaining a stable socioeconomic status. Compliance with group norms is rational as it helps coordinate actions, exchange information, and fosters cooperation (Chong, 2000; Chiotis, 2015).

The formation of social networks and interpersonal relationships enables individuals to share values, manage resources, build trust, and invest in the future. Social capital, defined as the aggregate of social networks, is thus indispensable for economic development and civic engagement (Putman, 1993). Overall, the theories and empirical findings presented here provide evidence that the need for belongingness is fundamental and universal. It is essential for sustaining human existence and facilitating cooperation, interaction, and trust.

Individuals who feel they belong to a group or society are more willing to behave prosocially and invest resources to maintain and enhance social welfare. However, mere belonging is not sufficient to enhance cooperation and prosocial behavior. Individuals also need acceptance and approval from their group or society for their distinct personality, characteristics, and abilities.

The Relational Need for Social Approval

The need for social approval corresponds to the desire for validation and appreciation from important others regarding one's personality, actions, and achievements. Social approval is crucial not only for each individual but also for social interactions. An economic model proposed by Holländer (1990) suggests that individual cooperative behavior not only depends on material gain but also on the strength of the approval incentive. This model posits that subjective preferences derive utility not only from private and public goods but also from social approval, which can significantly influence cooperative behavior in social dilemmas. Empirical research partially supports the idea that social approval or social punishment can affect cooperative behavior, the efficiency of teamwork, and decision-making in various contexts. Unlike purely economic exchanges, social exchanges involve the exchange of social rewards, which are not based on contractual obligations but are instead expressed through spontaneous positive or negative emotions. One notable example of the impact of social (dis)approval is the recruitment of volunteer soldiers during World War I. The British government used large-scale posters to convey the idea that nonparticipation was akin to free-riding and that such behavior would be socially disapproved and despised by British society (Gächter & Fehr, 1999).

Public disapproval and loss of social reputation are significant threats to individuals' social identity disapproval from loved ones or people with whom one frequently interacts is often more hurtful and threatening than disapproval from strangers (Grasmick & Green, 1980). Related experiments demonstrate that indirect social approval – such as the belief that someone dislikes one's behavior – can incite cooperation in public good games (Rege & Telle, 2004). Additionally, the awareness of being observed by others tends to enhance prosocial behavior (Kurzban et al., 2007; Bateson et al., 2006). Even a random, costless opportunity to approve or disapprove of another's decisions significantly increases contributions (Masclet et al., 2003). A study using fMRI examined the neural correlates of reward valuations when individuals decided whether or not to donate money in the presence or absence of observers. The presence of observers increased participants' willingness to donate, which was associated with increased activation in the ventral striatum. High striatal activations were particularly notable when a high social reward was expected (observed donation), as well as when there was an opportunity for personal enrichment without social costs (self-enrichment in the absence of observers). Among those who chose to donate, activation in the left striatum was significantly higher when the donations were observed. This suggests that the extrinsic reward of social approval is processed in the same striatal region as monetary rewards. Both social and monetary rewards thus enhance individuals' subjective utility (Izuma et al., 2010).

These findings suggest that social approval significantly enhances individuals' willingness to invest in and sustain their social communities, encouraging cooperative and prosocial behavior to ensure future positive appraisal. Acceptance of one's identity, choices, thoughts, and beliefs not only provides self-assurance but also positively impacts mental health. Conversely, societal or group rejection and disapproval profoundly affect individuals' mental well-being.

4.3 Agency Needs

Social identity theory, as described in the previous section, demonstrates that belonging to and identifying with a particular group – defined by nationality, ethnicity, gender, profession, or sport affiliation – shape individuals' perception of themselves and their environment (Tajfel, 1981). People not only derive their self-esteem and self-confidence from their personal characteristics but also from their membership of a particular group. This means that individuals form perceptions, attitudes, and preferences based on their affiliations with important others. They make choices and act in accordance with the shared group identity, values, and norms to receive social approval and feel accepted and included. To better understand how individuals make choices and shift their preferences under given conditions, it is essential to delve into both interpersonal and intrapersonal processes. Interpersonal processes involve interactions, events, and feelings between two or more individuals through which a person learns to interact with others and form social relationships. Intrapersonal factors operate within the individual, including the formation of an agent self, self-esteem, and self-perception. Individuals' behaviors, preferences, and choices are clearly influenced by both social-contextual (interpersonal) and self-conceptual (intrapersonal) factors (Moller et al., 2006).

The previous chapter focused on interpersonal, social-contextual factors, leading us to explore how intrapersonal factors matter – specifically, the impact of the agent self on subjective decision-making, attitudes, preferences, and behavior. In this regard, the self is perceived as the source of agency and regulation, meaning that individuals attribute the source of their perceptions, attitudes, thoughts, and actions to themselves (their body, mind, and abilities).

The Agency Need for Self-esteem

Self-esteem is considered one of the central and most important aspects of an individual's self-concept (Baumeister, 1993). The term refers to the assessment of one's worth and can be defined as "a self-reflexive attitude that is the product of viewing the self as an object of evaluation" (Campbell and Lavallee, 1993, p. 4). By this definition, individuals evaluate their qualities and characteristics, which are part of their self-concept, in a self-reflective manner. Self-esteem encompasses an individual's physical self-image, their view of their capabilities and achievements, values and beliefs, and their perceived success in living in coherence with them. The more positive the cumulative evaluation of the self-concept, the higher the self-esteem (Campbell, 1990).

Individuals generally strive for a positive self-evaluation and want to think well of themselves. Studies show that individuals aim to form consistent self-beliefs and often reject information that contradicts these beliefs, such as negative feedback (Slotter et al., 2015). Research also reveals that individuals alter their self-evaluations to maintain their self-esteem when it is threatened (Greenberg & Pyszczynski, 1985). For instance, people tend to underestimate or overestimate their performance, especially when it is relevant to their self-concept. When individuals perform poorly on a self-related task, they tend to overestimate the number of others who also performed poorly. Conversely, when they perform well, they tend to underestimate the number of others who also performed well (Campbell, 1986). Favorable self-beliefs and a positive self-evaluation enhance happiness and mental well-being and can predict a variety of positive outcomes, such as better adjustment to the environment, improved coping with life challenges, and even better physical health (Leary & MacDonald, 2003). Self-esteem also influences how individuals perceive themselves and their social environment, providing a foundation for information processing and behavior (Stinson et al., 2010). Thus, psychological research suggests that high self-esteem is essential for healthy psychological functioning.

One fundamental question that has been extensively debated across disciplines is why individuals vary in their levels of self-esteem. Psychological research consistently finds that individuals with low self-esteem do not invariably possess negative self-views; rather, their descriptions of themselves are often neutral (Tice, 1993). These individuals tend to have greater needs for certainty and ambiguity avoidance. They act to minimize potential losses, avoid risky choices and behaviors, set unchallenging goals to avoid failure, and are motivated to protect themselves from possible threats (Tennen & Affleck, 1993). While many researchers agree that individuals with low self-esteem appear more sensitive and reactive to their social environment (e.g., Campbell & Lavallee, 1993), they also note that high self-esteem individuals can exhibit high levels of instability. This means that individuals can have high self-esteem but still reflect fragility in their positive self-feelings and self-beliefs (Greenier et al., 1995). These fluctuations are particularly observed in individuals who base their self-worth heavily on evaluative information, whether externally received or internally generated, which can be inconsistent. In other words, the more individuals rely on information about themselves to determine their self-worth, the more likely these feelings are to fluctuate.

Another factor that contributes to unstable self-esteem is a poorly developed self-concept. It is argued that an inconsistent and fragile self-concept leads to greater susceptibility to evaluative information. This means that the less individuals know about their own characteristics, strengths, weaknesses, preferences, etc., the less stable their feelings of self-esteem may be. If unstable self-esteem is associated with a poorly defined self-concept, it should also reflect diminished functional flexibility and increased dependence on external events. This implies a decreased capacity to adjust easily to various situations, as individuals are less sure about their own capabilities and self-image, and depend more on situational information to form beliefs and perceptions of themselves (Dunlop, 2017).

The Agency Need for Self-determination/Autonomy

Self-determination is a concept that is widely debated across various academic disciplines. While the philosophical discourse often revolves around whether human behavior is predetermined or a result of free will, psychology focuses more on the internal and external factors that influence human behavior. One of the most influential contributions to the understanding of self-determination comes from psychologists Edward Deci and Richard Ryan (Deci & Ryan, 1986, 2008, 2012). In his early writings, Deci (1980) argued that self-determination is a fundamental human need to feel competent and autonomous, enabling individuals to use their will to choose how to fulfill their own needs and preferences. Self-determination theory posits that human beings are active organisms, motivated to adapt and integrate their experiences, knowledge, and abilities within their environment (Deci & Ryan, 2012). The theory emphasizes intrinsic, autonomous motivation as essential for healthy psychological adjustment and highlights the negative consequences that can arise when individuals are deprived of the ability to act autonomously or perceive themselves as driven mainly by external forces or rewards (Shogren et al., 2017).

Various empirical studies provide evidence that satisfying the need for autonomy enhances subjective mental well-being and supports the development of a consistent and stable self-concept. A true self develops when individuals act autonomously and consistently according to their own preferences, and when they are socially accepted for who they are rather than for conforming to external requirements. Acting freely according to one's own preferences, desires, and attitudes fosters the development of a genuine and consistent sense of self, as well as a stronger sense of self-worth. Autonomy is both a contributor to and a manifestation of high and stable self-esteem (Deci & Ryan, 1995). Conversely, when individuals feel obligated to conform to certain roles or social standards, and thus feel compelled to relinquish their autonomy and true sense of self, their self-concept becomes contingent on adhering to these imposed roles or rules. Clinical studies have shown that deprivation of the need for autonomy – meaning the lack or denial of resources or opportunities to fulfill this need – can result in personality or behavioral disorders.

Economic studies examine the relationship between socioeconomic factors and individuals' subjective sense of autonomy. They suggest that socioeconomically disadvantaged individuals often hold physically demanding jobs with limited opportunities to express autonomy and have fewer resources to make choices aligned with their needs and desires (Poleshuck & Green, 2008). Limited access to socially valuable resources that enable individuals to fulfill their needs and make autonomous decisions is perceived as hindering the development of self-regulatory mechanisms essential for managing various life tasks and challenges. In other words, a lack of environmental support and opportunities to make decisions based on personal preferences and goals can negatively affect individuals' psychological and physical well-being (Shogren et al., 2017; Rouse et al., 2011).

During adolescence, in particular, individuals require environmental support and opportunities to develop a stable self-concept and a positive self-view. Experiencing oneself as the originator of actions and decisions reinforces self-worth and boosts self-confidence (Hansen & Jessop, 2017). Developmental psychologists, therefore, emphasize that self-determination is achieved when individuals identify and pursue goals based on a thorough understanding and appreciation of themselves (Field & Hoffman, 1994).

However, cross-cultural psychologists emphasize that the manifestation and endorsement of autonomy (or self-determination) differ across cultures to varying degrees. Self-determination is often viewed as being characteristic of individualistic Western societies, which promote subjective independence rather than social interdependence. Thus, the need for autonomy is sometimes seen as conflicting with the need for belongingness and interdependence, both of which are highly valued in collectivistic societies. However, others argue that the need for autonomy is universal and present in all humans but may be expressed differently across cultures. In collectivistic cultures, the need for autonomy can be met through the internalization of choices made by significant others. For instance, a study of Chinese children found that those who had a close relationship with their mother showed less need for autonomy yet remained intrinsically motivated to complete tasks chosen by their mothers. By contrast, autonomy was a crucial factor for children without close relationships. The authors concluded that the importance of freedom of choice diminished in the context of an intimate and positive relationship (Bao & Lam, 2008). Another study involving Chinese students revealed that the need for autonomy was strongly linked to the need for belongingness, indicating that more autonomous support from parents enhanced the students' sense of connection with their parents (Hui et al., 2011).

The researchers involved in the former study posited that "the issue of autonomy is concerned with the extent to which one fully accepts, endorses, or stands behind one's actions. If Chinese children have internalized the choices made by trusted others, they might experience autonomy even if they did not make the choice" (Bao and Lam, 2008, p. 280). Individuals who base their self-concept on interdependent relationships perceive themselves as part of a social system and may thus regard close individuals as extensions of their own selves (Markus & Kitayama, 1991). These findings and assumptions suggest that the need for autonomy is a fundamental human need that persists across different cultures and values.

The Agency Need for Self-efficacy

The previous sections emphasized that the development of a true, stable, and consistent self is fostered by acting autonomously, being accepted for who one is (feeling a sense of belonging and approval from important others), and learning to appreciate and understand one's own capabilities, skills, attitudes, and preferences.

Another significant aspect of true self-development is the ability to experience an inner sense of self-efficacy, which is the perception of one's capacity to create, achieve, and produce something of personal significance and attain desired results. Individuals strive to feel competent, make effective decisions, solve problems, and overcome challenges (Gecas, 1989). Bandura (1977), Bandura (1986), the pioneer of self-efficacy theory, postulates that self-efficacy is the primary determinant of behavioral change and successful environmental adjustment. He distinguishes between efficacy expectations and outcome expectations. An efficacy expectation is the subjective belief that one is capable of successfully performing an action, while an outcome expectation is the estimate that an action will lead to a desired result. The former is a belief about one's own competence, while the latter is a belief about one's environment. Bandura argues that this distinction is crucial in understanding feelings of frustration and powerlessness, which can stem either from a low sense of self-efficacy or from a lack of responsiveness in one's social environment (e.g., lack of opportunities, lack of social support). To decrease efficacy-based feelings of meaninglessness, individuals need to develop their abilities and awareness of their personal effectiveness. Addressing outcome-based feelings of meaninglessness requires changes in the prevailing environmental structures, such as reducing social barriers and increasing social support.

The concept of self-efficacy has been expanded to refer more broadly to the subjective belief in one's capacity to mobilize resources to achieve specific outcomes. Self-efficacy judgments, in this context, are not about the skills one possesses but rather about evaluating what can be accomplished with those skills and resources. In this process, individuals assess, weigh, and integrate information from various sources regarding their capabilities (such as skills, resources, knowledge, etc.) and regulate their choices, actions, and effort expenditure accordingly. In experiments, self-efficacy expectancy has been observed as a viable and reliable measure for assessing an individual's likelihood of achieving certain outcomes. For example, one study demonstrated that the best predictor of a smoker's success in quitting is their self-efficacy expectancy. This means that assessing a smoker's perception of their own ability and determination to quit smoking under specific environmental conditions provides better predictive results than measuring their self-esteem or self-confidence (Maddux, 1995). An individual who believes they can abstain from smoking or other drugs – and thus achieve a desired outcome using their personal resources – is more likely to lead an active and self-determined life (Ilgen et al., 2005).

Stronger feelings of self-efficacy can significantly influence one's behavior, actions, and value priorities. When individuals believe they have the ability to achieve specific outcomes and effect change, they are more willing to act and adapt to their environment. Thus, self-efficacy plays a crucial role in psychological adjustment. Studies show that individuals with low self-efficacy are more likely to suffer from depression, as they often doubt their ability to behave effectively and reach desired outcomes. Low self-efficacy is also linked to dysfunctional anxiety and avoidant behavior. Individuals who lack confidence in their abilities are more likely to avoid difficult and stressful situations, and they tend to react with greater uncertainty and anxiety when faced with threats and unpredictability. Conversely, individuals with high self-efficacy are better equipped to manage threatening and uncertain situations and tend to react more calmly to stress and unexpected events (for a review, see Maddux, 2002).

There is also a long and rich tradition in sociology when it comes to dealing with self-efficacy. When individuals have the opportunity to create or achieve something of subjective significance, their sense of self is formed and affirmed. By contrast, individuals who feel estranged and alienated from their social and work environments experience a frustrated need for self-efficacy. Depriving individuals of the chance to perform effectively and achieve desired results can lead to long-term feelings of powerlessness and meaninglessness in life (Gecas, 1989).

Developmental psychology suggests that certain socioeconomic factors must be provided to develop the ability to act impactfully, efficaciously, and authentically. Although research on this issue is limited, a study by Bandura et al. (2001) examined the multifaceted sociocognitive origins of children's self-efficacy beliefs and their impact on career-related choices. The proposed conceptual model tested the influence of socioeconomic, familial, and self-related factors on self-efficacy and career choice. The study found that familial socioeconomic status and parental perceptions of their efficacy significantly shape children's personal efficacy, which, in turn, influences their decision-making regarding potential career paths. Another study by Boardman and Robert (2000) demonstrates that the socioeconomic level of a neighborhood – which is influenced by, for instance, high levels of unemployment or reliance on public assistance – can significantly impact an individual's self-efficacy. The findings suggest that neighborhood socioeconomic background can reinforce the relationship between socioeconomic status and self-efficacy beyond individual-level socioeconomic status. This means that individuals with similar socioeconomic status may report different levels of self-efficacy based on the socioeconomic conditions of their neighborhoods. The authors explain that limited resource flows into low socioeconomic neighborhoods mean that individuals with low socioeconomic status living in such environments have fewer resources to draw upon. In these contexts, where opportunities and resources are scarce, the perception of one's ability to achieve goals and act according to personal desires is diminished. Additionally, living in a social environment with limited exposure to others who engage in efficacious actions and achievements lowers individuals' perceptions of their own efficacy.

These theories and findings suggest that when individuals believe they can master their environment, act efficaciously, and make impactful choices, it encourages the formation of a consistent and stable self-concept. Acting autonomously and authentically according to one's own desires, preferences, and goals, coupled with opportunities and active encouragement from one's social environment, fosters a self-determined, stable, and consistent sense of self. Conversely, depriving individuals of these resources, options, and mental support can lead to maladjustment, frustration, and the development of an inconsistent self-concept.

References

Akerlof, G. A., & Kranton, R. (2010). Identity economics. *The Economists' Voice, 7*(2).

Amat, J., Baratta, M. V., Paul, E., Bland, S. T., Watkins, L. R., & Maier, S. F. (2005). Medial prefrontal cortex determines how stressor controllability affects behavior and dorsal raphe nucleus. *Nature Neuroscience, 8*(3), 365–371.

Arcidiacono, P., Beauchamp, A., & McElroy, M. (2016). Terms of endearment: An equilibrium model of sex and matching. *Quantitative Economics, 7*(1), 117–156.

Ashmore, R. D., Deaux, K., & McLaughlin-Volpe, T. (2004). An organizing framework for collective identity: articulation and significance of multidimensionality. *Psychological Bulletin, 130*(1), 80–114.

Bandura, A. (1977). Self-efficacy: Toward a unifying theory of behavioral change. *Psychological Review, 84*(2), 191–215.

Bandura, A. (1986). *Social foundations of thought and action: A social cognitive theory*. Prentice Hall.

Bandura, A. (1994). Social cognitive theory and exercise of control over HIV infection. In *Preventing AIDS: Theories and methods of behavioral interventions* (pp. 25–59). Springer.

Bandura, A., Barbaranelli, C., Caprara, G. V., & Pastorelli, C. (2001). Self-efficacy beliefs as shapers of children's aspirations and career trajectories. *Child Development, 72*(1), 187–206.

Bao, X.-H., & Lam, S.-F. (2008). Who makes the choice? Rethinking the role of autonomy and relatedness in Chinese children's motivation. *Child Development, 79*(2), 269–283.

Bateson, M., Nettle, D., & Roberts, G. (2006). Cues of being watched enhance cooperation in a real-world setting. *Biology Letters, 2*(3), 412–414.

Baumeister, R. F. (1991). *Meanings of life*. Guilford Press.

Baumeister, R. F. (1993). Understanding the inner nature of low self-esteem: Uncertain, fragile, protective, and conflicted. In *Self-esteem: The puzzle of low self-regard* (pp. 208–218). The Plenum Series in Social/Clinical Psychology. Springer.

Baumeister, R. F. (2005). *The cultural animal: Human nature, meaning, and social life*. Oxford University Press.

Baumeister, R. F. (2012). *Public self and private self*. Springer.

Baumeister, R. F., & Leary, M. R. (1995). The need to belong: Desire for interpersonal attachments as a fundamental human motivation. *Psychological Berlin, 117*(3), 497–529.

Becker, G. S. (1964). *Human capital: A theoretical and empirical analysis, with special reference to education*. Columbia University Press.

Becker, G. S. (1965). A theory of the allocation of time. *The Economic Journal, 75*(299), 493–517.

Becker, G. S. (1973). A theory of marriage: Part I. *Journal of Political Economy, 81*(4), 813–846.

Becker, G. S. (1974). A theory of marriage: Part II. *Journal of Political Economy, 82*(2), S11–S26.

Berns, G. S., McClure, S. M., Pagnoni, G., & Montague, P. R. (2001). Predictability modulates human brain response to reward. *Journal of Neuroscience, 21*(8), 2793–2798.

Boardman, J. D., & Robert, S. A. (2000). Neighborhood socioeconomic status and perceptions of self-efficacy. *Sociological Perspectives, 43*(1), 117–136.

Brandt, M. J., & Reyna, C. (2010). The role of prejudice and the need for closure in religious fundamentalism. *Personality and Social Psychology Bulletin, 36*(5), 715–725.

Campbell, J. D. (1986). Similarity and uniqueness: The effects of attribute type, relevance, and individual differences in self-esteem and depression. *Journal of Personality and Social Psychology, 50*(2), 281–294.

Campbell, J. D. (1990). Self-esteem and clarity of the self-concept. *Journal of Personality and Social Psychology, 59*(3), 538.

Campbell, J. D., & Lavallee, L. F. (1993). Who am I? The role of self-concept confusion in understanding the behavior of people with low self-esteem. In *Self-esteem: The puzzle of low self-regard* (pp. 3–20). The Plenum Series in Social/Clinical Psychology. Springer.

Campbell, J. D., & Tesser, A. (1983). Motivational interpretations of hindsight bias: An individual difference analysis. *Journal of Personality, 51*(4), 605–619.

Caplin, A., & Leahy, J. (2001). Psychological expected utility theory and anticipatory feelings. *The Quarterly Journal of Economics, 116*(1), 55–79.

Carlsson, K., Andersson, J., Petrovic, P., Petersson, K. M., Öhman, A., & Ingvar, M. (2006). Predictability modulates the affective and sensory-discriminative neural processing of pain. *Neuroimage, 32*(4), 1804–1814.

Carvallo, M., & Gabriel, S. (2006). No man is an island: The need to belong and dismissing avoidant attachment style. *Personality and Social Psychology Bulletin, 32*(5), 697–709.

Celinska, K. (2007). Individualism and collectivism in America: The case of gun ownership and attitudes toward gun control. *Sociological Perspectives, 50*(2), 229–247.

Chiotis, V. (2015). The morality of economic behaviour. *Journal of Global Ethics, 11*(2), 188–204.

Chong, D. (2000). *Rational lives: Norms and values in politics and society*. University of Chicago Press.

Cilliers, P. (2010). Difference, identity and complexity. In *Complexity, difference and identity* (pp. 3–18). Springer.

Cummins, R. A. (1998). *Directory of instruments to measure quality of life and cognate areas*. School of Psychology, Deakin University.

Cummins, D. D. (2000). How the social environment shaped the evolution of mind. *Synthese, 122*(1–2), 3–28.

Curley, S. P., Yates, J. F., & Abrams, R. A. (1986). Psychological sources of ambiguity avoidance. *Organizational Behavior and Human Decision Processes*, 38(2):230–256.

De-Wit, L., Machilsen, B., & Putzeys, T. (2010). Predictive coding and the neural response to predictable stimuli. *Journal of Neuroscience, 30*(26), 8702–8703.

Deci, E. L. (1980). *The psychology of self-determination*. Free Press.

Deci, E. L., & Ryan, R. M. (1986). The dynamics of self-determination in personality and development. In *Self-related cognitions in anxiety and motivation*, (pp. 171–194). Lawrence Erlbaum Associates.

Deci, E. L., & Ryan, R. M. (1995). Human autonomy. In *Efficacy, agency, and self-esteem* (pp. 31–49). The Springer Series in Social Clinical Psychology. Springer.

Deci, E. L., & Ryan, R. M. (2000). The "what" and "why" of goal pursuits: Human needs and the self-determination of behavior. *Psychological Inquiry, 11*(4), 227–268.

Deci, E. L., & Ryan, R. M. (2008). Self-determination theory: A macrotheory of human motivation, development, and health. *Canadian Psychology/Psychologie Canadienne, 49*(3), 182–185.

Deci, E. L., & Ryan, R. M. (2012). Self-determination theory. In *Handbook of theories of social psychology: Volume 1* (pp. 416–436). Sage Publications.

Degner, J., & Wentura, D. (2010). Automatic prejudice in childhood and early adolescence. *Journal of Personality and Social Psychology, 98*(3), 356–374.

De Cremer, D., & Van Vugt, M. (1999). Social identification effects in social dilemmas: A transformation of motives. *European Journal of Social Psychology, 29*(7), 871–893.

De Donder, L., De Witte, N., Buffel, T., Dury, S., & Verté, D. (2012). Social capital and feelings of unsafety in later life: A study on the influence of social networks, place attachment, and civic participation on perceived safety in Belgium. *Research on Aging, 34*(4), 425–448.

Diener, E., & Biswas-Diener, R. (2002). Will money increase subjective well-being? *Social Indicators Research, 57*(2), 119–169.

Dunlop, W. L. (2017). Situating self-concept clarity in the landscape of personality. In *Self-concept clarity: Perspectives on assessment, research, and applications* (pp. 416–436). Springer.

Edmondson, D., Chaudoir, S. R., Mills, M. A., Park, C. L., Holub, J., & Bartkowiak, J. M. (2011). From shattered assumptions to weakened worldviews: Trauma symptoms signal anxiety buffer disruption. *Journal of Loss and Trauma, 16*(4), 358–385.

Evans, G. W., Gonnella, C., Marcynyszyn, L. A., Gentile, L., & Salpekar, N. (2005). The role of chaos in poverty and children's socioemotional adjustment. *Psychological Science, 16*(7), 560–565.

Feather, N. T. (1996). Reactions to penalties for an offense in relation to authoritarianism, values, perceived responsibility, perceived seriousness, and deservingness. *Journal of Personality and Social Psychology, 71*(3), 571–587.

Feather, N. T. (2006). *Values, achievement, and justice: Studies in the psychology of deservingness*. Kluwer Academic Publishers.

Festinger, L. (1957). *A theory of cognitive dissonance*. Stanford University Press.

Field, S., & Hoffman, A. (1994). Development of a model for self-determination. *Career development for Exceptional Individuals, 17*(2), 159–169.

Fiske, S. T., & Taylor, S. E. (1991). *Social cognition*. Mcgraw-Hill Book Company.

Freeman, R. B. (1976). *The overeducated American*. Academic Press.

Frenkel-Brunswik, E. (1949). Intolerance of ambiguity as an emotional and perceptual personality variable. *Journal of Personality, 18*(1), 108–143.

Friedland, N., Keinan, G., & Regev, Y. (1992). Controlling the uncontrollable: Effects of stress on illusory perceptions of controllability. *Journal of Personality and Social Psychology, 63*(6), 923–931.

Friesen, J. P., Kay, A. C., Eibach, R. P., & Galinsky, A. D. (2014). Seeking structure in social organization: Compensatory control and the psychological advantages of hierarchy. *Journal of Personality and Social Psychology, 106*(4), 590–609.

Fuchs, V. R. (1982). Time preference and health: An exploratory study. In V. R. Fuchs (Ed.), *Economic aspects of health* (pp. 93–120). University of Chicago Press.

Gächter, S., & Fehr, E. (1999). Collective action as a social exchange. *Journal of Economic Behavior & Organization, 39*(4), 341–369.

Gawronski, B. (2012). Back to the future of dissonance theory: Cognitive consistency as a core motive. *Social Cognition, 30*(6), 652–668.

Gebhardt, W. A., & Brosschot, J. F. (2002). Desirability of control: Psychometric properties and relationships with locus of control, personality, coping, and mental and somatic complaints in three Dutch samples. *European Journal of Personality, 16*(6), 423–438.

Gecas, V. (1989). The social psychology of self-efficacy. *Annual Review of Sociology, 15*(1), 291–316.

Golman, R., & Loewenstein, G. (2018). Information gaps: A theory of preferences regarding the presence and absence of information. *Decision, 5*(3), 143–164.

Golman, R., Hagmann, D., & Loewenstein, G. (2017). Information avoidance. *Journal of Economic Literature, 55*(1), 96–135.

Grasmick, H. G., & Green, D. E. (1980). Legal punishment, social disapproval and internalization as inhibitors of illegal behavior. *The Journal of Criminal Law and Criminology, 71*(3), 325.

Greenberg, J., & Pyszczynski, T. (1985). Compensatory self-inflation: A response to the threat to self-regard of public failure. *Journal of Personality and Social Psychology, 49*(1), 273–280.

Greenier, K. D., Kernis, M. H., & Waschull, S. B. (1995). Not all high (or low) self-esteem people are the same. In *Efficacy, agency, and self-esteem* (pp. 51–71). The Springer Series in Social Clinical Psychology. Springer.

Grenier, S., Barrette, A.-M., & Ladouceur, R. (2005). Intolerance of uncertainty and intolerance of ambiguity: Similarities and differences. *Personality and Individual Differences, 39*(3), 593–600.

Gries, T., & Müller, V. (2020). Conflict economics and psychological human needs. Working Papers CIE 135, Paderborn University, CIE Center for International Economics.

Grossman, M. (1972). On the concept of health capital and the demand for health. *Journal of Political Economy, 80*(2), 223–255.

Hales, A. H., Williams, K. D., & Eckhardt, C. I. (2015). A participant walks into a bar…: Subjective intoxication buffers ostracism's negative effects. *Social Psychology, 46*(3), 157.

Hansen, D. M., & Jessop, N. (2017). A context for self-determination and agency: Adolescent developmental theories. In *Development of self-determination through the life-course* (pp. 27–46).

Haslam, C., Holme, A., Haslam, S. A., Iyer, A., Jetten, J., & Williams, W. H. (2008). Maintaining group memberships: Social identity continuity predicts well-being after stroke. *Neuropsychological Rehabilitation, 18*(5–6), 671–691.

Hirshleifer, J. (1983). From weakest-link to best-shot: The voluntary provision of public goods. *Public Choice, 41*(3), 371–386.

Hogg, M. A. (2000). Subjective uncertainty reduction through self-categorization: A motivational theory of social identity processes. *European review of Social Psychology, 11*(1), 223–255.
Holländer, H. (1990). A social exchange approach to voluntary cooperation. *The American Economic Review* 1157–1167.
Howell, R. T., & Hill, G. (2009). The mediators of experiential purchases: Determining the impact of psychological needs satisfaction and social comparison. *The Journal of Positive Psychology, 4*(6), 511–522.
Howell, R. T., Kurai, M., & Tam, L. (2013). Money buys financial security and psychological need satisfaction: Testing need theory in affluence. *Social Indicators Research, 110*(1), 17–29.
Hsu, M., Bhatt, M., Adolphs, R., Tranel, D., & Camerer, C. F. (2005). Neural systems responding to degrees of uncertainty in human decision-making. *Science, 310*(5754), 1680–1683.
Hui, E. K., Sun, R. C., Chow, S. S.-Y., & Chu, M. H.-T. (2011). Explaining Chinese students' academic motivation: filial piety and self-determination. *Educational Psychology, 31*(3), 377–392.
Ilgen, M., McKellar, J., & Tiet, Q. (2005). Abstinence self-efficacy and abstinence 1 year after substance use disorder treatment. *Journal of Consulting and Clinical Psychology, 73*(6), 1175.
Izuma, K., Saito, D. N., & Sadato, N. (2010). Processing of the incentive for social approval in the ventral striatum during charitable donation. *Journal of Cognitive Neuroscience, 22*(4), 621–631.
Janoff-Bulam, R. (1992). *Shattered assumptions: Towards a new psychology of trauma*. Free Press.
Jonas, E., Schulz-Hardt, S., Frey, D., & Thelen, N. (2001). Confirmation bias in sequential information search after preliminary decisions: an expansion of dissonance theoretical research on selective exposure to information. *Journal of Personality and Social Psychology, 80*(4), 557.
Kőszegi, B. (2010). Utility from anticipation and personal equilibrium. *Economic Theory, 44*(3), 415–444.
Kahan, D. M. (2012). Cultural cognition as a conception of the cultural theory of risk. In *Handbook of risk theory* (pp. 725–59). Springer.
Kasser, T. (2009). Psychological need satisfaction, personal well-being, and ecological sustainability. *Ecopsychology, 1*(4), 175–180.
Kiesler, S. B. (1973). Preference for predictability or unpredictability as a mediator of reactions to norm violations. *Journal of Personality and Social Psychology, 27*(3), 354.
Kluegel, J. R., & Smith, E. R. (1986). *Beliefs about inequality: Americans' Views of what is and what ought to be*. Aldine De Gruyter.
Koomen, W., & Van Der Pligt, J. (2015). *The psychology of radicalization and terrorism*. Routledge.
Kruglanski, A. W., & Freund, T. (1983). The freezing and unfreezing of lay-inferences: Effects on impressional primacy, ethnic stereotyping, and numerical anchoring. *Journal of Experimental Social Psychology, 19*(5), 448–468.
Kruglanski, A. W., & Shteynberg, G. (2012). Cognitive consistency as means to an end: How subjective logic affords knowledge.
Kurzban, R., DeScioli, P., & O'Brien, E. (2007). Audience effects on moralistic punishment. *Evolution and Human Behavior, 28*(2), 75–84.
Lambert, N. M., Stillman, T. F., Hicks, J. A., Kamble, S., Baumeister, R. F., and Fincham, F. D. (2013). To belong is to matter: Sense of belonging enhances meaning in life. *Personality and Social Psychology Bulletin, 39*(11), 1418–1427.
Lauriola, M., Foschi, R., Mosca, O., & Weller, J. (2016). Attitude toward ambiguity: Empirically robust factors in self-report personality scales. *Assessment, 23*(3), 353–373.
Leary, M., & MacDonald, G. (2003). Individual differences in self-esteem: A review and theoretical integration. In *Handbook of self and identity* (pp. 401–418). The Guilford Press.
Lee, R. M., & Robbins, S. B. (1998). The relationship between social connectedness and anxiety, self-esteem, and social identity. *Journal of Counseling Psychology, 45*(3), 338–345.
Leotti, L. A., & Delgado, M. R. (2011). The inherent reward of choice. *Psychological Science, 22*(10), 1310–1318.

Leotti, L. A., Iyengar, S. S., & Ochsner, K. N. (2010). Born to choose: The origins and value of the need for control. *Trends in Cognitive Sciences, 14*(10), 457–463.

Lerner, M. J. (1980). *The belief in a just world*. Springer.

Loewenstein, G., & Molnar, A. (2018). The renaissance of belief-based utility in economics. *Nature Human Behaviour, 2*(3), 166–167.

Lott, B. (2002). Cognitive and behavioral distancing from the poor. *American Psychologist, 57*(2), 100.

Lundberg, S., & Pollak, R. A. (1996). Bargaining and distribution in marriage. *Journal of Economic Perspectives, 10*(4), 139–158.

Maddux, J. E. (1995). Self-efficacy theory. In *Self-efficacy, adaptation, and adjustment* (pp. 3–33). Springer.

Maddux, J. E. (2002). Self-efficacy: The power to believing you can. In *Handbook of positive psychology* (pp. 277–287). Oxford University Press.

Majid, A., & Pragasam, J. (1997). Interactions of intolerance of ambiguity and of contingent liability on auditors' avoidance of litigation. *Psychological Reports, 81*(3), 935–944.

Makwana, A. P., Dhont, K., Akhlaghi-Ghaffarokh, P., Masure, M., & Roets, A. (2018). The motivated cognitive basis of transphobia: The roles of right-wing ideologies and gender role beliefs. *Sex Roles, 79*(3–4), 206–217.

Markus, H. R., & Kitayama, S. (1991). Cultural variation in the self-concept. In *The self: Interdisciplinary approaches* (pp. 18–48). Springer.

Masclet, D., Noussair, C., Tucker, S., & Villeval, M.-C. (2003). Monetary and nonmonetary punishment in the voluntary contributions mechanism. *American Economic Review, 93*(1), 366–380.

Maslow, A. H. (1943). A theory of human motivation. *Psychological Review*, 1.

McGuire, W. J. (1966). The current status of cognitive consistency theories. *Cognitive consistency: Motivational antecedents and behavioral consequents* (pp. 1–26).

Miller, S. M. (1979). Controllability and human stress: Method, evidence and theory. *Behaviour Research and Therapy, 17*(4), 287–304.

Moller, A. C., Friedman, R., & Deci, E. L. (2006). A self-determination theory perspective on the interpersonal and intrapersonal aspects of self-esteem (pp. 201–208).

Moskowitz, G. B. (1993). Individual differences in social categorization: The influence of personal need for structure on spontaneous trait inferences. *Journal of Personality and Social Psychology, 65*(1), 132.

Müller, V., & Gries, T. (2024). *Ideology and the microfoundations of conflict: From human needs to intergroup violence*. Oxford University Press.

Neuberg, S. L., & Newsom, J. T. (1993). Personal need for structure: Individual differences in the desire for simpler structure. *Journal of Personality and Social Psychology, 65*(1), 113.

Newman, A., Donohue, R., & Eva, N. (2017). Psychological safety: A systematic review of the literature. *Human Resource Management Review, 27*(3), 521–535.

O'reilly, J. X. (2013). Making predictions in a changing world inference, uncertainty, and learning. *Frontiers in Neuroscience, 7*, 105.

Pagnini, F., Bercovitz, K., & Langer, E. (2016). Perceived control and mindfulness: Implications for clinical practice. *Journal of Psychotherapy Integration, 26*(2), 91.

Paulus, M. P., Hozack, N., Zauscher, B., McDowell, J. E., Frank, L., Brown, G. G., & Braff, D. L. (2001). Prefrontal, parietal, and temporal cortex networks underlie decision-making in the presence of uncertainty. *Neuroimage, 13*(1), 91–100.

Payzan-LeNestour, É., & Bossaerts, P. (2012). Do not bet on the unknown versus try to find out more: Estimation uncertainty and unexpected uncertainty both modulate exploration. *Frontiers in Neuroscience, 6*, 150.

Pervin, L. A. (1963). The need to predict and control under conditions of threat. *Journal of Personality*, 31(4), 570–587.

Pew Research Center. (2017). Key takeaways on Americans views of guns and gun ownership fact tank. online erh ltlich unter https://www.pewresearch.org/fact-tank/2017/06/22/key-takeaways-on-americans-views-of-guns-and-gun-ownership/

Ploghaus, A., Becerra, L., Borras, C., & Borsook, D. (2003). Neural circuitry underlying pain modulation: expectation, hypnosis, placebo. *Trends in Cognitive Sciences, 7*(5), 197–200.
Poleshuck, E. L., & Green, C. R. (2008). Socioeconomic disadvantage and pain. *Pain, 136*(3), 235.
Powdthavee, N., & Riyanto, Y. E. (2015). Would you pay for transparently useless advice? A test of boundaries of beliefs in the folly of predictions. *Review of Economics and Statistics, 97*(2), 257–272.
Putman, R. (1993). The prosperous community: Social capital and public life. online erh ltlich unter http://www.prospect.org/print/vol/13 (accessed 7 April 2003).
Pyszczynski, T., Greenberg, J., & Solomon, S. (1997). Why do we need what we need? A terror management perspective on the roots of human social motivation. *Psychological Inquiry, 8*(1), 1–20.
Rege, M., & Telle, K. (2004). The impact of social approval and framing on cooperation in public good situations. *Journal of public Economics, 88*(7–8), 1625–1644.
Rodin, J., & Langer, E. J. (1977). Long-term effects of a control-relevant intervention with the institutionalized aged. *Journal of Personality and Social Psychology, 35*(12), 897.
Rouse, P. C., Ntoumanis, N., Duda, J. L., Jolly, K., & Williams, G. C. (2011). In the beginning: role of autonomy support on the motivation, mental health and intentions of participants entering an exercise referral scheme. *Psychology & Health, 26*(6), 729–749.
Rozin, P., Lowery, L., Imada, S., & Haidt, J. (1999). The cad triad hypothesis: a mapping between three moral emotions (contempt, anger, disgust) and three moral codes (community, autonomy, divinity). *Journal of Personality and Social Psychology, 76*(4), 574.
Ryan, R. M., & Deci, E. L. (2006). Self-regulation and the problem of human autonomy: Does psychology need choice, self-determination, and will? *Journal of Personality, 74*(6), 1557–1586.
Sampson, R. J., & Laub, J. H. (1993). *Crime in the making: Pathways and turning points through life*. Harvard University Press.
Sanbonmatsu, D. M., & Fazio, R. H. (1990). The role of attitudes in memory-based decision making. *Journal of Personality and social Psychology, 59*(4), 614.
Schaller, M., Boyd, C., Yohannes, J., & O'Brien, M. (1995). The prejudiced personality revisited: Personal need for structure and formation of erroneous group stereotypes. *Journal of Personality and Social Psychology, 68*(3), 544–555.
Schulz-Hardt, S., Frey, D., Lüthgens, C., & Moscovici, S. (2000). Biased information search in group decision making. *Journal of Personality and Social Psychology, 78*(4), 655.
Sen, A. (2017). *Collective choice and social welfare: Expanded edition*. Penguin UK.
Shapiro Jr., D. H., Schwartz, C. E., & Astin, J. A. (1996). Controlling ourselves, controlling our world: Psychology's role in understanding positive and negative consequences of seeking and gaining control. *American Psychologist, 51*(12), 1213.
Shogren, K. A., Wehmeyer, M. L., & Palmer, S. B. (2017). Causal agency theory. In *Development of self-determination through the life-course* (pp. 55–67). Springer.
Sicherman, N., Loewenstein, G., Seppi, D. J., & Utkus, S. P. (2016). Financial attention. *The Review of Financial Studies, 29*(4), 863–897.
Slotter, E. B., Winger, L., & Soto, N. (2015). Lost without each other: The influence of group identity loss on the self-concept. *Group Dynamics: Theory, Research, and Practice, 19*(1), 15–30.
Staub, E., Tursky, B., & Schwartz, G. E. (1971). Self-control and predictability: Their effects on reactions to aversive stimulation. *Journal of Personality and Social Psychology, 18*(2), 157.
Steele, C. M., Spencer, S. J., & Lynch, M. (1993). Self-image resilience and dissonance: the role of affirmational resources. *Journal of Personality and Social Psychology, 64*(6), 885.
Steptoe, A. E., & Appels, A. E. (1989). *Stress, personal control and health*. John Wiley & Sons.
Stinson, D. A., Logel, C., Holmes, J. G., Wood, J. V., Forest, A. L., Gaucher, D., Fitzsimons, G. M., & Kath, J. (2010). The regulatory function of self-esteem: Testing the epistemic and acceptance signaling systems. *Journal of Personality and Social Psychology, 99*(6), 993.
Sullivan, M. W., & Lewis, M. (2003). Contextual determinants of anger and other negative expressions in young infants. *Developmental Psychology, 39*(4), 693.

Tajfel, H. (1981). Human groups and social categories: Studies in social psychology. *Cup Archive*.

Tennen, H., & Affleck, G. (1993). The puzzles of self-esteem a clinical perspective. In *Self-esteem: The puzzle of low self-regard* (pp. 241–262).

Thompson, M. M., Naccarato, M. E., Parker, K. C., & Moskowitz, G. B. (2001). The personal need for structure and personal fear of invalidity measures: Historical perspectives, current applications, and future directions. In *Cognitive social psychology: The Princeton symposium on the legacy and future of social cognition* (pp. 19–39).

Tice, D. M. (1993). The social motivations of people with low self-esteem. In *Self-esteem: The puzzle of low self-regard* (pp. 37–53). Springer.

Timmer, M., Cordero, M. I., Sevelinges, Y., & Sandi, C. (2011). Evidence for a role of oxytocin receptors in the long-term establishment of dominance hierarchies. *Neuropsychopharmacology, 36*(11), 2349–2356.

Tricomi, E. M., Delgado, M. R., & Fiez, J. A. (2004). Modulation of caudate activity by action contingency. *Neuron, 41*(2), 281–292.

Van den Bos, K., & Maas, M. (2009). On the psychology of the belief in a just world: Exploring experiential and rationalistic paths to victim blaming. *Personality and Social Psychology Bulletin, 35*(12), 1567–1578.

Van Harreveld, F., Rutjens, B. T., Schneider, I. K., Nohlen, H. U., & Keskinis, K. (2014). In doubt and disorderly: Ambivalence promotes compensatory perceptions of order. *Journal of Experimental Psychology: General, 143*(4), 1666.

Weber, B. J., & Tan, W. P. (2012). Ambiguity aversion in a delay analogue of the Ellsberg paradox. *Judgment and Decision Making, 7*(4), 383–389.

Webster, D. M. (1993). Motivated augmentation and reduction of the overattribution bias. *Journal of Personality and Social Psychology, 65*(2), 261–271.

Webster, D. M., & Kruglanski, A. W. (1994). Individual differences in need for cognitive closure. *Journal of Personality and Social Psychology, 67*(6), 1049.

Webster, D. M., & Kruglanski, A. W. (1997). Cognitive and social consequences of the need for cognitive closure. *European Review of Social Psychology, 8*(1), 133–173.

Weinstein, N., & Stone, D. N. (2018). Need depriving effects of financial insecurity: Implications for well-being and financial behaviors. *Journal of Experimental Psychology: General, 147*(10), 1503.

Williams, K. D. (2007). Ostracism: The kiss of social death. *Social and Personality Psychology Compass, 1*(1), 236–247.

Williams, K. D., Cheung, C. K., & Choi, W. (2000). Cyberostracism: effects of being ignored over the internet. *Journal of Personality and Social Psychology, 79*(5), 748.

Willis, R. J. (1999). A theory of out-of-wedlock childbearing. *Journal of Political Economy, 107*(S6), S33–S64.

Zheng, Z., Gu, S., Lei, Y., Lu, S., Wang, W., Li, Y., & Wang, F. (2016). Safety needs mediate stressful events induced mental disorders. *Neural Plasticity, 2016*, 8058093

Chapter 5
Belief Systems and Ideologies, Their Functions, and Their Organizations

Belief systems and ideologies are an essential part of people's lives. This book explores the role of ideologies and belief systems in human decision-making using basic economic theory. In fact, studying "beliefs" and "narratives" with the help of economic approaches is not new, but the approach suggested here is different. If you want to talk about belief systems and ideologies, you quickly come across an interesting literature that links phenomena such as "beliefs", "narratives", or "moral behavior" with economic thought structures and models. The focus of these works is often on moral behavior and individual narratives that are processed and passed on in the context of communication interactions between different individuals. For example, there is a strand of literature that connects prosocial or norm-compliant behavior with signaling or moral and identity issues. Important contributions to this strand are, e.g., Bénabou and Tirole (2006, 2011a,b). Another strand of research focuses on interactions and learning in networks. Most of this literature focuses on agents learning from other agents and strategically passing data or narratives to others in their communication (see, e.g., Hagenbach & Koessler, 2010; Galeotti et al., 2013; Acemoglu & Mathew, 2015). Furthermore, there is a strand of research that focuses on motivated beliefs. This perspective emphasizes that beliefs often fulfill important psychological and functional needs of the individual. These include confidence in one's own abilities, moral self-esteem, hope and fear reduction, social identity, and more. It is explained that individuals want to engage in behaviors such as not knowing, wishful thinking, and refusing to face reality. Motivated beliefs make it possible to maintain different self-images and worldviews. Contributions that represent this strand are, among others, especially Bénabou (2015) and Bénabou and Tirole (2016), and the papers reviewed in their literature discussions. However, these approaches differ in their initial question from what is to be covered in this book.

In this book, we do not look at isolated narratives and/or how they are passed on in communicative interactions, but we look at the phenomenon of entire belief systems and ideologies which fulfill certain functions for people as individuals. Why do ideologies and belief systems exist and what functions do they fulfill for the

T. Gries et al., *The Economics of Ideologies*, Springer Studies in Alternative Economics, https://doi.org/10.1007/978-3-031-93514-5_5

individual? This question therefore starts with the individual and is actually even easier to discuss than the interactive multi-agent or network approaches.

Our discussion of belief systems and ideologies therefore begins with a definition of the terms and then in the first section of this chapter moves on to the functions that belief systems and ideologies fulfill for people. Based on an intuitive discussion and description of these functions, a model is then developed in the later sections of both the activity of an independent ideological organization (Sect. 5.2) and an individual that adopts a belief system or ideology (Chap. 6). In Chap. 7, we then describe how actions and decisions are ultimately made by subjectively rational individuals, taking into account the rules of their belief systems and ideologies.

However, before moving on to more detailed reflections on the functions of belief systems and ideologies, the terms themselves and the way they are used in this book first need to be clarified.

Belief systems and ideologies describe a similar phenomenon. However, in our use of the terms, a belief system is the more general term, and the term ideology refers more to a political belief system. A belief system or an ideology is a (largely consistent) set of narratives, beliefs, and attitudes that provide interpretations, explanations, evaluations and values, visions, or even utopias of and for a society. A belief system or an ideology is usually shaped by an organization, which dominates the current interpretation of the respective narratives, beliefs, evaluations, and attitudes. Ideologies usually convey first, a particular set of goals and desired states, including a value system closely associated with them and, second, a proposal for how to achieve those states. Thus, they also propose strategies and actions for achieving these desired states. Belief systems and ideologies therefore fulfill certain functions for humans. In the next section, we identify five functions and briefly introduce them.

5.1 Functions of Belief Systems and Ideologies

(1) Mitigating the Human Information Problem

In Chap. 2, we suggested that humans have a fundamental information problem. Rational decisions almost always have to be made with incomplete information. Belief systems and ideologies emerge as a direct response to the constraints imposed by incomplete information and the limited human capacity to fully understand the environment. At the same time, their function is also to mitigate this human problem of imperfect information and incomplete understanding and to bring about good solutions even without complete information.

Humans have the remarkable ability to think logically and gather infor- mation. This cognitive capacity enables them to theorize and understand the underlying mechanisms that are relevant to them and their environment. This analytical capacity enables humans to develop innovative technologies that improve their life and positively influence their living conditions. By continuously collecting and analyzing information in research and development, people use their intellectual potential to continually understand and sometimes improve the world around them. In the 19th century, humans had only a very rudimentary understanding of the world, and science only gradually began to understand natural phenomena. This decoding of the laws of nature and rationality in particular, which was also used as a basis to research social and economic relationships, led to the coining of the phrase "disenchantment of the world" in Weber (1919, p. 22). The term is used to describe a process in which traditional religious and metaphysical beliefs, including faith and spirituality, are replaced by rational and scientifically unambiguous explanations. Max Weber argued that in modern societies the world is increasingly dominated by a rational, scientific worldview that supplants the mystical and spiritual elements of earlier worldviews.

Weber was initially right about the fact that scientific methodology and thinking and its findings have improved many areas of people's lives. However, despite science's success in uncovering some of the basic mechanisms at work in our environment, we still only know and understand a relatively small part of them. We are a long way from fully understanding our natural environment. We are even further away from gaining a comprehensive understanding of our more complex social and economic systems even though we have made progress in explaining their underlying mechanisms. The permanent interaction between different variables and factors in these very complex systems also makes them structurally extremely dynamic. This makes it particularly difficult to uncover and understand stable relationships and causal mechanisms. Therefore, despite all the efforts and progress that have been made in research, our scientific understanding is still very limited. This is evident when considering the volume of scientific information that exists and, consequently, that could potentially be accessible to society; and this is even more evident when considering the amount of information available to individuals and their understanding of it.

Individuals often lack the accurate information and deep understanding that science provides about human-related mechanisms. While, for example, doctors, who rely on scientific knowledge, know more than we (as individuals) do, they do not know everything. We turn to doctors because they have a better understanding of these matters than we do, even though their knowledge is not complete. We seek out experts because we ourselves as individuals have even less reliable information because correct information is very expensive. This not only applies to the complex "human body system" but also to other complex systems such as social or economic systems. Overall, the amount of information available to societies, and even more so to individuals, is still quite small.

Despite the pervasive information problem that humans face, they continually strive to make decisions that will improve their lives and well-being. However, the fulfillment of this desire to make good decisions for their well-being is constantly undermined by the incomplete information and limited understanding they have of their environment. Under these conditions, how can they still make good decisions?

One possible solution is to use an alternative to real, robust information that fulfils the same function as real information and understanding and can help to fill the information gap. Given the high cost or even unavailability of information and knowledge, people tend to fall back on plausible narratives and thus use quasi-heuristic recommendations. Ideologies and belief systems serve as heuristics, and we have already shown in Sect. 3.3 and in (Burs & Gries, 2022) (in a different context) when the switch to a heuristic is subjectively rational.

The narratives disseminated by ideologies and belief systems thus offer a cost-effective alternative to nonexistent or expensive (but often only marginally helpful) additional real information, especially for an individual. Ideologies and belief systems are thus a rational substitute for the costly, genuinely far-reaching investigation of complex social and economic systems. Their narratives can provide rapid orientation in order to be able to make subjectively rational decisions based on them, even without comprehensive information acquisition. The available narratives replace the large amount of effort and high costs associated with complex real analyses of social and economic systems, which also come with the risk of providing uncertain results. The process of decoding and completely understanding is limited, at least in the short term.

In economic theories, "rational choice" models, which are based on the assumption of perfect information, are often at the center of the analysis. These models assume that actors have complete and free access to information and can therefore make rational decisions. However, in the real world, individuals often face an enormous information problem. Ignoring the human information problem in rational choice models is undoubtedly a fundamental assumption. It can be justified in simple situations. For example, if the acquisition of information is all but free of charge, the assumption of perfect information may seem justified. But this assumption begins to falter as soon as we find ourselves in a world of complex systems and high information costs. In a complex world where information costs are significant, the concept of rational choice must include the information problem (Burs & Gries, 2022). In this chapter, similar as in Sect. 3.4, it is also pointed out that there are certainly qualitative differences in the results of decisions when information is not available free of charge. As a substitute for real information, belief systems and ideologies provide the "guidance" that people would otherwise have hoped real information would provide. However, this "guidance" is sometimes so poor that it is obvious that someone would not have made the same decision if they had had complete information.

A first and also very fundamental function of belief systems and ideologies is that they offer an answer to the otherwise unsolvable human information problem. Ideologies and belief systems propose a cost-effective solution to the information problem by providing narratives that can replace the lack of real knowledge. Based on these belief systems and ideologies, it becomes possible for individuals to understand their individual situation, explain their circumstances, develop strategies, and ultimately make appropriate decisions under ideological guidance.

(2) Creating a Coherent View of the World and Providing Orientation and Identification

One of the functions of belief systems and ideologies is to help individuals to create a coherent view of the world by providing a structured interpretation of reality based on a firm foundation of norms, values, and attitudes. They provide norms and values that help individuals to create their individual view of the world. Hence, belief systems and ideologies form the moral and ethical framework that guides people's actions accordingly. Belief systems, ideologies, norms, and values serve as guidelines for the behavior of and decision-making by their adherents. Shared norms and values then create a common foundation for common views within a group that shares the same belief system or ideology.[1]

Further, belief systems and ideologies create and provide narratives and anecdotes. These narratives provide a framework within which followers of a particular belief system or ideology can interpret events and experiences in their lives. Belief systems and ideologies allow followers to interpret, connect, and understand the past, present, and future in a coherent way. They make it possible to integrate these coherent narratives into one's own life (and existence). Narratives give context and meaning to what is happening and help people integrate their individual stories into the larger narrative framework of their beliefs. By introducing a narrative framework, belief systems and ideologies create a coherent structure within which to interpret reality and promote shared understanding within the group.

In addition to integrating personal experiences, belief systems and ideologies also provide stability and meaning in an often unpredictable and uncertain world. By providing a clear answer to fundamental questions about the purpose and meaning of life, belief systems and ideologies give followers a sense of direction and purpose. They provide a framework within which followers can understand their experiences and convey a deep sense of connection to something bigger than themselves.

However, belief systems and ideologies also allow individuals to connect with others, identify with a group, and embrace shared values. Membership of a faith community or belonging to a group that follows a common ideology provides a strong sense of belonging and connectedness. One experiences a strong common bond because the shared values and beliefs within the ideological community create a sense of unity and solidarity. By identifying with these values, one feels connected to other members who share similar views. Members of a faith community often support each other in times of need, be it through dialogue, moral support, or practical help. This network of support can strengthen a person's ties with the belief system and the community. Shared rituals and traditions can further strengthen this sense of belonging and provide a sense of continuity and stability. All of this creates the possibility of identification and even a link to one's own identity.

Overall, these mechanisms enable belief systems and ideologies to foster a cohesive worldview, offering adherents a shared foundation for interpreting reality. By providing norms, values, narratives, and a framework for integrating personal experiences, belief systems and ideologies thus have the function of providing a structured, coherent, and meaningful interpretation of the world that provides stability, meaningfulness, orientation, and identification.

---

[1] For a broader discussion of this function, see MacKenzie and Baumeister (2014, pp. 25–37), or Jost (2017).

(3) Providing a Viable Option for Reconciling Psychological Human Needs
The third function of ideologies and belief systems is that they provide a viable need reconciliation option.

As we saw in Chap. 4, there is a broad spectrum of fundamental needs that are universal in themselves. However, the extent of individual needs is structured very differently for each person. In general, we find a wide variety of individual needs profiles in a society. For some people, needs such as security are of fundamental importance, while others have a stronger need for autonomy. Still others may be more focused on belonging and identity. Each individual is therefore unique in terms of their needs, and we can describe a whole range of individuals with different need structures. Given these many different need structures, there is also a multitude of desired conditions and states that can meet these needs. Staying with the economic jargon, these desires thus describe the demand for conditions and states that can serve underlying needs.

And so, if we have a demand side, how is this demand matched on the supply side? What is capable of addressing desires for abstract states, such as security or self-determination, which may not currently be experienced but which are to be striven for? The answer is very simple: Belief systems and ideologies propose solutions to these needs. Positioned on the supply side, they offer ideas on how these needs might be fulfilled. Using their rich narratives and stories, belief systems and ideologies initially meet these needs in an abstract, virtual manner.

A specific belief system or ideology offers a system of interpretation that addresses a certain group of needs. Ideologies and belief systems thus take up an individual's existential, epistemic, social-relational, and agency needs. They explain how these needs can be addressed and met. For example, ideologies commonly referred to as "conservative" emphasize the core values of tradition, social order, preservation of the status quo, role ascription, and acceptance of inequality (maintaining the organic structure of society). Conservative belief systems defend established institutions, social orders, and values and thus convey a sense of stability, order, consistency, and control over followers' lives, especially for security-oriented individuals. Empirical studies in social psychology, e.g., Jost et al. (2003), have shown that people who choose a conservative belief system have a stronger need for order, control, consistency, and ambiguity avoidance. They also perceive the environment or the unknown as dangerous or view people or events that challenge the traditional social order as threatening.

However, belief systems and ideologies not only offer explanations of how the observed and experienced reality of life relates to and interacts with one's own needs, they also develop ideas about possible societal and social conditions and states that could better serve one's own needs. Furthermore, they also show ways in which these social conditions can be achieved. Belief systems and ideologies therefore not only describe target visions and an associated value system, but they also offer solutions as to how these visions can be realized.

If an individual has specific needs and finds an ideology or belief system that can address these needs, through its detailed narratives – i.e., its interpretations, explanations, and proposed solutions – then this ideology becomes an effective tool for need reconciliation. It is, therefore, in the individual's interest to connect their individual need structure with a belief system or ideology that addresses and serves precisely this structure.

Therefore, there is a match between psychological needs and a particular ideology or belief system. How might we envision such a match developing? Young people typically start to form their worldviews and adopt ideologies as adolescents and young adults.[2] This process in which adolescents and young adults explore various explanations of the world and ideas about what makes a good world is complex. It often starts at home, where basic concepts are introduced, sometimes directly, sometimes subtly. As they grow, this exploration expands beyond their home environment, exposing them to various narratives from different belief systems and ideologies. These ideas might contradict each other and are weighed against the realities of their lives. Through this comparison, young people discern which narratives resonate with their personal needs. Over time, they discover that certain stories align with their desires and expectations. This ongoing process, where personal needs are matched with different narratives, is what we describe as finding a "match" between an ideology or belief system and an individual's needs. Ultimately, an ideology or belief system that fits well with a person's needs is likely to be adopted.

(4) Propose Essential Forms of Togetherness, e.g., Creating Trust

Another function that ideologies and belief systems provide is that they propose essential forms of interaction and togetherness. For example, they recommend whether a society should be hierarchical – egalitarian, exclusive – participatory, authoritarian – democratic, individualistic – social, competitive – cooperative, controlling – trusting, polarizing – balanced, self-centered – social caring, etc. Basic societal conditions, orientations and formal as well as informal institutions are shaped by belief systems and ideologies.

One important basic aspect of interpersonal as well as personal-institutional relationships is trust. The significance of trust is often only briefly mentioned, so we want to highlight once more how crucial this relationship is both between individuals and between people and institutions. Ideologies and belief systems can create or destroy interpersonal and intergroup trust. In a complex world characterized by imperfect, incomplete, or unevenly distributed information, trust – or the lack of it – is a vital component of the information system and plays a key role in how individuals coordinate themselves within society. Trust is an effective means of reducing the complexity and information costs of individuals' interactions.

Arrow addressed the role of trust in various of his works, particularly in relation to uncertainty and asymmetric information and transactions. Although his focus was not on trust, it is clear from his arguments that trust has an economic function in the transaction process. In Arrow (1974), he examines the influence of uncertainty and asymmetric information on the functioning of organizations. He argues that trust can play a role in overcoming information asymmetries by facilitating exchange and

[2] For a review of political socialization, see Sapiro (2004) or recently van Ditmars (2023).

cooperation. Arrow (1984) also addresses the effect of uncertainty and asymmetric information on the efficiency of markets. As a result, reputation and trust can help to solve information problems.

Akerlof (1970) also analyzes how asymmetric information impairs the market mechanism. He illustrates this using the used car market, where sellers often have more information about the quality of a vehicle than potential buyers do. Because buyers do not know whether a vehicle on offer is actually of the quality they are hoping for, they are reluctant to pay a reasonable price for it, fearing that the vehicle may be of inferior quality ("a lemon"). As a result, "lemons" (bad used cars) can accumulate in the market as buyers are unwilling to pay the price for a vehicle whose quality they cannot judge with any certainty. Akerlof argues that trust plays a key role in overcoming asymmetric information. If buyers have confidence in the quality of a product, they are more willing to pay a reasonable price even if they do not have all the relevant information. Trust can thus help to improve the market mechanism and avoid inefficient outcomes due to asymmetric information.

Trust also plays an important role in institutional economics in relationships between companies and in contractual relationships. Trust plays a particularly important role in the "transaction cost theory approach", which deals with the costs and efficiency of different forms of organization. The term was coined by Oliver Williamson. For example, Williamson (1979) analyzes the importance of trust as a decisive factor in the design of contractual relationships and the choice of governance structure. Trust enables companies to reduce transaction costs and promote efficient economic interactions. Williamson (1985) argues that trust is a fundamental prerequisite for economic transactions and cooperation between companies. Companies that have confidence in the integrity and reliability of their business partners are more willing to enter into long-term relationships and complex contracts. Various institutional arrangements – such as contract law, company law, and property rights – serve to create and maintain trust between contracting parties. These institutions provide mechanisms for minimizing risk, overcoming information asymmetries, and ensuring contract enforcement, which ultimately promotes trust in economic transactions.

Trust is also identified as an important fundamental principle of social interactions outside of economic theory. Coleman (1990) identified trust as an important part of "social capital". "Social capital" is defined as a resource consisting of social relationships, norms, and trust. Trust between individuals facilitates communication, cooperation, and coordination and plays an important role in the functioning of organizations, communities, and societies as a whole. Communities with high levels of social capital and trust tend to be more efficient and better able to achieve common goals.

Fukuyama (1995) also regards trust as a fundamental social virtue that lays the foundation for a successful society. He looks at different forms of trust, including trust between individuals, institutional trust in governments and organizations, and social trust within communities and societies. Fukuyama argues in this book that trust is a crucial factor for economic prosperity. When people trust each other and have confidence in their institutions, economic transactions are conducted more efficiently and innovation is encouraged. However, trust is also important for political stability and democratic participation. In societies where citizens trust their governments and where there is a high level of social trust, there is less likelihood of social conflict and political crises.

In Putnam (2000), the decline of social capital and community ties in the United States is described. Putnam coined the term "bowling alone" to refer to the fact that more and more people in the United States are bowling alone rather than in organized groups or clubs. This trend is symbolic of the decline in social interactions and cohesion in U.S. society. Putnam argues in his book that the decline in social ties and trust reduces a society's social capital, which has a negative impact on the common good and democratic participation. He shows how the decline in membership of clubs, churches, and other social groups leads to a loss of trust, cooperation, and commitment.

What is described here in the various disciplines is ultimately a special type of public good in the form of a club good that can be implemented in a society.[3] If trust is widespread in a society, everyone can benefit from its positive effects without competing for them. When one person uses trust, it does not reduce the ability of others to also benefit from trusting relationships. The question of excludability as a second criterion of a public good is somewhat more complicated. If a group of people decides to act in mutual trust, people in the group who abuse that trust can certainly be excluded. However, for all the remaining group members, trust may be maintained. Further, the group itself can also have no trust in other groups or it can include other groups in this system of trust. Thus trust as a club good can be defined for a well-defined group of people, so that this state can in principle apply to a small social group as well as to a large group such as an entire society.

Scandinavian societies are often cited as examples of societies in which a state of high trust prevails (Svendsen & Svendsen, 2015). Trust is an important social condition in Scandinavian countries that is characterized by strong social ties, pronounced community orientation, and a sense of solidarity among people. This manifests itself in a tolerant and inclusive society. Trust in the social system creates an atmosphere of mutual respect and cooperation. There is little corruption, which indicates that trust in institutions and public servants is high. Citizens trust the state to act effectively and transparently and to use resources for the good of society.

So how is trust established? Williamson (1985) refers to various institutional arrangements such as contract law, company law, and property rights. They serve to minimize transaction risks, overcome information asymmetries, and ensure contract enforcement, so that ultimately trust is created in the feasibility of economic transactions as desired. However, even the drafting of legally sound contracts and their subsequent enforcement is not a low-cost activity or even free of charge.

The agreement to trust each other and the cooperative and trusting execution of a transaction would then be free of charge. Even for such purposes, narratives and thus also normative stipulations that the involved parties agree on and follow

[3] Note, a public good usually has two properties, no rivalry and no excludability.

can establish conditions that establish trust as a public/club good. The narrative of the "honorable merchant", for example, goes back to the time of the medieval Hanseatic League. "Honorable merchants" were an ideal that emphasized the importance of honesty, integrity, fairness, reliability, and respect in trade and business relationships. They were part of a belief system that generated trust among honorable merchants. Trade was to generate mutual benefit and not involve any attempt to take advantage of one's business partner from the outset.

This example already shows that the way in which trust is handled between individuals within a group and between groups is significantly influenced by their belief systems and ideologies. Ideologies and their narratives can promote trust, and if many people follow these narratives, this will also lead to a state of trust. Ideologies and belief systems whose narratives emphasize cooperation and solidarity as positive or which believe that interactions between individuals can give rise to shared positive externalities view the establishment of trust as important. If individuals trust each other, they will, for example, follow the assumption that neediness will not be faked and financial transfers to poor people, for instance, will not be acquired by deceit. They trust that help is actually needed.

Examples of ideologies and belief systems that aim to build trust include humanism and those that advocate for liberal democracy as a key principle for political organization. In liberal democracies, trust is seen as fundamental to the functioning of a free society. The idea that individuals and institutions are capable of making their own decisions and exercising personal freedoms is based on a certain degree of trust in the abilities and integrity of others. In liberal democracies, trust in the social, legal, and governmental institutions is both assumed and encouraged through relevant narratives. In humanism, trust is seen as fundamental to interpersonal relationships and the development of each individual. Humanism emphasizes the dignity and worth of each human being and the importance of empathy, respect, and mutual trust for a society's well-being. But there are also ideologies and belief systems that disparage trust and spread respective narratives. In the following, we will look at three examples in which trust is systematically discredited: conspiracy theories, extreme individualism and libertarian ideologies, and extreme economic neoliberalism.

Let us start with conspiracy theories, in which complex events are seen as the result of secret machinations and conspiracies. Conspiracy ideologies use systematic strategies to destroy trust. They interpret certain complex events as being the result of secret machinations or conspiracies. Their narratives propagate mistrust of established institutions and official explanations. The spread of disinformation and the rejection of real facts give rise to mistrust. This mistrust of established, often public, institutions is then attempted to be redirected into a new trust in the organization of the conspiracy ideology and its own purposes.

Extreme individualism and extreme libertarian ideologies can also lead to mistrust of communities and institutions. Libertarian ideologies that emphasize the absolute autonomy of the individual and focus their central narratives exclusively on this value and deny social and societal responsibility can undermine trust in society and cooperation between its members.

The same applies to the ideology of economic neoliberalism. Extreme economic neoliberalism, which propagates unrestricted market competition and the deregulation of the state as a dogma and whose narratives emphasize competitive behavior as exclusively positive, sees interactions between individuals primarily as a zero-sum game. Trust is not regarded as an efficient coordination tool for reducing transaction costs. In these narratives, state institutions and their activities are not to be trusted as they only hinder free competition and market forces. This explicitly creates mistrust of precisely these state institutions and public services. The idea that an unrestricted market alone offers the best solutions to societal problems can lead to a lack of trust in state interventions and social welfare programs.

These are all examples of the fact that one function of ideologies and belief systems is to recommend fundamental ideas and coordination principles about how to live together in a society. Trust is one such principle. There are ideologies and belief systems that want to promote this principle and others that reject it or even sow distrust.

(5) Providing Orientation for Everyday Decisions

In addition to function (2), belief systems and ideologies not only offer a general and sometimes abstract understanding of the world, but they often also provide specific, detailed rules and recommendations for everyday behavior. Belief systems and ideologies thus help individuals to process information, understand reality, and organize their values and beliefs in such a way that they are incorporated into their lives and decision-making. They help to explain why people want to do what they do and how they incorporate their values and judgments, which are determined by their beliefs, into everyday decision-making. Individuals can therefore rely on their belief system or ideology to help them behave correctly, cope with life's problems, and deal with threatening and uncertain situations. This function of belief systems and ideologies was already discussed by Max Weber (1905). Weber examines the role of religion and belief systems in society and analyzes how they define norms and values that guide their adherents' behavior and decisions.

Ideologies and belief systems are usually associated with organizations that claim to have the sole ability and power to correctly interpret a particular ideology or belief system. These organizations set rules of behavior based on their own interpretation. Followers are willing to obey these rules because they want to be consistent with their beliefs Burs et al. (2023). Let us take the simple example of a consumption decision: A person who adheres to an ecological ideology is guided by the recommendation that they should consume organic food. In their daily shopping decisions, that person will try to limit the amount of conventionally produced food they buy and will instead buy more organic products even if they cost more. Another example related to the theme of this book is career choice. In times of conflict, an individual may decide to join a militia because he or she feels committed to an ideological narrative and the organization representing them has issued a call to arms. The individual will follow this call, even if he or she is poorly paid, and will accept a high personal risk. Both examples show that decisions are influenced by psychological effects that guide our everyday behavior.

Hence, individuals not only make decisions based on purely physical preferences. Their decisions are also influenced by the rules and judgments of the ideology or belief systems they have adopted. Following the rules and norms of a certain ideology or belief system when making decisions has the function of ensuring that concrete decisions are made under the "guidance" of the respective belief system or ideology. This creates consistency, order, and meaning in life, even when making concrete decisions. If people follow an ideology, the assessments, behavioral recommendations, and guidance of that ideology will also influence their daily decisions.

Looking at all these five functions of belief systems and ideologies, it appears that belief systems and ideologies are a natural part of our psychological functioning. Three of these functions are addressed in this book. Chapter 2 looked at the human information problem. Ideologies and belief systems can mitigate of the information problem (function (1)). Function (2) of ideologies and belief systems is to provide a coherent view of the world and to give values, evaluations, and overall orientation in the world. However, this function is not explicitly addressed in detail in this book. Function (3) of ideologies and belief systems is to address and serve human psychological needs in relation to states of the world. Belief systems and ideologies outline social conditions and states that serve psychological needs, and they also explain how to achieve these states. Through their interpretations, explanations, and proposed solutions, they depict a state of the world where these needs are recognized and fulfilled. Consequently, individuals seek out ideologies or belief systems that match their individual need structure such that it provides narratives that address and serve that very structure. Hence, in Chap. 6, we show how humans are attracted by the ideology or belief system that matches an individual's particular need system, and thus how it is a viable reconciliation option for psychological human needs. Function (4), even though it addresses the basic forms of togetherness that ideologies or belief systems propose and hence is important, it is not explicitly addressed in this book. Function (5) is discussed in Chap. 7. In this chapter, we will see how belief systems and ideologies provide orientation for everyday decisions and, hence, provide guidance for subjectively rational decision-making. Ideologies and belief systems transfer beliefs and attitudes into "reality" by providing guiding narratives, principles, or categorizations about how to process information and how to behave.

Further, a belief system or ideology is usually shaped by an organization, which dominates the current interpretation of narratives, beliefs, evaluations, and attitudes. Thus, the belief system/ideology and its organization provide permanent interpretations, evaluations, visions, and, if necessary, utopias or dystopias about society, they formulate goals, and propose strategies and actions for achieving these goals. Thus, the organization representing an ideology or belief system is extremely important for understanding its role in human societies. Organizations decide about objectives, narratives, and even strategies for achieving goals. They can act for the good of their followers or for their own benefit. They can be agreeable or aggressive, bad or good, peaceful or violent. Therefore, Sect. 5.2 takes a closer look at how such organizations behave.

5.2 Ideologies and Belief Systems Are Shaped by Organizations

So far, we have analyzed the role of ideologies and belief systems for an individual's needs and preferences. We have thus studied the "consumers" of ideologies and belief systems. But we also need to take a look at the organizations that shape ideologies and belief systems, that is, the "suppliers" of ideologies and belief systems. To simplify, we assume that an organization can be described by means of two elements: the leader or head of the organization and the adherents or followers of that organization. The two elements each play a different role that needs to be considered if we want to understand how such organizations function and what role the ideology or belief systems play in them.

Leaders Leaders dominate organizations. To simplify again, we assume that leaders determine the content of the ideology or belief system through their key narratives and value system, and they define the organization's goals, set its strategies and policies to reach those goals, and develop means of recruiting adherents. They know that a large number of followers are needed in order to reach whatever goals they have.

Adherents and Followers Adherents and followers search for need reconciliation that an ideology or belief system can provide. Note that we are making the stylized assumption here that people become adherents of an ideology or belief system as the narratives address and reconcile the needs of the individuals. Further, the extent of need reconciliation by an ideology is measured by the magnitude of the match value between individual's needs and an ideology. This mechanism will be described and discussed in detail in Chap. 6. Thus, anyone who wants to understand in detail how an individual becomes a follower of an ideology should read Chap. 6 before continuing with this current chapter. If the concept of need reconciliation and match values as an abstract concept is sufficient at this point, you can continue directly with this current chapter.

However, once the ideology or belief system is adopted, it provides guidance and has all the functions that were described in the above. Followers support the ideology and believe that this support will bring the organization and them personally closer to achieving their goals. This support can be provided in many different forms. It can take the form of minor support through membership fees paid to the organization, or it can be a generous donation; it can take the shape of support through public demonstrations or discussions, volunteering for the organization, or direct professional activities up to that of a military fighter. The important point is that each of these activities will increase public awareness, manifest the importance of the organization and its ideology or belief system, and bring it closer to achieving the goals of the ideology or belief system and its organization. Against the backdrop of this varying distribution of roles within organizations, we can now examine the functioning of these organizations and their ideologies.

The central and dominant player in such organizations is its leader (or leading group). He or she holds responsibility for all its key activities. And so let us start with the leader and his or her motivations. What motive do leaders have for directing and forming an organization and its ideology? To understand this motivation, we refer to Collier and Hoeffler (2004) and their discussion of "greed" versus "grievance" as two possible causes of armed conflict. The "greed" explanation refers to the materialistic causes of war, such as the exploitation of economic resources (e.g., oil) or profits from businesses related to war or simply power. By contrast, according to the "grievance" explanation, organizations and their leaders seek to gain some kind of sociopolitical improvement that is often related to discriminated groups, ethnicity, age, religion, or gender. "Grievance" refers to a complaint or protest against perceived injustice or unfair treatment. Although we are not only analyzing the role of ideologies and belief systems in the context of social conflict but also in a more general sense, we can still derive leaders' motivations from these ideas.

However, the point of reference in our interpretation is not necessarily an objective point but the narrative adopted by an ideology or belief system. Something is considered unfair because one's own ideological beliefs are not fully recognized. The commitment to one's own ideology or belief system, along with the goals, values, and strategies that come with it, often motivates the leaders of an organization. This means that the leadership of an organization can in principle pursue its activities for two very different motives. Either it is greedy for income and/or power or it actually wants to help its own ideological belief to prevail. When questioning top officials in real-world organizations, we are likely to uncover a variety of individual and specific motivations. However, for the purposes of this discussion, we are concentrating solely on these two motivations.

Next, organizations understand that they require followers and resources to achieve their goals, regardless of what those goals are. Thus, recruiting and retaining followers is crucial for building this base of resources. This brings us back to the role of ideologies and belief systems, and the human pursuit of fulfilling psychological needs. We return to the concept that the narratives within ideologies can meet these needs, leading individuals to adopt the belief system or ideology that aligns best with their personal needs.

What implications does this have for an organization's efforts to attract followers? Organizations must craft narratives that resonate with the needs of potential followers. Sometimes, they might even create narratives that highlight threats to certain needs as a strategy to engage potential supporters. Crucially, it is vital for them to disseminate their narratives broadly to maximize their reach and connect with as many people as possible. Followers can only be recruited if a message resonates with them.[4]

When is an ideological message especially effective? (1) When people are dissatisfied and feel they are being treated unfairly, they often perceive that their needs are being ignored or unmet. In such situations, individuals are likely to seek out narratives that acknowledge their concerns and propose strategies for positive

[4] Here, the term resonance is related to the concept of Rosa (2016). We believe that the mechanism that we technically refer to as "match" manifests itself through a form of resonance in Rosa's sense.

change. This demand for recognition and resolution drives people to align with ideologies that promise to address and serve their needs. The search for and adoption of a new ideology therefore reflect the perceived disregard for their needs.

(2) Adolescents and young adults go through an orientation phase. During this phase, they are particularly open to all kinds of narratives that interpret and explain the world they observe, that evaluate the conditions and states they discover, and suggest what should change and what should remain. They are looking for a belief system or ideology that provides explanations and answers to their questions in relation to their own need structures. They are, therefore, also particularly sensitive to the narratives proposed by ideologies and belief systems.

(3) Even when people adhere to their ideology or belief system for a longer period of time after initially adopting it and base their everyday decisions on recommendations made (see Chap. 7), it is still possible to change one's orientation. This is particularly the case when an individual realizes that the previous recommendations have led them to make bad decisions. For this reason, people who realize that they are following an ideology or belief system that does not actually suit them are also open to new offers.

Hence, it is in particular the three groups described in the above that are open to such narratives and may join a movement or even an organization with a shared belief system or ideology. Furthermore, ideologies and belief systems also provide a basis for identification. Members of a particular organization share values, norms, and beliefs, creating a sense of community that is another function of ideologies and belief systems.

Organizations fully understand these dynamics. They know what actions are necessary and what an effective recruitment process entails. However, adequate resources are essential to fund such a process. Even with a clear understanding of the mechanisms involved, the primary limitation for an organization is its resource base. An organization can only disseminate its narratives widely and ensure they have the desired impact if it has sufficient resources and a robust communication strategy.

Based on this description of organizations, we can see that they have to solve a typical, even complex, economic problem. They have an objective that can only be achieved with the help of resources, but available resources are limited. Thus, organizations have a resource constraint because they only have access to resources through their followers. These followers, in turn, can only be attracted through a recruitment process, which in turn absorbs resources. Further, recruiting followers is a time-consuming process. It usually takes many years. This means that organizations have an intertemporal decision-making problem. In each period, they have to decide whether to choose to use resources to pursue their objective or whether to prefer to recruit more followers who will then make more resources available and improve the pursuit of their objective. The solution to such an intertemporal problem is an optimal time path for devoting resources to the respective objective and recruitment process, and an optimal final number of followers.

In the next section, we develop a model that incorporates these elements. An organization and its leader define an objective that can be achieved by means of an intertemporal optimal path of recruitment and promoting the organization's objective.

Model of an (Ideological) Organization

The model will be discussed in three steps: First, we describe the formalization of the organization's objectives. Second, we outline the recruitment process and intertemporal constraints. Third, we solve the model and identify the path of an organization's development as well as the final number of followers and achievements of its objectives.

Objectives Proponents of the "greed" explanation, such as Collier and Hoeffler (2004), argue that personal profit is the primary cause of conflict. Thus, greed is already a motivation for taking the lead in an organization and shaping its objectives. In this modeling, we adopt this suggestion and assume that greed on the part of an organization's leaders is directed toward disposable income and the exercise of power. Disposable income can then be used either directly for consumption purposes or for purposes that lead to the exercise of power. Leaders of such organizations therefore try to assert their personal interests and use the organization for their own purposes.

Formally, we assume that in each period an organization has disposable income $\mathfrak{d}(t)$ that generates a flow of benefit b for the organization and for its leaders. We specify the benefit function as

$$b(\mathfrak{d}(t)) = \frac{\mathfrak{d}(t)^{1-\sigma}}{1-\sigma} \text{ with } b'(\mathfrak{d}) > 0 \text{ and } b''(\mathfrak{d}) < 0. \tag{5.1}$$

Further, as we are considering a full time path of organizational development, we can look at more than a single period. We have to consider the whole lifetime of the organization and add up all future periods to get the total benefit B. The objective is to maximize this total benefit

$$\max: B = \int_0^\infty b(\mathfrak{d}(t))e^{-\rho t}dt. \tag{5.2}$$

Generating Income The goal of maximizing the organization's benefit can be better achieved if the number of that organization's followers F is high. Followers' membership contributions and donations lead to gross revenue for the organization, denoted by y. The larger the number of followers, the more revenue can be generated. This revenue is the basis for all the organization's other activities and benefits. Therefore, the organization's headquarters will try to recruit a large number of supporters. However, the supporters are not all the same and are not all equally committed to the organization.

Organizations use their narratives to appeal to potential followers. Thus, the first adherents are likely to have a high match value and, hence, become highly committed members who are willing to invest in the organization's success (Weinstein, 2005). Individuals with a lower match value show lower levels of commitment and, hence, less willingness to contribute financially. Thus, the larger the total number of an organization's followers the less the additional income that is generated by additional adherents will be. Hence, from the organization's perspective, income is generated as a function of the total number of followers F,

$$y = y(F) = F^a \text{ with } y'(F) = \alpha F^{a-1} > 0 \text{ and } y''(F) = \alpha\,(a-1)\,F^{a-2} < 0. \tag{5.3}$$

Parameter $a < 1$ represents the organization's income elasticity with respect to followers.[5] This means that if the number of followers F increases by 1%, income increases by about a%. Hence, a high value for parameter a means that the followers generate a relatively high income. Thus, the number of followers is of great importance for an organization, and recruitment is crucial. However, this is a task that requires some effort, which is why we need to look at this process in more detail.

Recruitment Recruitment is defined as the gross marginal increase in followers in a period $\dot{F}^g = R$. In Müller and Gries (2024), we suggest that organizations use two channels of recruitment: the channel of the narrative as well as the channel of providing direct transfers or social welfare benefits as a reward for commitment to that organization. As discussed in detail in Chap. 6, narratives are important because they can match with a potential follower's need structure and then turn that follower into a real adherent. Adherents become convinced that the ideology or belief system can guide and support them by serving their needs. The second channel, which is more common in poorer countries, refers to the fact that an organization provides concrete financial and social support to its followers and their families in addition to the narrative it proposes. People become followers because the organization provides for them or at least contributes to their care.

We do not, however, want to pursue this second channel any further. We will concentrate on the narratives and the need to find supporters using these narratives. Gaining followers is not an automatic process. To recruit adherents, organizations have to invest time, effort, and financial resources in the recruitment process. To do this, people first have to get to know the respective narratives in order to then check whether they serve their needs. Organizations will therefore disseminate information or even propaganda, P_R, about their ideology or belief system. Disseminating information or propaganda is, therefore, a first essential part of the recruitment process.

In addition, organizations have to reach out to people and convince them by making sure that the messages they are sending serve the needs of those people. However, a population has very different people in it who have very different need structures. Therefore, a certain narrative, let us say one that – on the left-right political spectrum – tends to address and serve people with a preference for the political right cannot at the same time also appeal to people who have quite strong preferences for politically left-wing narratives.

[5] The income elasticity with respect to the number of followers is $\frac{\partial Y}{\partial F}\frac{F}{Y} = a$, and the elasticity with respect to the average match value is $\frac{\partial Y}{\partial \bar{M}}\frac{\bar{M}}{Y} = b$.

From the organization's point of view, this means that its ideological positioning determines how high the maximum match value of its narrative is for a given distribution of preferences in the population as a whole. This positioning therefore determines how well the ideology or belief system matches the preferences in the population as a whole and what the maximum level of acceptance is. $\bar{\mathfrak{M}}_i$ denotes this maximum match value between the narratives of an organization i and the total population's preferences.

In this simple model, we now assume that only these two elements are decisive for recruitment success. We can thus describe the recruitment of new followers for the organization i as a function of the maximum match value $\bar{\mathfrak{M}}_i$ of this ideology with the population's preferences and the information or propaganda this organization can generate by disseminating P_R. For the sake of simplicity, we specify this function as

$$\dot{F}_i^g = R_i = R\left(P_R, \bar{\mathfrak{M}}_i\right) = P_R \bar{\mathfrak{M}}^b,$$

where b is the elasticity of recruitment (new followers) with respect to the maximum match value of ideology i.[6] Further, while R describes gross recruitment, there are at the same time some supporters who stop supporting the organization at a constant exogenous rate δ. Thus, the net change in followers can be described and specified as

$$\dot{F}_i = P_R \bar{\mathfrak{M}}_i^b - \delta_i F_i(t). \tag{5.4}$$

In order to understand this recruitment process and how an organization manages it in more detail, we need to take a closer look at the two central elements of recruitment. We first look at the dissemination of information and/or propaganda P_R, before turning to the concept of the maximum match value $\bar{\mathfrak{M}}_i$ in more detail.

Information Dissemination and Propaganda Since a potential follower will only turn into a real follower if the organization's narratives match that follower's need structure at least to a certain degree, the organization has to disseminate its narratives to reach potential followers and convince them that its narratives match the individual's need structure. Therefore, organizations need to spend revenue on professionally managing the dissemination of their narratives. The reach of propaganda is determined by expenditure on propaganda activities. This expenditure is defined by the income of the organization $y(t)$ minus the income the organization wants to spend on consumption or its purposes, that is, the revenue the organization and its leaders would like to have at their disposal $\mathfrak{d}(t)$,

$$P_R(t) = \varphi(y(t) - \mathfrak{d}(t)). \tag{5.5}$$

[6] The recruitment elasticity describes the percentage rate of new followers that can be recruited when the maximum match value of the ideology increases by a particular percentage: $b = \frac{\partial R}{\partial \bar{\mathfrak{M}}} \frac{\bar{\mathfrak{M}}}{R}$.

In Eq. (5.5), φ is a parameter of propaganda effectiveness with respect to propaganda expenditure. This parameter depends on the leaders' ability to efficiently propagate the organization's ideology or belief system to the population. The higher φ is, the more successful the propaganda is in terms of recruitment. Later, we will see that this parameter of propaganda effectiveness or propaganda reach will play an important role in the organization's success. The range of information, for example, strategies for using the Internet to disseminate information and disinformation, can be discussed with the help of this parameter.

Match Value with the Population's Preferences Next to the number of followers, maximum acceptance of and support for an ideology or belief system in the population are important for an organization's recruitment. As already defined, $\bar{\mathfrak{M}}_i$ is the maximum match value between the population and the organization's belief system. Each organization i and its narratives have its own value $\bar{\mathfrak{M}}_i$ in a given population. The higher this match value, the higher the share of the population that at least to some extent matches with the organization, and the more easy it is to recruit followers. To understand the concept of the maximum match value of the population $\bar{\mathfrak{M}}_i$, we look at the population and how an ideology or belief system relates to the preferences and the distribution of preferences among the population. Figure 5.1 describes this distribution of preferences.

In our standard discussions, each individual has an n-dimensional system of needs and preferences (see Chap. 4) that are to be served. This is why we generally avoid a one-dimensional left-right political spectrum, because we want to model multidimensional needs and reconcile them by means of multidimensional narratives. However, at this point, a one-dimensional left-right representation is advantageous for reasons of simplification, and it also allows a comparison with the "median voter model" later on. The curve in Fig. 5.1 illustrates the distribution of the population's desire for left- or right-wing ideologies. In this example, the distribution has the shape of a Gaussian curve: Only a few individuals have a very high preference for either extreme right-wing or extreme left-wing ideological narratives, while many individuals have neither extreme left-wing nor extreme right-wing preferences.

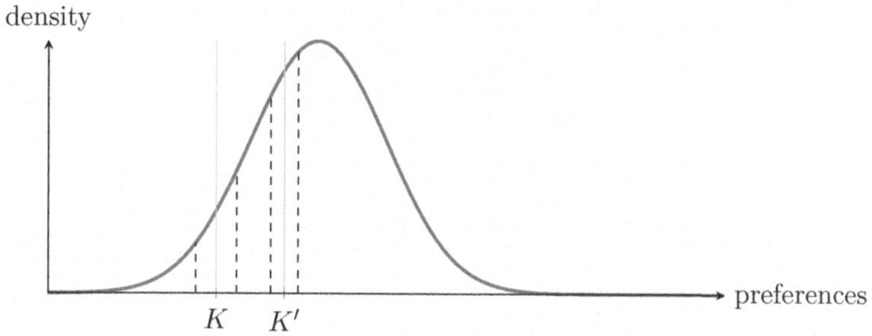

Fig. 5.1 Distribution of preferences: left preferences (left), right preferences (right)

Now let us turn to the ideologies themselves. Each ideology i consists of values, norms, and narratives that serve people's need. Some ideologies and their narratives serve the preferences of left-wing-oriented people more, others right-wing-oriented people. Thus, each ideological organization i has a position on the horizontal axis in Fig. 5.1. If we assume that ideology $i = K$ stands for narratives that are quite left-leaning, individuals who have the same or a very close positions to K have the highest match value. The greater the distance to that position, the lower the individual's match value with that organization. Thus, the maximum match value $\bar{\mathfrak{M}}_K$ that an ideology K reaches in a population can be calculated using the population's preference distribution. In Fig. 5.1, organization K' has a higher maximum match value $\bar{\mathfrak{M}}_{K'}$ than organization K because there are more individuals with preferences close to K'.

To illustrate how we can depict an ideology in Fig. 5.1 and determine the corresponding match value of this ideology, we briefly discuss the following example. An approximation of the distribution in Fig. 5.1 ought to be the representation with discrete values in Fig. 5.2.

Within the left-right political scheme, the preference category L10 could represent a preference for the extreme far left and the preference R10 for the extreme far right. As in Fig. 5.1, we see a discrete representation of a frequency distribution of preferences in the total population in the columns in Fig. 5.2. The distribution resembles a normal distribution, i.e., only a relatively small proportion of the population (0.5%) has preferences for L10 (extreme left-leaning narratives) or R10 (extreme right-leaning narratives), but almost half of the total population (44%) has

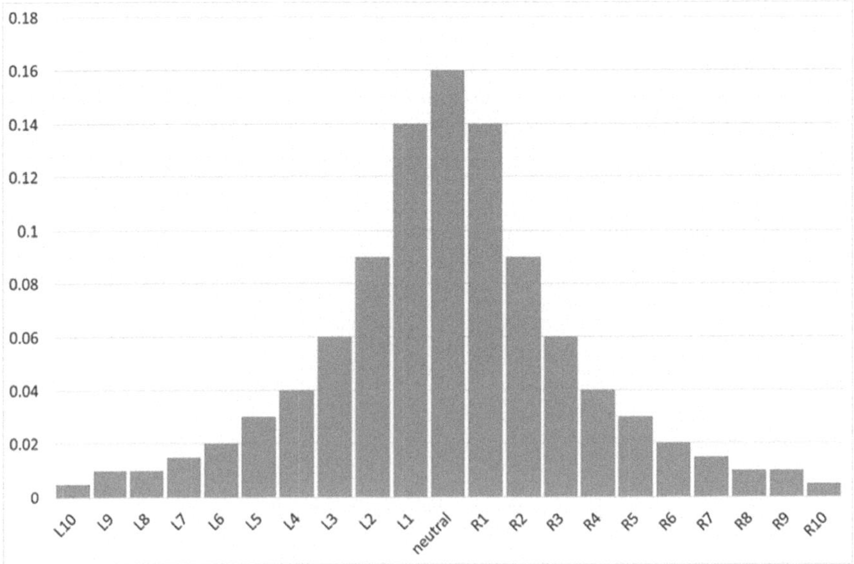

Fig. 5.2 Example: Discrete left/right preference distribution in a population

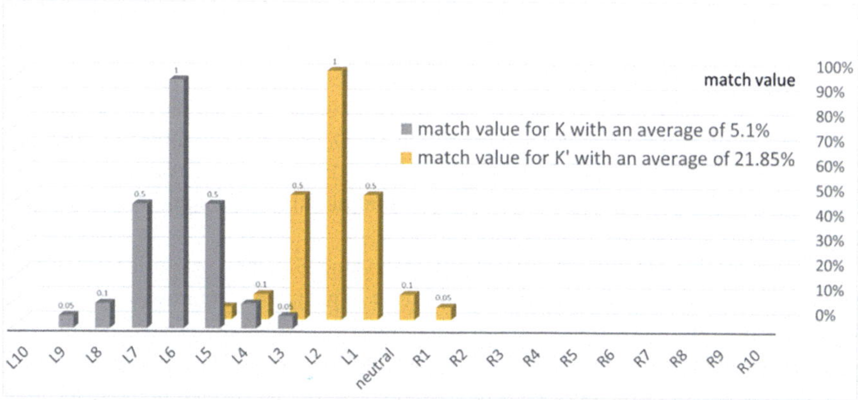

Fig. 5.3 Example: Calculated maximum match values for ideologies perfectly matching L6 and L2

preferences for moderate narratives ranging from L1 to R1. If this represents the population's preferences, and thus the demand side for ideological narratives, we can now look at the supply side and describe how an ideology K, whose narratives are located at the interval L6 in Fig. 5.2, i.e., relatively to the left, can be included in our considerations. If K serves the category L6 and a number of people are looking for these narratives, then there is a perfect match for these people. If the value of a perfect match equals 1, and no match is 0, then the people whose preferences are categorized as L6 will be perfectly served by K, and the match value for these people with ideology K is 1. If we now assume that the match value of K with the preferences of the people in the neighboring categories L7–L9 and L3–L5 decreases with increasing distance, this can be illustrated by Fig. 5.3. While the match value in L6 is 100%, the match values with the people in L5 and L7 are assumed to be only 50%, and the match values with the preferences of the people in L4 and L8 are assumed to be only 10%, and for further distances, it turns to 0. If we take these values for the respective match values as an example, the maximum match value that ideology K can achieve with this distribution of preferences in this population is $\mathfrak{M}_K = 5.1\%$ (maximum level of approval in the population)).[7]

[7] Calculation of the maximum match value ideology K can obtain in this population

	L9	L8	L7	L6	L5	L4	L3
Match value of K with	0.05	0.1	0.5	1	0.5	0.1	0.05
Frequency	1%	1%	1.5%	2%	3%	4%	6%
Contribution	0.05%	0.1%	0.75%	2%	1.5%	0.4%	0.3%
Maximum match value of K In population	5.1%						

That is, maximum acceptance of this ideology K in this society, and therefore the general approval for this ideology that can be found in this society, is therefore relatively weak. The situation is different if we look at ideology K'. Ideology K' is a 100% match for category L2. Since category L2 already comprises a relatively high proportion of the population (9%), and the neighboring category L1 also represents a very high proportion (14%), and the match value is still 0.5, the maximum match value in relation to the total population is significantly higher, namely $\bar{\mathfrak{M}}_{K'} = 21.85\%$. [8]

This means that ideology K' with this match value $\bar{\mathfrak{M}}_{K'}$ has a significantly higher level of acceptance in the population and can expect more approval on average. Applying this preference distribution, ideologies in the center ground can expect more approval from the population as a whole. In this example, Fig. 5.4 describes the match values of all those ideologies that would be perfectly located in the respective preference category (from L10 to R10).

Using this part of the model and this interpretation of the aggregated maximum match value of an ideology as a measure of acceptance and approval of this ideology in the population, we are close to the well-known *median voter model*. However, we will see further below that the model presented here allows for completely different patterns than just a movement toward the center. For the moment, we can indicate the position of each ideology K in Fig. 5.1 and calculate the maximum match value for the population.

Thus, returning to Fig. 5.1, we can see that the organization's position reveals information about how to recruit followers. As mentioned above, those individuals whose needs perfectly match the ideology of organization K have the highest match value, and, thus, we assume that these individuals are the first to become its followers. But the match value of individuals still close to K (see the dashed interval in Fig. 5.1) is also high, and these therefore individuals will also tend to follow the organization. Recruiting additional followers means widening this symmetrical interval to reach more individuals. This can be done through propaganda. The more followers an organization recruits, the lower the match value of additional followers is. Therefore, they must be convinced of the organization's ideology through propaganda and other benefits. Note that the width of the interval for organization K' is narrower than the width of the interval for organization K in

[8] Calculation of maximum match value ideology K' can obtain in this population

	L5	L4	L3	L2	L1	Neutral	R1
Match value of K' with	0.05	0.1	0.5	1	0.5	0.1	0.05
Frequency	3%	4%	6%	9%	14%	16%	14%
Contribution	0.15%	0.4%	3%	9%	7%	1.6%	0.7%
Maximum match value of K' In population	21.85%						

Note also that maximum match values do not need to add up to 1.

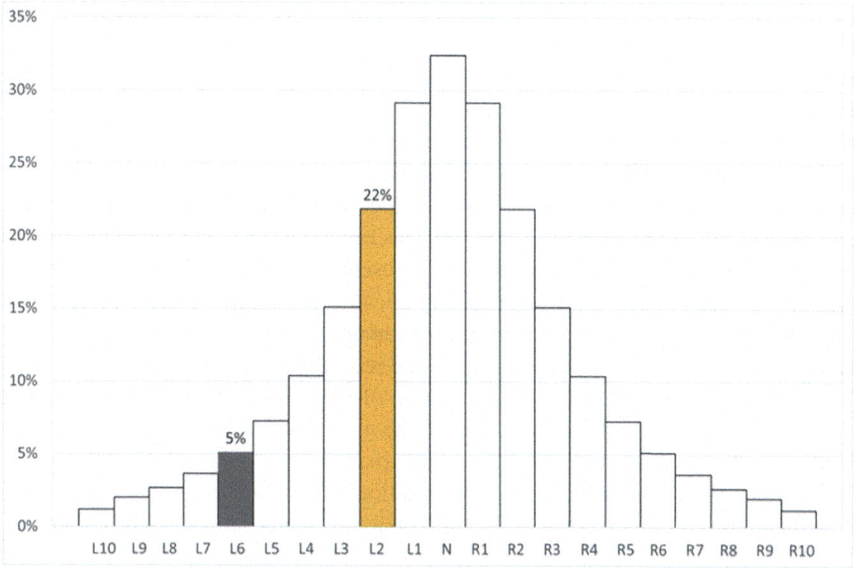

Fig. 5.4 Example: Calculated maximum match values for each category Li

Fig. 5.1. Since there are more individuals with high match values for organization K' than for organization K, organization K' already has more followers with a smaller recruitment interval than organization K. It is, therefore, actually easier for organization K' to successfully recruit followers. However, we will see below that this is not a sufficient condition, only an advantage that can easily be squandered.

Intertemporal Optimization In our model, we have assumed greed for income and/or power as the leadership's key motivation. The organization's leadership thus pursues the goal of maximizing its benefits from the organization's income and that that income remains available to it over a long period of time. At the same time, the leadership knows that its income is only generated by the number of the organization's followers. It needs supporters. However, these can only be gained by the organization spending income on information dissemination and propaganda. This means it needs an optimal expenditure path for information dissemination and propaganda. This optimization problem will be formally formulated below.

Before we turn to a formal description of the organization's intertemporal optimization model, it is still important and interesting when it comes to a political interpretation of the organization's actions and the resulting implications not to confuse objectives and constraints. It is, therefore, already possible to see at this point how such an organization will act politically, for example, whether it will be prepared to make political compromises. If the objective – as in our model – is greed for power and income, the narrative is primarily a means of acquiring resources. Any narrative and positioning – even of extremist ideas – that mobilize followers are worth using as long as they actually do mobilize followers. Although followers are recruited through narratives, leaders will have other intentions based on their objectives that sometimes have little to do with the pronounced ideology. This can mean both that they present themselves as more willing to compromise in terms of their ideology and are more extremist in terms of their narratives. Ultimately, the ideological outcome is irrelevant, as the leaders are pursuing other goals anyway.

The situation is different, however, if the organization actually pursues ideological goals and perhaps even has an extremist ideological vision. In this case, it must also recruit supporters. However, if it only succeeds in doing so by showing itself to be more tolerant of other narratives, it will present a trivialized version of its actual extreme ideology for as long as necessary because it is opportune for recruitment reasons. When we look at organizations, we can only correctly assess them and their behavior if we correctly assess their goal and recruitment mechanism. However, at this point, we do not yet have the full picture of what optimal behavior on the part of organizations is, which is why, for now, the model will be developed further and these and other interpretations will be taken up again later on (see Sect. 8.2).

Formally, we can now define the organization's optimization problem described at the beginning of this section as the following intertemporal control problem:

$$\begin{aligned}
&\text{maximize} \int_0^\infty b(\mathfrak{d}\,(t))e^{-\rho t}dt \\
&\text{subject to } \dot{F} = R\left(P_R\left(F\left(t\right), \mathfrak{d}\left(t\right)\right), \bar{\mathfrak{M}}\right) - \delta F\left(t\right) \\
&F(0) = F_0 \\
&\text{and } 0 \leq \mathfrak{d}(t) \leq y(F),
\end{aligned}$$

where ρ is the personal rate of time preference of the organization's leaders. This is an infinite horizon optimal control problem where $\mathfrak{d}\,(t)$ is the control variable and $F\,(t)$ is the state variable. The Hamiltonian for this problem is

$$H := b(\mathfrak{d}(t))e^{-\rho t} + \lambda(t)\left(R\left(P_R\left(F\left(t\right), \mathfrak{d}\left(t\right)\right), \bar{\mathfrak{M}}\right) - \delta F\left(t\right)\right).$$

Model Solution and Interpretations As this problem is autonomous, we can simply use the current-value Hamiltonian and plug in the specified functions

$$H_c := He^{\rho t} = \frac{\mathfrak{d}\,(t)^{1-\sigma}}{1-\sigma} + \mu\,(t)\left(\varphi\left(F(t)^a - \mathfrak{d}(t)\right)\bar{\mathfrak{M}}^b - \delta F\,(t)\right). \tag{5.6}$$

First order condition (FOC) With $\mu = \lambda e^{\rho t}$, the maximum principle requires

$$\frac{\partial H_c}{\partial \mathfrak{d}} = \mathfrak{d}^{-\sigma} - \mu\varphi\bar{\mathfrak{M}}^b = 0 \tag{5.7}$$

$$\dot{F} = \frac{\partial H_c}{\partial \mu} = \varphi(y(F) - \mathfrak{d})\bar{\mathfrak{M}}^b - \delta F \tag{5.8}$$

$$\dot{\mu} = -\frac{\partial H_c}{\partial F} + \rho\mu = -\mu\left(\varphi\alpha F^{\alpha-1}\bar{\mathfrak{M}}^b - \delta - \rho\right). \tag{5.9}$$

Determine Optimal Dynamics (Two Differential Equations) From the FOC, we obtain the Ramsey rule for the organization

$$\frac{\dot{\eth}}{\eth} = \frac{\varphi\alpha F^{\alpha-1}\bar{\mathfrak{M}}^b - \delta - \rho}{\sigma}. \tag{5.10}$$

Using (5.10) and (5.9), we obtain a system of two differential equations and thus can perform a qualitative analysis using a phase diagram. For calculations, see Appendix A.5.

$$\dot{F}(t) = \varphi(F(t)^\alpha - \eth(t))\bar{\mathfrak{M}}^b - \delta F(t), \tag{5.11}$$

$$\dot{\eth}(t) = \frac{\varphi\alpha F(t)^{\alpha-1}\bar{\mathfrak{M}}^b - \delta - \rho}{\sigma}\eth(t). \tag{5.12}$$

In phase diagram Fig. 5.5, we draw the $\dot{F} = 0$curve and the $\dot{\eth} = 0$ curve.

The $\dot{F} = 0$ curve is defined by $\eth = F^\alpha - \frac{\delta}{\varphi\bar{\mathfrak{M}}^b}F$. In Fig. 5.5, this curve starts in the origin with an infinite slope $\frac{d\eth}{dF} = \alpha F^{\alpha-1} - \frac{\delta}{\varphi\bar{\mathfrak{M}}^b}$, reaches a maximum at $F = \left(\frac{\alpha\varphi\bar{\mathfrak{M}}^b}{\delta}\right)^{\frac{1}{1-\alpha}}$, and intersects the F-axis at $F^{\max} = \left(\frac{\varphi\bar{\mathfrak{M}}^b}{\delta}\right)^{\frac{1}{1-\alpha}}$. Thus, $F^{\max}$ is the maximum number of followers that can be generated.

The $\dot{\eth} = 0$ curve is defined by $y'(F) = \frac{\delta+\rho}{\varphi\bar{\mathfrak{M}}^b}$. Due to the assumptions $y'(F) > 0$ and $y''(F) < 0$, $y(F)$ is upward sloping and concave. The slope is unique for each F, and therefore, only one choice of F can satisfy $y'(F) = \frac{\delta+\rho}{\varphi\bar{\mathfrak{M}}^b}$. Consequently, the $\dot{\eth} = 0$ curve is a vertical line in the (F, y^d)-space.

In phase diagram Fig. 5.5, the intersection of the two isoclines at $(F^*, \eth^*)$ determines the system's intertemporal equilibrium of the system. This point is a steady state because neither F nor $\eth$ change over time.

In addition, we can analyze the dynamics of the system by starting at a point other than in equilibrium. From the differential equations (5.11) and (5.12), we can derive

$$\frac{\partial\dot{F}}{\partial\eth} = -\varphi\bar{\mathfrak{M}}^b < 0 \text{ and } \frac{\partial\dot{\eth}}{\partial F} = \frac{\eth}{\sigma}\varphi y''(F)\bar{\mathfrak{M}}^b < 0.$$

Since $\frac{\partial\dot{F}}{\partial\eth}$ is negative, we have $\dot{F} < 0$ for all points above the $\dot{F} = 0$ isocline and $\dot{F} > 0$ for all points below the $\dot{F} = 0$ isocline. Similarly, since $\frac{\partial\dot{\eth}}{\partial F}$ is negative, we have $\dot{\eth} < 0$ for all points to the right of the $\dot{\eth} = 0$ line and $\dot{\eth} > 0$ for all points to the left of the $\dot{\eth} = 0$-line. Thus, the $\dot{\eth} = 0$ line and the $\dot{F} = 0$ curve divide the phase diagram into four regions whose dynamic directions are represented by the blue and gray arrows in Fig. 5.5. The dashed green lines are examples for adjustment

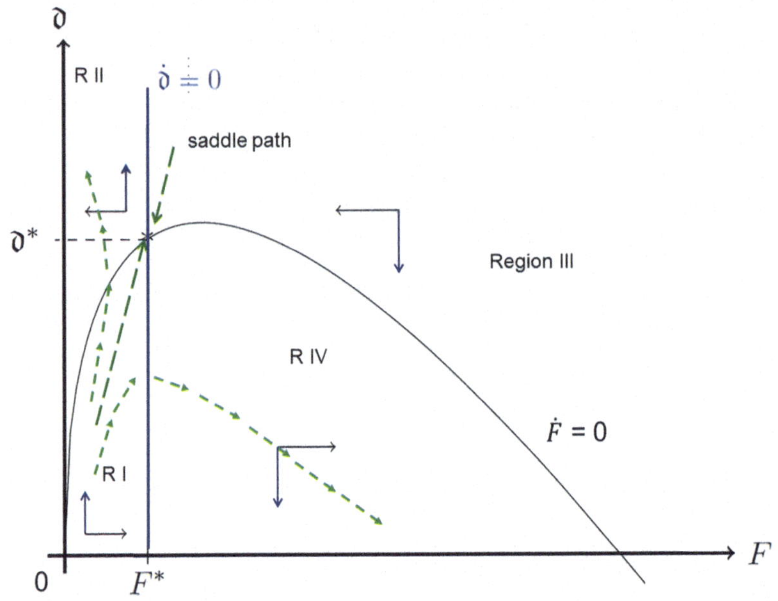

Fig. 5.5 Phase diagram: stationary point and potential dynamic adjustment paths of an organization

paths. From the directions of the arrows, we can conclude that the equilibrium point $(F^*, ð^*)$ is a saddle point. If the system starts in one of the regions where both variables ð and F move in the same direction (lower-left region or upper-right region), they will eventually reach the steady state on a saddle path. However, if the system starts in one of the other regions, it will end up with either $ð = 0$ or $F = 0$ – both of which will lead to the organization collapsing, either because its objective cannot be fulfilled or it no longer has any followers.

What does this mean for our understanding of how organizations develop and their dynamics? The first implication we obtain from this model is that an organization needs some time to develop. The appearance or disappearance of an organization is a dynamic process. Secondly, there is a stationary size toward which an organization moves. We will see in the following which factors determine an organization's success in a stationary dynamic equilibrium. Thirdly, it can be steered along an optimal growth path. However, it can also drift away if this steering is not actively carried out. We can illustrate this in the following descriptions of different paths.

Once an organization has been founded, its leadership must actively guide it along an optimal path toward steady-state dynamic equilibrium. If it fails to do so, the organization will either dissolve or it will have many members but will not achieve its goals.

Let us look at two such unstable development paths. An organization starts in origin and moves in region I [RI] with an increase in followers and an increase in disposable income in a north-easterly direction. However, if the path is steeper than the saddle path, i.e., if too many resources are used for the target system, the development path will drift into region II [RII]. As a consequence, the organization will have fewer and fewer followers and will ultimately dissolve due to a lack of followers – unless this process is actively counteracted. The situation is different if the movement path is flatter than the saddle path. In this case, the organization will move into region IV [RIV], in which it will gain many followers but will hardly pursue its actual goals. Its disposable income will shrink toward zero. However, since the organization's leaders can always adjust its path and adapt their policies, a definitively unstable development is unlikely. The leadership can always aim for dynamic equilibrium.

After this initially technical discussion, the next section will look at what political implications can be drawn from this.

Political Interpretation and Implications Now that we know how an organization develops, it is interesting in terms of a political interpretation to discuss what reach such an organization has, where it is located on the political spectrum, and what parameters it will use if it acts strategically.

Reach of the Organization Within the Population At the steady-state equilibrium, the organization has F^* followers. This is derived in Fig. 5.5 and also shown in Fig. 5.6. In Fig. 5.6, we assume that organization's first followers are those with the highest match value and who are, hence, closest to the position of K. Now, the optimal number F^* defines a symmetrical interval of recruited followers around K. In Fig. 5.6, the blue interval represents how many followers could be recruited and their distance to the position of the organization K. The higher F^*, the wider this interval is because more income is generated, which can be used for propaganda to recruit more followers. Formally,

$$F^* = \int_{K-b}^{K+b} f_K(x)dx = F_K(K+b) - F_K(K-b). \tag{5.13}$$

Thus, F^* determines the distance b between the follower with the lowest match value (in both directions) and the position of the organization K, and thus the width of the recruitment interval.

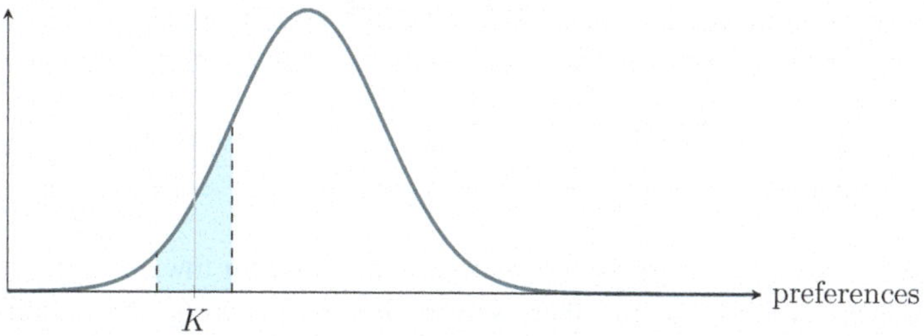

Fig. 5.6 Recruited followers of organization K in equilibrium

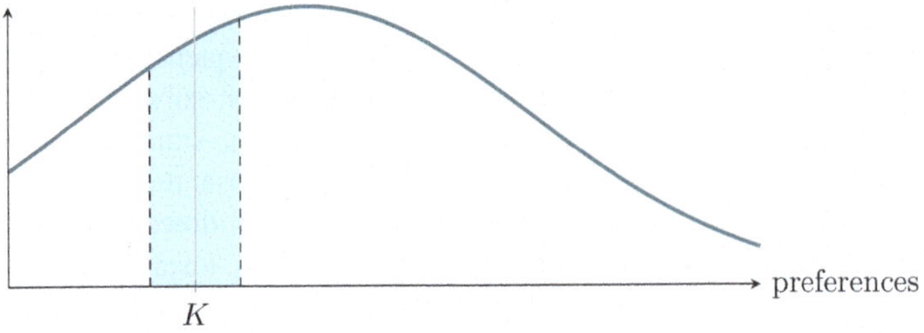

Fig. 5.7 Recruited followers of organization K with different population distributions

To obtain more intuition for the mechanisms of the model, we consider a variation of the variance in the preferences of the population. Figure 5.7 shows the recruitment interval of organization K when the population distribution is different. Now there is higher variance in the population's preferences. Therefore, the recruitment interval is wider than that in the population in Fig. 5.6. That is, for the same number of followers, the range of narratives found in these followers is wider. An ideology thus reaches a broader spectrum of followers with neighboring ideological preferences.

Determinants of Reach: The Position of the Ideological Narrative After having described optimal organizational development under given conditions, we can now turn to examining what effect changes to various parameters have. These parameters can be characteristics of certain organizations, but they can also describe technical conditions that have changed or that an organization deliberately uses to improve its position.

Three parameters can be easily interpreted and categorized from the political perspective: the positioning of the organization's narrative on the right-left political spectrum; the organization's time preference; and the effectiveness of its propaganda. We start by looking at the narrative's orientation. The narrative's position on the left-right spectrum translates into the characteristic match value $\bar{\mathfrak{M}}_i$ for each ideology i. In Fig. 5.4, we showed that ideologies that tend to be located on the edges of the spectrum have lower match values. If an ideology moves more toward the center, the match value increases. Therefore, we now want to examine what it means in terms of an organization's success if it aligns its narrative to be less extreme and more toward the center. From the differential equations (5.11) [$\dot{F} = 0$ isocline] and (5.12) [$\dot{\mathfrak{d}} = 0$ isocline], we can derive changes in the two curves

$$\left.\frac{d\mathfrak{d}}{d\bar{\mathfrak{M}}}\right|_{\dot{F}=0} = \frac{b(F^{\alpha} - \mathfrak{d})}{\bar{\mathfrak{M}}} > 0, \qquad \left.\frac{dF^{*}}{d\bar{\mathfrak{M}}}\right|_{\dot{\mathfrak{d}}=0} = \frac{bF}{(1-\alpha)\,\bar{\mathfrak{M}}} > 0.$$

Figure 5.8 shows the shift in the stationary equilibrium toward more followers and a higher level of income that is available for meeting the organization's objectives.

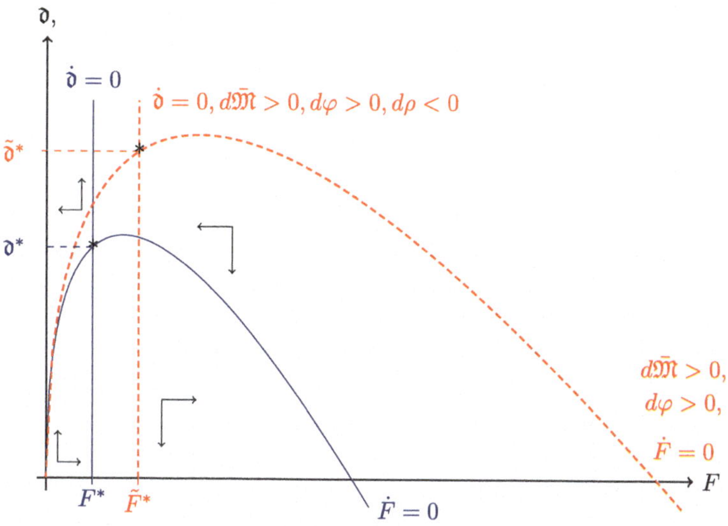

Fig. 5.8 Phase diagram in the $(F, \mathfrak{d})$-space with new equilibrium $(\tilde{F}^*, \tilde{\mathfrak{d}}^*)$ after an increase of the propaganda efficiency φ

Thus, this result confirms, within this model framework, the suggestions made on the basis of the median voter model, namely that political organizations tend to move toward the center of the distribution of preferences. However, as we will see further below, there are other ways to operate successfully as an organization. In particular, if we look at the effectiveness of information or propaganda dissemination, we see that moving toward the center is not the only way to achieve high numbers of followers or the organization's goals to a high degree.

Determinants of Reach, Low Time Preference Rate The time preference rate is a parameter that can be used to characterize the type of organization. If an organization is indeed motivated by greed and short-term benefits, the time preference rate can be expected to be quite high. An organization's leaders will want to realize its benefits soon and will not want to wait for long.

By contrast, organizations that believe in their mission and are significantly motivated by it are often convinced that their beliefs will prevail in the short or long term. Examples of this are religiously motivated belief systems and derived political ideological interpretations of such belief systems. For these organizations, it makes little difference whether they will govern in 5 or 50 years. The most important thing is that they actually govern in the end. Such organizations have staying power. It is, therefore, interesting to examine what chances organizations with such staying power will have when it comes to gaining followers and achieving their goals.

Formally, time preference is expressed in the parameter ρ. Religiously motivated belief systems often have a relatively low time preference. Therefore, we can analyze the effect of a lower ρ as regards this question.

Let us look again at the two stationarity conditions. Parameter ρ is only present in the $\dot{\mathfrak{d}} = 0$ curve in Fig. 5.8. We therefore only need to examine the shift of this curve,

$$\left.\frac{dF}{d\rho}\right|_{\dot{\mathfrak{d}}=0} = -\frac{1}{\varphi\alpha\,(1-\alpha)\,\bar{\mathfrak{M}}^{b}\,F^{\alpha-2}} < 0. \tag{5.14}$$

This means that a reduction in time preference shifts the $\dot{\mathfrak{d}} = 0$ line to the right and the steady-state equilibrium value increases. So patience pays off. A careful, patient policy of continually recruiting more followers will lead to greater achievement of the organization's goals in the long term and will increase the number of followers.

Determinants of Reach, Propaganda, and Internet Use However, the most interesting parameter that we can examine here is the effectiveness of information and propaganda dissemination. The parameter φ describes how spending on information and propaganda leads to additional followers. It is, therefore, a parameter that describes the effectiveness of the communication technology and strategy employed. Since information and belief play an essential role in this book, the effectiveness of the means of communication used for a specific purpose is particularly interesting. But also in practical terms we see that the nature of communication and the use of communication technologies and strategies have changed significantly over the past two decades. Organizations extensively use these new technologies and strategies for information dissemination and propaganda purposes. And so the question is this: How has this parameter φ changed over the past two decades and what does this change mean for organizations and their ability to establish themselves in the population, gain supporters, and achieve their goals?

Let us start with a technical interpretation of this parameter. One central change in social, political, and public communication is the change in communication structures that have been brought about by the Internet. Internet technology has led to a massive decentralization of information dissemination – for better or for worse. How? The Internet has facilitated access to potential recipients of information and even allows them to be used as multipliers of a message through decentralized networking.

This makes it much easier to provide recipients with information. Recipients of information via the Internet are often simply part of a communication network. The mere fact of belonging to a network, however, leads to a permanent random receipt of information – including in the form of the narratives of ideologies and belief systems. Hence, every member of such a network automatically participates in the exchange of information, at least passively. Every network member is automatically exposed to this provision of information or potential propaganda. Members of the network do not need to actively collect information – as was the case before the Internet age – but they are permanently involved in the flow of information through the social network. Information is not only provided almost free of charge but also, to a certain extent, automatically if recipients have not actively refused to receive information.

This means that the costs of receiving information have been reversed. In the past, receiving information required active effort, such as dedicating time to read newspapers or watch television. Today, however, those who participate in social networks are constantly bombarded with ideological messages, and they must actively choose to ignore them. The reach of messages has potentially expanded significantly, but it is not just the recipients' situation that has changed; the capabilities available to the senders of ideological messages have transformed dramatically. The decentralized nature of information input, often anonymous, enables any type of information – whether accurate, misleading, or entirely – to achieve a broad reach. What is communicated and perceived is not necessarily reality; rather, the perceived reality is the one which is most widely disseminated. Thus, the Internet can be exploited using the right resources. Decentralized access allows for the use of social bots and Internet trolls to manipulate these dissemination channels, spread disinformation, and execute ideological campaigns. This shift in dynamics marks a significant change in how information influences society. It is an invitation to organizations to make use of these technological possibilities.

Up to this point, φ only represented the technical effectiveness of the dissemination method. But organizations' communication strategies have also changed on account of the decentralized provision of information. Since in the pre-Internet age, information reach was only guaranteed by analog media such as newspapers, magazines, or analog television and radio stations, information channels were centralized. The dissemination of information by organizations required access to these media. This led to a certain degree of media power hold by traditional media, but also to mutual control. As there were only a few media outlets, they controlled each other in an oligopolistic system. Genuine false reports, disinformation, and propaganda were therefore uncovered relatively quickly by good journalism. There was a kind of quality competition for good journalism. The central narratives were the subject of public debate, and these were observed and scrutinized. Public service media, such as the BBC, which were supposed to process and prepare information exclusively according to journalistic professional ethics, were also of great importance for the credibility of the system. However, this type of media concentration was not all good, as media power also meant that issues and groups were not always sufficiently heard in public discourse. Nevertheless, a common control of what is fact or fake was more ease possible. The perceived realities of the different groups of people in a society were not as different as they are today. Today public verification of information has become much more diffuse as a result of decentralization. Disinformation already has a wide reach before it is even exposed as such, or it is not exposed at all. It is quite rare for the public to correct false information, as it usually refers less to major scandals and more to subliminal misinformation, which often only turns into massive manipulation of the perception of reality when seen as a whole.

This possibility also has an influence on organization's communication strategies. If there is no strong public control around propaganda claims, misinformation, or disinformation, it is easy for organizations to spread their propaganda subliminally and continuously. They can thus manipulate the recipients of their propaganda and paint a false picture of reality, reaching a wide range of recipients with their matching narratives. In Sect. 8.2, we show how disinformation, half-truths, and propaganda turn fake news into fake reality in the perception of those absorbing it.

However, at this point, we do not want to model the entire mechanism involved in what has been described in the above but rather to look at its effect on how organizations develop. Utilizing the technological changes brought about by the Internet and adjusted communication strategies as a result will significantly increase the effectiveness of spending on information and propaganda. This increases the parameter φ in our formal analysis. What does this increase mean for an intertemporally optimally acting organization?

Formally, this means we have to find out how the $\dot{F} = 0$ isocline and $\dot{\mathfrak{d}} = 0$ isocline react when φ increases. The $\dot{\mathfrak{d}} = 0$ line in our phase diagram (see Fig. 5.5) is described by the equation $\varphi \bar{\mathfrak{M}}^b \alpha F^{\alpha-1} = \delta + \rho$. Deriving the change in F with respect to φ, we obtain

$$\left.\frac{dF}{d\varphi}\right|_{\dot{\mathfrak{d}}=0} = \frac{F}{\varphi(1-\alpha)} > 0. \tag{5.15}$$

Thus, an increase in φ moves the $\dot{\mathfrak{d}} = 0$ line to the right, which implies a larger number of followers F^* in equilibrium. This is again depicted in Fig. 5.8.

Furthermore, the $\dot{F} = 0$ curve is described by $\mathfrak{d} = F^{\alpha} \frac{\delta}{\varphi \bar{\mathfrak{M}}^b} F$. Thus,

$$\left.\frac{d\mathfrak{d}}{d\varphi}\right|_{\dot{F}=0} = \frac{\delta}{\varphi^2 \bar{\mathfrak{M}}^b} F > 0.$$

This means that the $\dot{F} = 0$ curve is higher when φ increases, which implies that in equilibrium we have a higher $\mathfrak{d}^*$ (see Fig. 5.8).

In Fig. 5.9, we see the effect of an increase in propaganda effectiveness φ on the recruitment interval. The more effectively the propaganda is spread, the more followers are recruited and the wider the recruitment interval is. This means

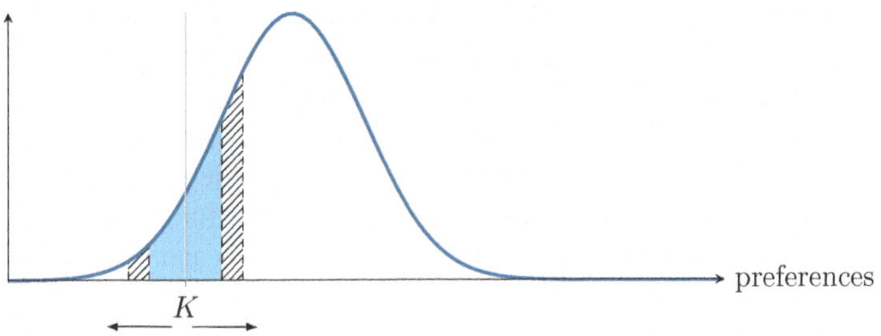

Fig. 5.9 Equilibrium expansion of recruited followers of organization K before (blue area, see also Fig. 5.8) and after an increase in propaganda efficiency φ (hatched area)

propaganda also reaches people who do not very closely match the ideology such that even they become followers.

Multiple Organizations and Overlapping Narratives In a next step, we move from an individual organization to multiple organizations vying for followers. Each organization uses propaganda to recruit its followers, and we assume that this process is independent of the recruitment process of other organizations. If there are two organizations, K and K', we could observe a scenario like the one shown in Fig. 5.10. Both organizations reach followers that are also within the reach of the other organizations. The recruiting intervals of the two organization overlap. What does this mean? It is possible that some individuals follow more than one organization. Individuals feel that certain needs are better served by narratives of one ideology, while they feel that other needs are better served by narratives of another ideology. There is no need to clearly assign each individual to just one ideology and its organization. In Sect. 6.2, we see that individuals can adopt a mixture of ideologies, which means that they become followers of more than one organization: They become followers of both K and K'.

Comparison with the Median Voter Model In Fig. 5.11, we see the recruitment intervals of two organizations, K and R, which have quite different positions on the left-right political spectrum. Both organizations have their optimal way of

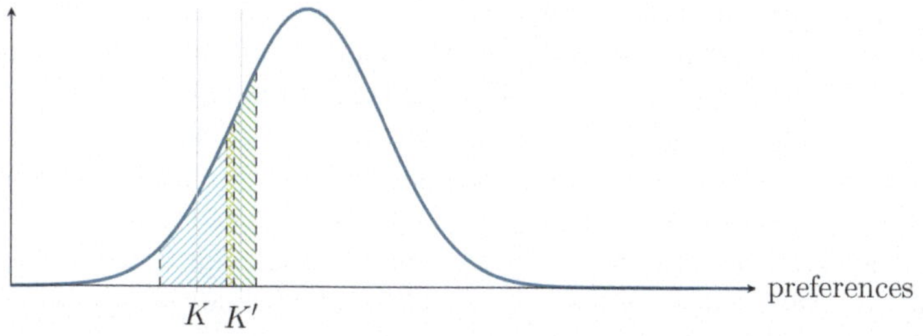

Fig. 5.10 Equilibrium of recruited followers of organizations K (blue rising hatched area) and K' (green sloping hatched area) with an overlapping area in the middle

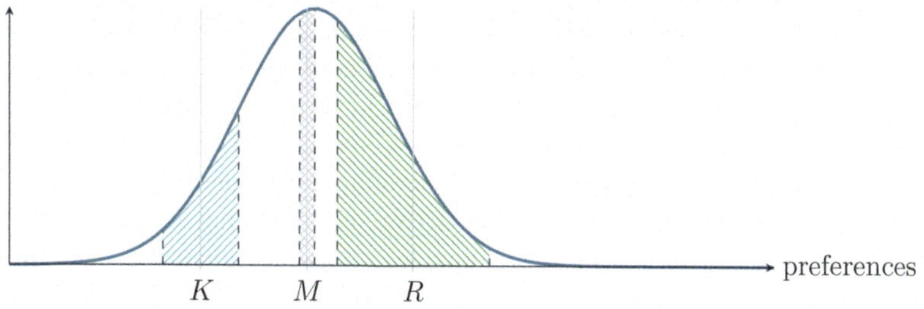

Fig. 5.11 Recruited followers of organizations K (blue rising hatched area), M (gray crosshatched area), and R (green sloping hatched area) in equilibrium

using propaganda to reach their optimal number of followers F^* in Eq. (5.13). Organization R recruits more followers than organization K.

What is important for a greater understanding at this point is that the match value leads to an interval around the respective organization's ideological position. Only those who are sufficiently close to the ideology of R or K will become followers if the respective organization's information campaign reaches them. Individuals who adopt extreme preferences beyond these intervals will no longer be reached by these ideologies. They will not follow either of the two ideologies. This has implications for an ideology's positioning, especially if one considers that the number of followers above all depends on the reach of its information strategy and propaganda. Increasing expenditure on propaganda increases the number of followers and thus also the width of the interval. Thus, recruiting additional followers simply requires greater effort in terms of propaganda activities or making it more efficient to reach more individuals with lower match values. Hence, what is needed is not a change in the narrative's positioning but above all the provision of more information and propaganda. Even if an organization's positioning on the ideological spectrum does not change, additional followers can be won over, for example, by means of more efficient information technology and concepts. The use of information and propaganda channels in recruitment thus enables a completely different strategy of expanding the organization than that which is, for example, possible in the median voter model (Black, 1948). In the median voter model, preferences are also usually interpreted as right-wing or left-wing political positions, and parties choose their position on the horizontal axis. Organizations' or parties' goal is to obtain the vote of the median voter, as this means they win the majority of votes. They can do so by adjusting their political program and changing their position. It is assumed that they receive the votes of those individuals at the tails anyway. So, their position converges toward the median voter. In our model, it is not necessary to change position toward the median voter. Followers are recruited based on their match values. This includes both individuals with high and lower preferences in relation to an organization's position. The decisive factor is that the respective narratives are widely disseminated and reach potential followers.

This model can therefore be used to easily explain polarization in a population. If the distribution is relatively flat, with a wide spread and therefore high variance, as in Fig. 5.7, and if the central positions are already largely occupied, or if there is a communicative vacuum there, ideologies can establish themselves on the fringes of the distribution. Through their communicative reach, they win over many supporters who would actually be located in the center. Social media have led to a significant increase in the effectiveness of information dissemination. Above all, algorithmically amplified, attention-generating fake news, false claims, and half-baked narratives, together with the active use of resources by social bots, Internet trolls, and fake accounts, easily enable communication dominance through propaganda, disinformation, and information manipulation. Added to this, there is a communication strategy that utilizes all the possibilities of deliberate and targeted misinformation. With such intensive use of these technical and communication strategy possibilities, it is also possible to reach peripheral potential followers. The interval in Fig. 5.11 increases. Insufficient communication and vision in the political center ground allow extreme ideologies to expand. People turn to a communicative ideology because it is primarily through this communication that they perceive their needs being addressed and potentially served. Even if people are in principle closer to "moderate" ideologies, their perception and knowledge of this ideology are too weak for them to turn to it. Therefore, ideology M in Fig. 5.11 has only generated a very small interval (gray crosshatched area) due to a lack of information reach, although this ideology in the center of the political spectrum has great potential.

In political competition without controlled competition rules, the ideology that achieves the highest maximum match values in a society will therefore not necessarily succeed in gathering many followers. Ideologies that have large amounts of resources and whose organizations translate this resource wealth into effective information and propaganda strategies will also have the opportunity to gain large followings and even majorities.

References

Acemoglu, D., & Mathew, J. (2015). History, expectations, and leadership in the evolution of social norms. *Review of Economic Studies, 82*(2), 423–456.

Akerlof, G. A. (1970). The market for "lemons": Quality uncertainty and the market mechanism. *The Quarterly Journal of Economics, 84*(3), 488–500.

Arrow, K. J. (1974). *The limits of organization*. W.W. Norton & Company.

Arrow, K. J. (1984). *The economics of information*. Number Bd. 4 in Arrow, Kenneth J.: [Collected papers]. Harvard University Press.

Bénabou, R. (2015). The economics of motivated beliefs. *Revue déconomie politique, 125*(5), 665–685.

Bénabou, R., & Tirole, J. (2006). Incentives and prosocial behavior. *American Economic Review*.

Bénabou, R., & Tirole, J. (2011a). Identity, morals and taboos: Beliefs as assets. *The Quarterly Journal of Economics, 126*(2), 805–855.

Bénabou, R., & Tirole, J. (2011b). Laws and norms. *NBER Working Paper*, 17579.

Bénabou, R., & Tirole, J. (2016). Mindful economics: The production, consumption, and value of beliefs. *Journal of Economic Perspectives, 30*(3), 141–164.

Black, D. (1948). On the rationale of group decision-making. *Journal of Political Economy, 56*(1), 23–34.

Burs, C., & Gries, T. (2022). Decision-making under imperfect information with Bayesian learning or heuristic rules. *Working Paper, Center for International Economics (CIE)*, Paderborn University, 149.

Burs, C., Gries, T., & Müller, V. (2023). The choice of ideology and everyday decisions. *Journal of Organizational Psychology, 23*(1), 134–153.

Coleman, J. (1990). *Foundations of social theory*. Belknap Press of Harvard University Press.

Collier, P., & Hoeffler, A. (2004). Greed and grievance in civil war. *Oxford Economic Papers, 56*(4), 563–595.

Galeotti, A., Ghiglino, C., & Squintani, S. (2013). Strategic information transmission in networks. *Journal of Economic Theory, 148*(5), 1751–1769.

Fukuyama, F. (1995). *Trust: The social virtues and the creation of prosperity*. Free Press.

Hagenbach, J., & Koessler, F. (2010). Strategic communication networks. *Review of Economic Studies, 77*(3), 1072–1099.

Jost, J. T. (2017). Ideological asymmetries and the essence of political psychology. *Political Psychology, 38*(2), 167–208.

Jost, J. T., Glaser, J., Sulloway, F., & Kruglanski, A. W. (2003). Political conservatism as motivated social cognition. *Psychological Bulletin, 129*, 339–375.

MacKenzie, M. J., & Baumeister, R. F. (2014). Meaning in life: Nature, needs, and myths. In *Meaning in positive and existential psychology*, (pp. 25–37). Springer.

Müller, V., & Gries, T. (2024). *Ideology and the microfoundations of conflict: From human needs to intergroup violence*. Oxford University Press.

Putnam, R. (2000). *Bowling alone: The collapse and revival of american community*. A Touchstone book. Simon & Schuster.

Rosa, H. (2016). *Resonanz: Eine Soziologie der Weltbeziehung*. Suhrkamp Verlag.

Sapiro, V. (2004). Not your parents' political socialization: Introduction for a new generation. *Annual Review of Political Science, 7*, 1–23.

Svendsen, G. L. H., & Svendsen, G. T. (2015). The puzzle of the scandinavian welfare state and social trust. *Issues in Social Science, 3*(2), 90–99.

van Ditmars, M. M. (2023). Political socialization, political gender gaps and the intergenerational transmission of left-right ideology. *European Journal of Political Research, 62*(1), 3–24.

Weber, M. (1905). Die protestantische ethik und der 'geist' des kapitalismus. *Archiv für Sozialwissenschaft und Sozialpolitik, 20 und 21*, 117–156.

Weber, M. (1919). Wissenschaft als beruf, vorträge vor dem freistudentischen bund. In *Geistige Arbeit als Beruf*. Duncker & Humblodt.

Weinstein, J. M. (2005). Resources and the information problem in rebel recruitment. *The Journal of Conflict Resolution, 49*(4), 598–624.

Williamson, O. E. (1979). Transaction-cost economics: The governance of contractual relations. *The Journal of Law and Economics, 22*(2), 233–261.

Williamson, O. E. (1985). *The economic institutions of capitalism*. Free Press.

Chapter 6
The Individual Choice of an Ideology

Why do people adopt a particular ideology or belief system? Why do some adopt one kind of belief system or ideology while others opt for another? These questions take us back to the third of the five functions (Sect. 5.1) that ideologies and belief systems have for humans. We argue that adopting a particular belief system or ideology is rooted in one's individual psychological structure. Specific psychological needs can be served by the characteristics and narratives of belief systems and ideologies. More precisely, we suggest that depending on an individual's socioeconomic environment and their personal and genetic disposition, they have non-tangible, psychological preferences (needs) of varying intensities. To serve these needs, individuals seek reconciliation options. We adopt the idea prevalent in the psychological literature[1] that beliefs, belief systems, and ideologies can serve psychological needs and provide need reconciliation. Further and more specific, we turn to what Jost et al. (2009) referred to as "elective affinities hypothesis". Following Jost et al. (2017), we suggest that belief systems or ideologies can serve such needs and that this is one reason why people adopt certain belief systems or ideologies based on their specific psychological structure. Thus, individuals adopt the belief system or ideology that best serves their personal psychological needs. In this chapter, we develop two models that can be used to describe the adoption of an ideology or belief system by means of an optimal choice. Accordingly, the choice of belief system or ideology can be explained in a subjectively rational manner. Further, we can then discuss how the structure of psychological preferences affects the adoption of a particular belief system or ideology.

In Chap. 4, we described the human need and preference system. We found four clusters of needs: existential and epistemic needs (e.g., the need to feel safe or the need to have order); relational needs (e.g., the need for belongingness); agency needs (e.g., the need to act autonomously); and consumer needs (e.g., the need to

[1] For example Jost (2006), Kruglanski and Orehek (2009), Knight (2006), Hogg et al. (2007) and Jost et al. (2013).

T. Gries et al., *The Economics of Ideologies*, Springer Studies in Alternative Economics, https://doi.org/10.1007/978-3-031-93514-5_6

feel well-equipped with resources to serve one's own consumer preferences). That is, humans desire to live in states that are aligned with their need system. Since we are all different and have different need structures, our desires for the world's states also differ. Need and preference structures – across individuals in a society – translate into a demand for a variety of desirable states of the world.

The above describes the demand side, but what about the supply side? Ideologies or belief systems can help individuals navigate volatile, uncertain, complex, and ambiguous (VUCA) environments by minimizing the great effort and high costs associated with a detailed analysis of social and economic systems. As the costs of information and real knowledge are high, individuals rely on narratives and heuristic rules to understand their environment and make decisions (Burs & Gries, 2022). Furthermore, ideologies and belief systems provide alternative interpretations and explanations of reality (i.e., the social, political, and economic environment) and of human existence. That is, belief systems and ideologies provide narratives that enable individuals to understand and link the past, present, and potential future and then to integrate this coherent story into their own life (and existence). Such integration and understanding of (life) events, circumstances, and information forms coherent patterns of reality, which generates stability and a sense of meaning in life. Another important feature of belief systems and ideologies is their capacity for need reconciliation, i.e., their capacity to serve a variety of psychological human needs. In this context, ideologies and belief systems can be understood as mental meaning-making systems that address individual's existential, epistemic, relational, and agency needs, that is, needs that address the human drive to survive, to understand and control one's environment, to find one's role and purpose in life, and to feel accepted and efficacious in one's choices and actions. Therefore, in this chapter, we suggest that beliefs, belief systems, and ideologies describe the supply side in relation to the described psychological demands. Beliefs do not play a role in traditional microeconomic decision-making. However, as mentioned before (beginning of Chap. 5) in recent years, economists have started to look at beliefs and have realized that they are indeed an element in decision-making that is worth considering. Recently, Bénabou (2015) and Bénabou and Tirole (2016) reviewed a large number of articles that focus on the role of (motivated) beliefs in economic thinking.[2] They suggest that "... beliefs often fulfill important psychological and functional needs of the individual. Economically relevant examples include confidence in one's abilities, moral self-esteem, hope and anxiety reduction, social identity, political ideology and religious faith" (Bénabou & Tirole, 2016, p. 141). Even though formalized economic modeling that includes such elements is expanding, this way

[2] Their reviews in Bénabou (2015) and Bénabou and Tirole (2016) focus on – what they call – "motivated beliefs". "... motivated beliefs are by definition directed toward some end, though generally not consciously so. As an example, consider the opposite predictions of confirmation bias and self-enhancement for how someone who is initially insecure about his skill, attractiveness, or health will respond to feedback about these qualities in himself"(Bénabou & Tirole, 2016, p. 144). Even if there is some overlap, in this strand of the literature, the motivation for using beliefs and the categorization is somewhat different from the definition of "motivation" used in this book.

of thinking relates to a strand of the literature that developed in disciplines other than economics, including psychology, sociology, and political science.

According to the definition we provide at the beginning of Chap. 5, ideologies and belief systems consist of a coherent set of narratives that provide (1) explanations, interpretations, evaluations and attitudes, norms, values, visions, or even utopias of/to a society; and (2) provide strategies for how (political) actions lead to achievement of the desired objectives.

In Sect. 5.1, we also discussed the functions ideologies and belief systems perform for humans. The function that ideologies and belief systems serve human needs is most relevant for our discussion. Driven by their needs, humans ask for desirable states of the world. Narratives serve individuals' need system by describing what the state of the world could look like, how it could function, and what could lead to achieving that state. Thus, ideologies and belief systems reconcile human needs through their respective narratives. By having a set of narratives that describes a desirable state of the world, ideologies and belief systems provide interpretation and orientation through how the need system is served and matched.

Hence, in this chapter, we focus on the idea that belief systems or ideologies provide a set of narratives, beliefs, and visions that can reconcile an individual's set of needs. How? Belief systems and ideologies offer perspectives and narratives on how the real world functions. For example, (1) they help people make sense of threats, uncertainties, and perceived injustices by providing clear explanations. These ideologies allow individuals to perceive their world in a consistent manner, fulfilling their need for consistency. Additionally, they propose solutions and offer a sense of control over these situations. (2) Ideologies and belief systems address the needs of humans as social beings by offering individuals opportunities to identify and form their identities. When someone aligns with an ideology, they become part of a community of like-minded individuals. This community's beliefs, ideas, and norms create a stable, consistent, and reliable setting that members can rely on. Within this group, individuals find their place, identify with the group's values, and distinguish themselves from those outside the group. This affiliation provides direction in life, allowing individuals to identify not only with the group but also with their role and traits within it. (3) Ideologies also address the human needs for autonomy and self-realization. They outline scenarios where individuals can act independently and shape their surroundings with minimal restrictions. Alternatively, they might promote a vision of a prosperous society where the narrative suggests a high standard of living for everyone. Consequently, with the wide array of ideologies and belief systems available, various ones may resonate with different personal dispositions. The interpretations and narratives of these belief systems and ideologies closely reflect the psychological needs of individuals.

Figure 6.1 describes the concept behind this approach. In the next two sections, we present two models that can be used to describe an individual's optimal choice of ideology or belief system. The first model describes this choice as if an individual could choose an ideology from a variety of alternatives, like from a menu. This model is static and represents an optimal choice, particularly illustrating the concept of making a rational decision when adopting an ideology. The second model then

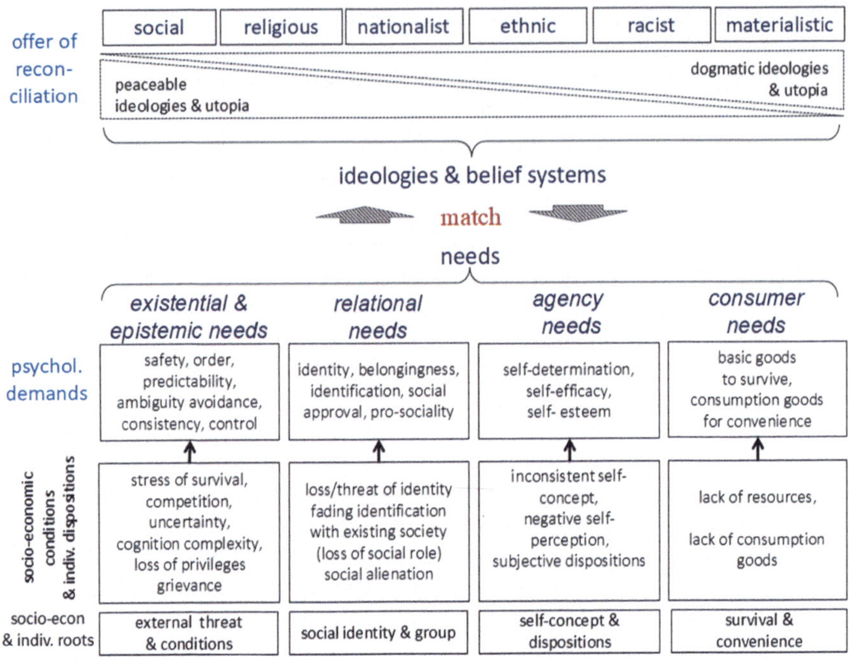

Fig. 6.1 Human needs are matched by ideologies, demand, and supply

describes the dynamic process of adopting an ideology or belief system over a longer period of time. This is a process of Bayesian Learning in which the individual learns more and more about the ideology or belief system and finally adopts it in an optimal manner.

6.1 A Simple Choice from a Menu

In this section, we introduce a theoretical model that allows us to describe the choice of a belief system or ideology as a consistent and subjectively rational behavior.[3] We do not claim that individuals behave in the derived way. However, we do claim that adopting a belief system or ideology can be consistent with rational choice behavior. The adoption of an ideology or belief system may then be considered to be a rational choice decision, even though the real decision procedure is different.

As a point of departure, we suggest for an individual j that she or he has a set of psychological, intangible needs and tangible consumer needs for physical goods

[3] This model is based on Gries et al. (2020). Another version of this model was published as Gries et al. (2022).

and services. We divide j's entire system into two sets of needs: (1) a subset of needs that is more related to physical desires for goods and services (consumption demand) and (2) a second subset that is more related to psychological or mental, intangible needs, as described above. We begin by examining subjective, intangible psychological needs before proceeding to the material dimension.

Intangible, Psychological Needs

In Chap. 4, we identified various universal psychological needs. In our model, each individual – marked by superscript j – is assumed to have a set of psychological needs. Each element of the set of needs indicates a need category (subscript i) and is described by an index number $N_i^j \in [0, 1]$. For instance, if need i stands for "self-determination", the value in the interval [0, 1] indicates the individuals' desired degree of self-determination. If N_i^j is close to zero, the individual's need for self-determination is quite low, meaning that this individual has a demand for states in which he or she is often guided by other people. If N_i^j is close to one, this individual has a very strong demand for states in which he or she can make his own decisions and in which he is fully self-determined. While N^j describes a vector with the dimension n of $j's$ psychological needs, j has a natural motivation to find the means to serve these needs. Individuals strive for settings that best serve their psychological needs in all the relevant dimensions. They will try to find means that serve all the elements of the vector in the best possible way and to actively seek states of need reconciliation.

Matching Intangible, Psychological Needs, and Need Reconciliation Need reconciliation is provided by narratives that address an individual's needs in a way that is appropriate for that particular individual. We model this idea by suggesting that a potential imaginary ideology or belief system labeled with subscript K provides a set of narratives that characterizes it. The narratives used by this ideology can be clustered to address n need categories. Each of these categories i corresponds to a need in the individual's need system. For such an imaginary ideology K, we describe each category that is addressed using an index number $S_{Ki} \in [0, 1]$. This index number indicates to what extent (at what level) ideology K addresses and serves category i by providing the relevant narratives. If S_{Ki} is close to one ideology, K reaches a maximum level of addressing and serving the need category i. If the narratives of ideology K do not address this need category, S_{Ki} may be close to zero ($S_{Ki} = 0.1$). Thus, S_K is the vector with the dimension n that describes all categories i that are served by ideology K at level S_{Ki} for each category.

As individuals strive for need reconciliation, they experience ideologies or belief systems as providing narratives that can serve their demand by describing states of the world that address and serve their various need categories. For example, if the need category i stands for "self-determination" and the particular individual is seeking states in which this need is addressed and served at a high level $N_i^j = 0.9$, there may be an ideology K that propagates freedom and autonomy as a major narrative, meaning that this ideology K serves this need category at a high level,

$S_{Ki} = 0.9$.[4] That is, for the need category i, we can measure the distance D^j_{Ki} between the demand for the desired state N^j_i and the level of serving this needs through the relevant narratives provided by imaginary ideology K, S_{Ki} as

$$D^j_{Ki} = |N^j_i - S_{Ki}|. \tag{6.1}$$

As the individual's need system is a vector with dimension n, he or she seeks an ideology that serves and reconciles the whole set of categories in the best possible way. But how can a whole system be assessed in terms of how it serves the subjective need vector of individual j? While indicating the distance (6.1) for each single category i seems possible, the challenge is how it is possible to determine the distance between a complete set of narratives provided by an hypothetical ideology with vector S_K and the complete set of psychological needs of person j.

We meet this challenge by using a multidimensional measure of distance. Distance measures are widely known in political choice and voting theory.[5] However, in our approach, we adopt a slightly different perspective. We are interested in understanding why individuals choose a particular ideology or belief system. Therefore, our focus is more on the structure of this individual choice process. To that end, we choose a more general and even modified Minkovski distance measure to identify how close an ideology or belief system is to an individual's preferences. Most contributions to distance voting theory look at political issues and attitudes. As discussed for example in Hinich and Munger (2010, chapter 4), ideologies and belief systems represent a more fundamental interpretation of the world.[6] However, in our model, we relate individual psychological needs to the narratives that ideologies and belief systems provide. The appeal of an ideology or belief system depends on the distance between individual j's psychological needs in various need categories and the respective narratives. So distance here directly relates to psychological need categories and the way an ideology or belief system serves each of these need categories. What holds for each category also holds for the whole need system and

[4] Another example can be described using another imaginary ideology R and the need category i ="order". Narratives of the category i ="order" are provided by this other ideology R in an extreme way. In ideology R, there are very strict hierarchies, and all its rules are strictly enforced such that index S_{Ri} is extremely high and R served the need for [i ="order"] at the perfect level of [$S_{Ri} = 1$]. However, if the narratives of another imaginary ideology L are close to anarchy, the state provided by the narratives of L in category i ="order" has a value close to $S_{Li} = 0$; the category "order" is not served.

[5] The literature on the distance theory of voting and political choice goes back to Downs (1957), Davis et al. (1970) and Caplin and Nalebuff (1988), Caplin and Nalebuff (1991) and is still applied in more recent contributions like Schofield (2007), Berry and Pakes (2007), and Hinich and Munger (2010). Jackson (2014) provides a recent review of the Davis-Hinich model.

[6] Hinich and Munger (2010, p. 62) define an ideology as " .. an internally consistent set of propositions that make both proscriptive and prescriptive demands on human behavior. All ideologies have implications for (a) what is ethically good; (b) how society's resources should be distributed; and (c) where power appropriately resides".

the whole set of narratives of a particular ideology or belief system. The shorter the distance, the better an ideology or belief system serves the system of individual j's psychological needs.

In Eq. (6.2), the distance measure is defined, and D_K^j is the distance between the need system of individual j and the narratives that address and serve the needs provided by an imaginary ideology or belief system, for instance, K.[7] We describe preferences for matches. This distance measure tells us how far away the perceived narratives provided by hypothetical ideology K are from the desired ideal states indicated by individual j's need vector. Further, we use (6.2) to modify the standard Minkovski definition and include potential weights α_i^j for the various need categories. Parameter γ is interpreted in detail in one of the following subsections:

$$D_K^j = \left(\alpha_1^j \left(D_{K1}^j\right)^{\gamma} + \ldots + \alpha_i^j \left(D_{Ki}^j\right)^{\gamma} + \ldots + \alpha_n^j \left(D_{Kn}^j\right)^{\gamma}\right)^{\frac{1}{\gamma}}. \tag{6.2}$$

However, in order to determine the ideology that best serves the individual's psychological needs, we need a measure for matching of ideology rather than one for distance. Accordingly, we have to indicate to what extent ideology K serves individual j's need system and matches j's psychological needs through the narratives provided by K. Thus, we define the inverse of the Minkovski distance to measure the effectiveness with which ideology K serves and matches j's psychological needs. Thus, in each need category i, the reverse of the distance between the respective narratives and the individual's demand to serve the need category i is measured as a match value in each category

$$M_{Ki}^j = \left(D_{Ki}^j\right)^{-1}. \tag{6.3}$$

Thus, M_{Ki}^j is the match value with which K serves $j's$ need category i. If the match value M_{Ki}^j is high ideology, K matches and thus serves individual j's need category i well, while a weak match M_{Ki}^j indicates that K does not. According to (6.3), the inverse of the distance, the matching measure $M_{Ki}^j\,(K)$, expresses the effectiveness with which ideology K serves – and thus matches – j's psychological needs in category i. Thus, inserting (6.3) in (6.2), the modified Minkovski distance can be rewritten as $D_K^j = \left(\alpha_1^j \left(M_{K1}^j\right)^{-\gamma} + \ldots + \alpha_n^j \left(M_{Kn}^j\right)^{-\gamma}\right)^{\frac{1}{\gamma}}$.

Moreover, if the inverse of the Minkovski distance is the measure for the match between an ideology K and the system of j's psychological needs, the extent of the match can be described by the overall match value $M_K^j = \left(D_K^j\right)^{-1}$. As a result,

[7] Note that K is not yet a real ideology offering a service. We merely use this example to introduce the concept of preferences for matches. An individual can appreciate that a potential ideology matches their needs.

we can write the overall match value of a hypothetical ideology with the individual need system as

$$M_K^j = \left(\alpha_1^j \left(M_{K1}^j\right)^{-\gamma} + \ldots + \alpha_i^j \left(M_{Ki}^j\right)^{-\gamma} + \ldots + \alpha_n^j \left(M_{Kn}^j\right)^{-\gamma}\right)^{-\frac{1}{\gamma}}. \tag{6.4}$$

With M_K^j, we obtain a specific match value for an imaginary ideology K. It is one value, and (6.4) describes how this value is determined. Taking the example of a hypothetical ideology K was the easiest way to introduce the concept of match values. However, now that we know how a total match value can be calculated for a hypothetical ideology, we can use this concept to describe the preference system of individual j.

The CES Match Value Function and Its Interpretation[8] Equation (6.4) indicates how the narratives provided by an imaginary ideology K serve individual j's vector of needs and how this match is appreciated by j. However, K was a hypothetical ideology. What happens if there are slight changes in the match values of some of the components, regardless of whether these changes can be associated with K or another hypothetical ideology? And more generally, what would happen to the individual j's total match value if some of the components were to match better and others less so? M^j could increase if, seen overall, this new combination of components serves the needs of individual j better. If not, it could decrease or even stay the same. Thus, regardless of a specific ideology, we can apply this concept to the specific case in (6.4) to determine total match values based on the need components and can describe a general match value function as

$$M^j = \left(\sum \alpha_i^j \left(M_i^j\right)^{-\gamma}\right)^{-\frac{1}{\gamma}}. \tag{6.5}$$

This overall match value function indicates the total appreciation of any given set of narratives (that an ideology may provide) in all the categories that serve the psychological needs of individual j. A high match value indicates that the narratives serve the individual's need categories in a way that is highly appreciated. Thus, (6.5) describes how all kinds of potential combinations of matches in components aggregate to an overall match value. The equation describes the general aggregation rule for individual j's preference system. Taking a closer look at the match value function reveals some interesting mechanisms.

As the match value function is, formally, a CES function, it can be easily interpreted similar to a CES utility function. And so we can easily describe the role of the CES parameters for this evaluation. Below we provide a general interpretation of such match value functions, how they work, and how they reveal preferences and evaluations.

[8] Constant Elasticity of Subsitution: CES.

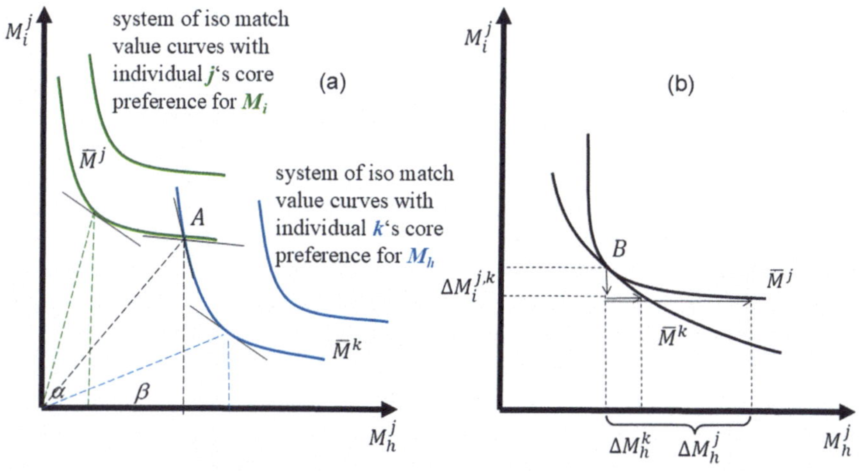

Fig. 6.2 Match value indifference curves for psychological needs

Iso Match Value (Indifference) Curves For economists, the interpretation of a CES function is a well-known exercise in microeconomics. In Fig. 6.2, we first look at curves with constant match values, that is, these curves are indifference curves, for example, the curve $\bar{M}^j$. For illustrative purposes, we consider a need system with only two need categories, i and h. M_i and M_h indicate the match value potentially realized in these two need categories. All the combinations of match values of curve $\bar{M}^j$ serve j's needs at an identical level. That is, the same appreciation can be generated under various combinations of M_i and M_h. Being served in one need category can substitute for being served in another need category – at least potentially. Thus, individuals can be characterized by their particular preference for a certain category or the ease with which they substitute one need category with another. This property is discussed more extensively in the next section.

Need Profile and Core Preferences Using indifferent curves, we can identify a first interesting characteristic of the match value function as an instrument for evaluating an ideology. It is important to recall that, even though the need system described in Chap. 4 is assumed to be universal, each individual has a different need profile. This means that the match value of an ideology is different for different individuals and their particular need profiles, such that the match value of category i may be high for individual j and low for individual k. If an individual has "core needs", it is particularly important that these need categories are served. Figure 6.2a illustrates how core needs translate into the system of indifference curves for individual j. If i is a core need that must be served with a particular emphasis based on individual j's preference system, ratios M_i^j/M_h^j must also be relatively high. Hence, for any given overall match value indifference curve $\bar{M}^j$ and a given slope of this indifference curve, j desires a relatively high ratio M_i^j/M_h^j. This indicates a stronger desire to experience a high match for need i compared to the other need

h. Thus, the system of indifference curves for individual j in Fig. 6.2a reflects a high desire to match need category i. As a consequence, the location of the whole system is relatively close to the important need category i in Fig. 6.2a, such that angle α indicates a high need intensity for dimension i. Individual k's preference system exhibits a core need for category h, as angle β with $\tan\beta$ indicates that a relatively high match value with respect to need h is desired. Therefore, we use the term "core needs" to identify an emphasis on a particular category and define a particular need profile. Individuals with a cluster of core needs greatly appreciate narratives that match these needs even though certain other needs remain practically unserved. Or they may appreciate narratives by which only a very specific need is served extremely well, while other need categories remain practically unaddressed.

This preference can also be illustrated by the marginal rate of substitution at for instance point A in Fig. 6.2a. At point A, both individuals realize the same ratio of match values M_i/M_h. However, when they are asked how much of need category i they are willing to give up to obtain a better match for need category h, we see that both individuals provide different answers: Individual j signals that only a very large improvement in the match value h can compensate for giving up some i to stay at the same indifference curve, while individual k indicates a willingness to easily give up a lot of i to obtain a small improvement in the match value for category h.

Substitutability of Need Categories This characterization of the indifference curve system describes how serving and matching in one category can be substituted by that in another need category, that is, whether need categories are complements to each other instead of substitutes. Substitutability and complementarity are depicted in Fig. 6.2b. We reduce our discussion to two need categories. The two indifference curves describe the shape of the system representing individual j's and individual k's preferences. The shape of k's indifference curve $\bar{M}^k$ implies that this individual would easily substitute a good match in category i by category h without there being any impact on for the overall match value. For individual j with indifference curve system $\bar{M}^j$, however, there is a complementary relationship between the two categories. In the case of an L-shaped indifference curve, the two need categories are pure complements. Identifying these properties is important, as it helps us understand that individuals may be willing to accept that certain needs may go unmet if this means another need can be served instead. Serving some needs can substitute for serving others (substitutability), which is illustrated in Fig. 6.2b. Again, axis M_i indicates the match value for need category i, and axis M_h indicates the match value for need category h. Being at point B and moving along individual k's indifference curve $\bar{M}^k$ indicate that, without a loss of overall match value, individual k may easily forgo some match value and, thus, serve need i (ΔM_i^k) if, in return, the need category h is met and served a little better (ΔM_h^k).

However, for another individual j, we can observe another preference scheme. In Fig. 6.2b, we again start at point B. In this case, we move along individual j's indifference curve $\bar{M}^j$. We observe that the overall match value for individual j is not reduced (i.e., it remains on the indifference curve), only if j achieves a much greater match for need category h (ΔM_h^j) when forgoing some match value of need category i (ΔM_i^j). A small increase in match value and, hence, serving need category h is not sufficient and lowers the overall match value. The two need categories cannot be easily substituted; instead, they are complementary.

Interpretation The above discussion implies three things: (1) We have a first tool for describing how belief systems and ideologies can reconcile psychological or intangible needs. (2) The evaluation of ideologies and belief system can be described using a CES match value or match utility function. (3) When reversing the perspective, we have a model that indicates the existence of belief systems and ideologies that mirror our psychological needs. Humans have psychological needs, and, accordingly, they invent belief systems and ideologies that match these needs. Organizations representing these ideologies and belief system can leverage the demand for need-serving states and conditions to tie individuals to them by (ostensibly) providing such states and conditions, at least in their narratives.

However, before we turn to the role organizations play in regard to the choice of an ideology or belief system, we want to look in more detail at the idea of a match between an individual's needs and ideologies. What do we mean when we say that an ideology or belief system matches an individual's needs and thus the ideology or belief system aligns with the individual, who may even become its follower.

Again, let us take an individual k who has a strong preference for conditions in which they feel safe, in which the surrounding structures are recognizable in the form of a clear order and the environment is manageable and predictable. Further, let us assume that this individual currently lives in an environment in which they believe these needs are well met. Everything is in order, clear, predictable, and safe.

If this individual is asked to imagine the conditions in which they could live in the future, they will be confronted with different narratives describing possible future conditions and states. One ideological description could be: "There is a possible future state of your world that looks very similar to the one you know, and even if certain policies need to be implemented what is important for you now will remain". This is to be a traditional conservative narrative, a narrative that preserves the familiar security, order, and predictability of a society. When this narrative is encountered by individual k who has their need structure, individual k feels that this ideology is speaking to them, k feels a resonance, because it describes not only the state that k desires but also the way in which this desired state can be achieved. For individual k, this conservative ideology thus offers an opportunity to achieve living conditions and states that correspond to his or her preferences. It thus enables individual k to think his or her way to a future that is good for him or her. There is a blueprint for a good future, all that individual k needs to do is follow the relevant narrative.

This is the central idea we want to model further in the next two sections. However, before presenting the actual selection process, we need to introduce another dimension of the utility function. This dimension is usually the central and, unfortunately, often the only subject of economic decision models: the utility of tangible consumer goods and services.

The Full Preference System

Much microeconomic modeling is based on the philosophical thinking of utilitarianism. One of the most important founders of Utilitarianism was Bentham (1789). In Jeremy Bentham's early writing on utilitarianism, utility is generated by everything that generates well-being or happiness. With our approach, we somehow go back to this original view that also immaterial states that meet psychological needs are part of a preference system and generate utility. We assume that everything that serves human needs (be it tangible or non-tangible) generates utilities. In the previous section, we focused on a set of subjective, psychological, or intangible needs. The discussion at the beginning of the previous section showed there is a second relevant set of needs, that is, tangible, or consumption, preferences. We thus extend this discussion by adding tangible needs for wealth or general states that allow for consumption. Now, j's preferences are characterized by two sets of needs: (1) intangible or psychological needs and (2) the need for material consumer goods that can be served by this wealth. To extend the discussion and include this additional set of needs, we first have to decide how these two sets interact with each other. To start with, we assume we can continue to keep the immaterial, intangible or psychological sphere separate from the material, tangible world of consumables. Ideologies and belief systems serve individuals' intangible, psychological needs, while material wealth provides the means for the consumption of goods and services that serve individuals' material needs.[9] As these two sets and their potential interactions determine overall well-being as well as choices and behavior, we have to include the material dimension in our general choice model. We assume that a utility function can serve as an instrument that describes individual well-being in a broad utilitarian interpretation. Thus, the two relevant dimensions are the match value of an ideology M^j with respect to intangible or psychological needs and the level of consumable wealth (an amount of tangible consumption goods) as promised by the narrative C^j. Thus, we can simply write the utility function as

$$U^j = U^j \left(M^j, C^j \right).$$

This utility function looks formally similar to utility functions in standard microeconomic decision-making. The match value of intangible services is nested in the simple specification of a utility function. We assume a CES utility function, with β_M^j and β_C^j describing the weights assigned to the two elements and *gamma* being a parameter that determines the substitutability of the two dimensions in a

[9] This is a simplified assumption because we can also think of examples where a mere purchase of consumption goods may serve psychological needs. Buying weapons could serve the need for control, etc.

CES utility function

$$U^j = \left[\beta_M^j \left(M^j\right)^{-\gamma} + \beta_C^j \left(C^j\right)^{-\gamma}\right]^{-\frac{1}{\gamma}}. \tag{6.6}$$

At this point, we do not claim that this specification is particularly justified. There is no specific reason for keeping consumption needs separate from psychological needs. However, this division into a dual system provides a simplification that allows for a straightforward yet interesting interpretation. While this interpretation is formally symmetrical to the above discussion of the match value function, it might give some interesting implications and insights.

Consumption Preferences Versus Intangible Need First, we consider an individual j who has relatively strong preferences for consumption such that their indifference curve system in Fig. 6.3 is located closer to the C-axis. We refer to such a strong preference as a "core preference". A high level of consumption is more important for this individual than a high match value of intangible needs. When searching for an ideology, individual j would be particularly attracted to one that promises high levels of consumable wealth. Matching the intangible needs is of less importance, j's interests are more materialistic, and he or she appreciates more materialistic ideologies.

Substitutability Individual j not only has materialistic preferences but would also easily substitute consumption for intangible needs. This is interesting, as it tells us something about the individual's willingness to appreciate states of the world that do not serve specific intangible or psychological needs. In authoritarian states, we sometimes observe a simple example of easy substitutability of intangible or psychological needs and consumption. If an ideology promises high consumable wealth and economic growth while signaling states of oppression and repressive

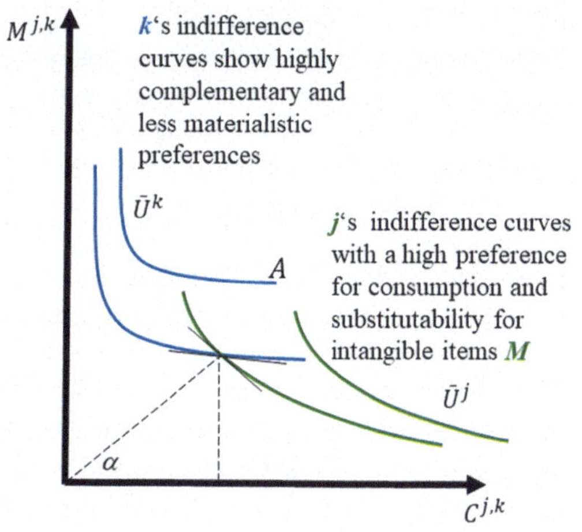

Fig. 6.3 Preference system, psychological match values, and consumption

policies, people may not feel significantly negatively affected because they accept the increase in consumable wealth as compensation for the fact that some intangible, psychological needs (e.g., agency needs) are met less well. In Fig. 6.3, we move along the indifference curve toward more consumption and a lower match value for psychological needs.

However, for strongly complementary preferences, as indicated by individual k's indifference curve in Fig. 6.2b, or – even more extreme in the case of an L-shaped indifference curve – the overall utility only increases if both consumption and the serving of intangible or psychological needs improve simultaneously. An increase in consumption does not improve overall utility (well-being) if the serving of intangible needs does not simultaneously improve as well. In our example, more consumption cannot easily compensate for repression and/or serving psychological needs like agency needs to a lesser degree.

Set of Consistent Efficient Option

So far we have described the evaluation system at the individual level. The utility function depicts a formalization and graphical representation of the evaluation system. While one dimension of the utility function, consumption C, is the purely material dimension, the second dimension of the utility function, match value M, is the purely psychological, immaterial, or intangible sphere and covers the serving of psychological needs.

If we can assume that people have ideas about the states of the world and the conditions under which they would like to live in the future, it is clear that they are looking for propositions of realization that correspond to their preference system. These propositions take the form of narratives which clearly address their need structure, which describe that and how their needs are to be met, and what the path into the world of these good states will look like. In other words, humans strive for need reconciliation with respect to (future) states of the world. Need reconciliation is done through narratives that explain and interpret the past and present world and one's position in it, that describe what a good world would look like for an individual, and how to get there. Striving for need reconciliation determines the individual demand side for narratives.

The supply of such narratives is determined by ideologies. As discussed in Sect. 5.1, ideologies can fulfill various functions, and providing sets of narratives for need reconciliation is one important one. How can we model the fact that ideologies provide options for an individual's need reconciliation?

After describing the preference system using utility (6.6) and providing a graphic description of the indifference curve system in Fig. 6.3, we can now turn to the set of options this individual has. That is, we have to identify the set of options available to individual j. From individual j's perspective, ideology K is characterized by two elements. First, K's narratives generate a specific match value with respect to j's intangibles or psychological needs at the level M_K^j. Second, ideology K's narratives also refer to the state of consumable wealth. Individuals know that consumption possibilities are not available independent of an ideology. The choice of an ideology may have consequences for j's consumable wealth, C_K^j, and j takes this into

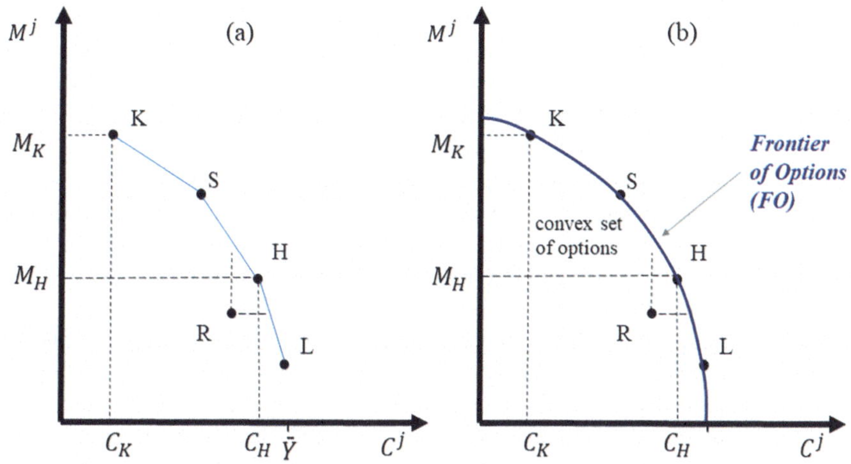

Fig. 6.4 Frontier of option

account. For example, if an individual chooses an egalitarian ideology, they know – if they are rich – that they will be taxed, which reduces their total consumable wealth. Similarly, they may receive transfer payment if they are poor.

Returning to the example of the egalitarian ideology, in Fig. 6.4a, individual j has a wealth $\bar{Y}^j$ and individual j is rich. However, they still like the egalitarian ideology K (high match value) and are aware that this ideology would tax a rich person at level τ_K. Thus, K implies a strong reduction of given wealth $\bar{Y}^j$ to the consumable level.

$$C_K^j = Y_K^j = \bar{Y}^j - \tau_K^j.$$

Thus, the pair (M_K^j, C_K^j) defines the true option for states of the world that ideology K offers to j in Fig. 6.4, $K^j = (M_K^j, C_K^j) \in R^+ \times R^+$. Moreover, more ideologies are available, and so individuals can explore the attractiveness of these other options. Staying with this example, another ideology S might be less egalitarian, so for j the match value M_S^j is lower than M_K^j, but still high. Further, because it is less egalitarian, the tax burden on the wealthy is smaller, and a rich individual will find another option for potential choice at point S. A third ideology on offer is a more market-liberal ideology L with few egalitarian elements. Tax revenue is only used to provide basic public services. Individual j does not find a high match value M_L^j but can consume more due to low taxation. So this option is described by point L, and ideology H is somehow in between the ideas of S and L. Staying with this example in Fig. 6.4a, we find four points that describe the set of options $\Omega = \{K, S, H, L\}$. There may be many more options on offer. However, some of them can be excluded, as they are an inefficient combination of M_i^j and C_i^j as we can see as regards point R in Fig. 6.4a. R is an option, but not an efficient one, because H can provide a better state that serves more psychological needs, generates a larger match value $M_R^j < M_H^j$, and allows for more consumption $C_R^j < C_H^j$ than option R. Even a linear combination of H and L would serve individual j's needs better than R. The way to interpret a linear combination is that the elements of two ideologies are mixed. This interpretation can be understood best if we think of ideology H and L as being dominated by two organizations who claim to be the sole representatives of each ideology and its narratives. However, individuals do not necessarily have to be out and out believers of an ideology and its narratives. They may combine existing ideologies to create something in between and to some extent follow the interpretations of one ideology and to another extent the interpretations of another ideology. Individual j may combine the narratives provided by H and L, generate some belief system of his or her own in between these two pure ideological positions. Graphically, all the linear combinations on line H to L are efficient.

We now assume that the existing set of efficient ideologies on offer forms a convex set $\Omega = \{K = (M, C) \in R^+ \times R^+\}$, such that the enveloping edge of this set can be described as a continuous and differentiable concave function $M^j = M^j(C^j)$. This function is indicated by the curve in Fig. 6.4b, which we refer to as the efficient *Frontier of Options (FO)*. This 'frontier of options' identifies the set of ideologies that best address both categories of need, psychological needs and consumption needs, and thus potentially offers the best options for need reconciliation for this person. For an individual, it describes the best options for need reconciliation that exist through the available ideologies.

Some Standard Choices

In the initial discussion of the rational adoption of an ideology, we establish the fundamental reasoning behind the adoption of ideologies and illustrate the normal reasoning using a few examples. We call this the "standard choice model" because it covers the most straightforward case. We assume that the efficient Frontier of Options describes a trade-off for the two components of the utility function. That is, at the efficient frontier of ideological options, narratives about states that allow for a higher match value for psychological, intangible needs go along with narratives about states of lower consumption possibilities. Again we note that these options are identified from j's individual perspective. It is the match value that j would realize with respect to his particular need system. In other words, at the efficient frontier of ideological options, ideologies either proclaim conditions that serve more consumer needs or they serve more psychological needs. Figure 6.5 depicts this assumption. We turn now to discuss which belief system/ideology individual j would adopt. The first result is that this choice clearly depends on the core preference j may have. If j's preference system emphasizes the psychological need system, j will choose ideology K and point K in line with the importance of their psychological preferences.

However, in this example, j has balanced preferences. Neither psychological needs nor consumer needs play a dominant role. Thus, given the Frontier of Options available for j, FO^j, individual j chooses the ideology that generates highest the greatest utility. Under the current conditions, $\bar{U}_3^j$ is the greatest utility that

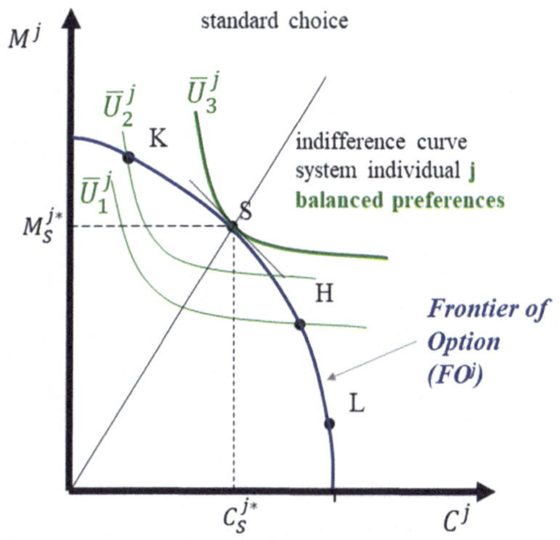

Fig. 6.5 Standard choice of an ideology

can be achieved by choosing ideology S with the promised match value M_S^{j*} and consumption C_S^{j*}. Individual j could choose ideology K, that is, K is an option. However, given j's preferences as described by the system of indifference curves, K leads to a lower level of utility than S, since $\bar{U}_2^j < \bar{U}_3^j$. The same holds for ideology H. For instance, if j believes that K is already a suitable ideology that serves his or her needs well and now considers S as another suitable ideology, j will move from ideology K to ideology S. j will then learn that S is more beneficial, since the utility gain from improved consumption possibilities overcompensates for the utility losses from a psychological component that is served less well. That is, the utility loss from living in a less egalitarian society such that j's psychological needs are served less well is overcompensated by the utility gain from a state with higher consumption.

Even if j generally likes egalitarian ideologies because they serve their psychological needs, they will still choose S. This graphic discussion can also be represented as a formal choice problem. Individual j maximizes utility U^j subject to the constraint of their individual efficient frontier of options:

$$\max : U^j = \left[\beta_M^j \left(M^j\right)^{-\gamma} + \beta_C^j \left(C^j\right)^{-\gamma}\right]^{-\frac{1}{\gamma}}$$

$$s.t. : M^j = M^j \left(C^j\right).$$

The solution to this standard choice problem is stated in Proposition 6.1.

Proposition 6.1 *With the assumption that* $M^j = M^j\left(C^j\right)$ *is a concave function, and* $U^j = U^j\left(M^j, C^j\right)$ *follows the standard characteristics, we obtain the optimal* *choice of match value* M^* *and consumption* C^* *as*

$$M^{j*} = M^j\left(\bar{Y}, \beta_C, \beta_M\right)$$
$$C^{j*} = C^j\left(\bar{Y}, \beta_C, \beta_M\right).$$

As each pair, (M^j, C^j) *represents an ideology, and* (M^{j*}, C^{j*}) *stands for the respective ideology with the pair* $(M^{j*} = M^j_K, C^{j*} = C^j_K)$ *such that an ideology* K *is identified*

$$K \leftarrow \begin{cases} M^j_K = M^{j*} \\ C^j_K = C^{j*} \end{cases}.$$

For a proof, see the appendix.

In the next two examples, we illustrate the fact that some ideologies manage to generate perceptions that both consumer needs and psychological needs can be served simultaneously, such that the Frontier of Options can slightly vary in shape. We also illustrate how this model can be applied to existing ideologies.

Choice of Imperialist Ideology In this section, we show how we can explain why people are attracted to and follow ideologies that we would consider unpeaceful and aggressive. Imperialism, which is based on the notion that one group or nation can dominate another, is such an ideology. How can we explain why people follow these narratives? If we go back to the system of needs described in Sect. 5.1, we find that imperialist narratives serve a variety of psychological and consumption needs. Imperialist narratives often talk about their own nation as a special, often superior, entity. An example of such a narrative could go something like this: As the chosen nation, our nation has a very special role among all other nations and in history. Our nation is morally and culturally superior. It knows its destiny and fulfills its divine task. Because of its uniqueness, however, it has many enemies who do not come close to its superior culture and are morally underdeveloped or even degenerate. These enemies threaten our culture and the self-determination of our people. Our nation must, therefore, defend itself against this threat from its enemies. Moreover, our own superior morals and culture should also set the standard for others, and its superior culture and morals can be enforced even with military vigor if necessary.

Even if, from today's perspective, this kind of thinking seems strange, it used to be common and represented the mindset of many people during the period of European Imperialism. "Am Deutschen Wesen soll die Welt genesen" (The world shall be healed by the German spirit) was an imperial propaganda slogan used during the German Empire. Strange enough that more than a hundred years later Russian propaganda when evading the Ukraine used similar narratives.

However, one reason for the existing of imperialism is that these narratives can be successful in recruiting followers, as they can meet the need structure of individuals. Let us describe j's need structure in the following way: Individual j has a strong need for belonging, for identity and identification, for social recognition, and for ambiguity avoidance and order. All of these needs are addressed and served by the elements of imperialist narratives. For example, the needs for belonging, identity, and identification are served by unconditional belonging to that nation. I am – just as I am – part of our nation. I belong to the "we and us" without reservation, and we form this group of our own accord and describe what makes us who we are. We are different from other people and groups; we are something special. We can identify ourselves and differentiate ourselves from other groups.

Further, social recognition and appreciation are generated through an appreciation of one's own group and, thus, also through an appreciation of oneself as a member of that group. That nation (group) is not just something special in the sense of "being different"; it is superior or even divinely chosen. There is, thus, a clear order and even a hierarchy of societies. One's own nation, to which one belongs, undoubtedly stands at the top of the hierarchy. In addition, the narrative of a threat to which this nation is exposed is often conjured up. This also addresses this group's need for safety.

Imperialist expansion and the need for safety justify massive spending on security and the military, even if this reduces private consumption opportunities. Thus, the match value generated by such an imperialist ideology M_{IP}^{k} may be high for those individuals whose needs are addressed (like individual k), while the consumption opportunities on offer, C_{IP}^{k}, are relatively low. In Fig. 6.6a, point IP (M_{IP}^{k}, C_{IP}^{k}) characterizes the imperialistic ideology for k. If k's preference system is now characterized by a strong emphasis on his or her psychological needs and less on consumption needs, it is quite possible that k will respond positively to these imperialist narratives, i.e., resonate positively with k, and k will follow these narratives. k can become a follower of these narratives. Serving psychological needs is a priority for k, even if he or she has to forego consumer opportunities. That

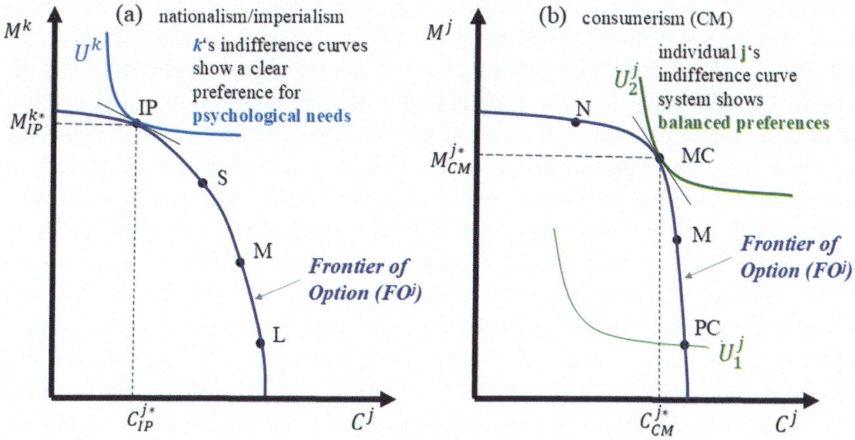

Fig. 6.6 Further examples: (**a**) strong nationalism/imperialism, (**b**) consumerism

is, restricting consumption options is not particularly problematic if individual k's preferences are dominated by psychological needs. As psychological needs are the core preference for k, the indifference curve system is relatively close to the vertical axis. Indifference curve U^k touches (M_{IP}^k, C_{IP}^k) such that the imperialist ideology generates the highest possible utilities, and k becomes a follower.

Choice of Consumerism Another example that can be used to illustrate the functioning of this model is consumerism. Obviously, the narratives of consumerism are completely different than the imperialistic narratives. However, they again address and serve the needs of individuals. To illustrate how different ideologies and their narratives affect their attractiveness for individuals, we will consider two versions of an ideology that focuses on consumption.

We suggest two versions of consumerism: pure consumption and meritocratic consumerism. Pure consumption is the kind of thinking about consumption as it is usually described in traditional economics. The benefit of consumption is generated by the provision of a consumption good. A car is a means of transportation with a degree of reliability and some comfort. The focus is on the material consumer good and the material services it provides for us. Cars provide mobility, home a place to live and sleep, and tables and chairs the comfort of not having to sit on the floor. In this version of consumerism, we only consider the material services goods provide and are thus not referring to the psychological associations we might have with consumer goods, only the material services themselves. A purely materialistic narrative thus addresses and serves only rudimentary consumer services. Although the availability of consumer goods is high, the match value for psychological needs remains low, as there is a lack of interpretations of this. In Fig. 6.6b, point PC, which describes pure material consumerism, is therefore at the bottom right of the Frontier of Options curve.

The matter is entirely different when we look at the ideology of meritocratic consumerism (MC) in Fig. 6.6b, which explicitly addresses and serves people's psychological needs. MC combines the availability of goods with a story that serves psychological needs. In these narratives, the possession of material goods or access to luxury goods indicates personal success. It is not the physical good itself and the service it provides that is important, rather it is the symbolism of the good in terms of success, social prestige, self-efficacy, etc. MC often emphasizes individualistic values by focusing on personal success and personal satisfaction. The acquisition of consumer goods is a means of self-realization and identity formation. Unlike many ideologies, there is not necessarily any directly dominant ideological organization that provides the relevant narratives. The promotion of the ideology of consumerism is the result of competition in the consumer goods industry. Companies want to sell their products and invent narratives that link human psychological needs to these products. Like other ideologies, these narratives reflect our needs. The advertising industry plays a key role when it comes to the expansion of the ideology of consumerism. Linking products and services to certain needs gives people the feeling that buying certain brands or products can serve such needs. MC can, therefore, also generate a high match value for psychological needs. In Fig. 6.6b, this means that when people adopt this narrative, in addition to a high level of consumption that is also generated by pure consumerism, a high match value is also generated for psychological needs. The point MC is almost vertically above PC.

Implications and Conclusions

At this point in a rather conventional method of modeling, we obtain an answer to our questions of why individuals chose a particular belief system or ideology.

The answer is this: The choice of a belief system or ideology is driven by a set of psychological, intangible needs and tangible needs: "We choose the belief system that best serves our needs!" This answer is derived by the following reasoning: Depending on individuals' socioeconomic environments and their personal and genetic dispositions, they develop an individual structure of psychological needs or demands in various dimensions. To serve these needs, individuals tend to search for reconciliation options. We claim that belief systems and ideologies provide viable "conditions" that serve these individuals' subjective psychological and tangible needs. Belief systems/ideologies can fulfill psychological demands and are thus options for reconciliation. This implies that individuals adopt those belief systems/ideologies that most closely match their subjective demands.

6.2 Adopting an Ideology Through Bayesian Learning

Individuals need to find those ideologies or belief systems that best match their subjective need systems. This was addressed in the previous section. However, a choice from a menu – the ideological opportunity frontier – is not a particularly realistic way of describing how an ideology or belief system is adopted. Adopting an ideology or belief system is a process of acquiring information and learning about ideologies and finding out if a particular one matches. Therefore, we again use the Bayesian Learning framework to model the process of finding those ideologies that best match an individual's needs and preferences.

Just because a given culture may offer a wide variety of ideologies (MacKenzie & Baumeister, 2014), individuals do not necessarily choose to adopt only a single one. Instead, they choose a mix that best suits their specific needs (Kay & Eibach, 2012). The Bayesian Learning framework allows for the adoption of such a mix of ideologies in the same it is used to make a decision about optimal product allocation. Therefore, we go through the information acquisition process symmetrically to find the optimal mix of ideologies that is consistent with the underlying needs structure.[10]

Bayesian Learning About Ideologies and Belief Systems

We include both the match value M_K, which indicates the degree of match between the individual's needs and a particular ideology K, and the level of consumption

[10] The following discussion is based on Burs et al. (2022).

C in the individual's utility function U. We skip the superscript because we are only interested in one individual and do not need to compare that individual with others. As before, we consider a choice between two ideologies: A and B. Utility is generated by the match values M_A and M_B with ideologies A and B, and consumption C,

$$\mathfrak{U} = \mathfrak{U}(M_A, M_B, C). \tag{6.7}$$

We assume that the match values M_A and M_B are unknown to the individual and use the Bayesian Learning framework for normally distributed parameters. So we assume that each match value M_K is normally distributed with mean μ_K and variance σ_K^2. Using Bayesian updating, the expected match value can be revealed as more information is observed.

As a first step, individuals form a prior belief about their match with each ideology. We assume that this prior belief is normally distributed, i.e.,

$$M_K \sim \mathcal{N}(\mu_{K,0}, \sigma_{K,0}^2).$$

This illustrates the fact that individuals tend to adopt those ideologies they observe in their social environment (Golman et al., 2016). That way, they are able to form prior beliefs from, for example, the ideologies adopted by their family and friends.

As a next step, individuals learn from noisy information signals

$$M_{K,T_{Info}} = M_K + \varepsilon_{K,T_{Info}} \text{ with } \varepsilon_{K,T_{Info}} \sim \mathcal{N}(0, \eta_{K,0}^2),$$

where $\eta_{K,0}^2$ represents signal precision and T_{Info} is the number of signals that are received, i.e., the number of information acquisition steps.

After receiving T_{Info} pieces of information, the distribution for each match value conditional on the obtained information set is a normal distribution

$$M_K | I_{K,T_{Info}} \sim \mathcal{N}(\mu_{K,T_{Info}}, \sigma_{K,T_{Info}}^2)$$

with

$$\mu_{K,T_{Info}} = \frac{\sigma_{K,0}^2}{T_{Info}\sigma_{K,0}^2 + \eta_K^2} \sum_{s=0}^{T_{Info}-1} M_{K,s} + \frac{\eta_K^2}{T_{Info}\sigma_{K,0}^2 + \eta_K^2} \mu_{K,0} \text{ and} \tag{6.8}$$

$$\sigma_{K,T_{Info}}^2 = \left(\frac{1}{\sigma_{K,0}^2} + T_{Info} \frac{1}{\eta_K^2} \right)^{-1} = \frac{\sigma_{K,0}^2 \eta_K^2}{T_{Info}\sigma_{K,0}^2 + \eta_K^2}, \text{ with } \frac{\partial \sigma_{K,T_{Info}}^2}{\partial \eta_K^2} > 0. \tag{6.9}$$

Choosing Optimal Ideologies

As discussed earlier, individuals have to find ideologies that best match their subjective needs and preferences. Each individual has a variety of needs that may not be well served by adopting only one ideology. Therefore, we allow individuals to choose a mix. That is, individuals agree, for example, with certain of the beliefs held by ideology A and with certain beliefs held by ideology B, depending on which needs are addressed by their respective narratives. Thus, a fraction α, respectively $1-\alpha$, of each ideology is optimally adopted, so that

$$\mathfrak{U} = \mathfrak{U}\left(\alpha M_A, (1-\alpha)M_B, C\right) \text{ with } \alpha \in [0, 1].$$

Note that this is a slight deviation from the utility function of product variations. In the following, we use the sequential optimization strategy to find the optimal fraction α. The extreme cases $\alpha = 0$ and $\alpha = 1$ are possible if someone fully adopts only one ideology.

Utility is also derived from consumption which is defined as the product of the consumption amount $\mathfrak{c}$ and consumption time T_C

$$C = \mathfrak{c} T_C.$$

Income Y is defined as the product of the given working time T_W and the hourly wage rate w. It is entirely spent on consumption at price p, so that

$$Y = T_W w = p\mathfrak{c}.$$

This is the income budget constraint that can be rearranged, so that $\mathfrak{c} = T_W \frac{w}{p}$ and consumption is

$$C = T_W \frac{w}{p} T_C.$$

Additionally, there is a time budget that can be divided into time for information acquisition T_{Info}, consumption time T_C, and work time T_W. We assume that there is a disposable time $\bar{T}$ per period that is already reduced by a fixed working time T_W, so that the time budget is

$$\bar{T} = T_{Info} + T_C.$$

The objective is to maximize utility under the budget constraint. Symmetrically to the consumer choice model, we use an exponential utility function with a constant absolute risk aversion (CARA)

$$\mathfrak{U} = 1 - \exp\left(-R\left(\alpha M_A + (1-\alpha)M_B + C\right)\right), \tag{6.10}$$

where $R > 0$ is the risk aversion parameter. Expected utility is

$$\mathbb{E}[\mathfrak{U}] = 1 - \exp\Big(-R\Big(\alpha\mu_A - \alpha^2 \frac{1}{2} R\sigma_A^2 + (1-\alpha)\mu_B - (1-\alpha)^2 \frac{1}{2} R\sigma_B^2 + C\Big)\Big).$$

As the stochastic parameters for M_K are unknown to the individual, they can only consider the conditional expected utility after T_{Info} information acquisition steps

$$\mathbb{E}[\mathfrak{U}|I_{T_{Info}}] = 1 - \exp\Big(- R\Big(\alpha\mu_{A,T_{Info}} - \alpha^2\frac{1}{2}R\sigma^2_{A,T_{Info}} + (1-\alpha)\mu_{B,T_{Info}} - (1-\alpha)^2\frac{1}{2}R\sigma^2_{B,T_{Info}} + C\Big)\Big),$$

where $I_{T_{Info}} = I_{A,T_{Info}} \cup I_{B,T_{Info}}$ is the current information set for both ideologies A and B. Note that $\mathbb{E}[\mathfrak{U}|I_{T_{Info}}]$ is maximized if the reduced objective function

$$\mathbb{E}[U|I_{T_{Info}}] = \alpha\mu_{A,T_{Info}} - \frac{\alpha^2}{2}R\sigma^2_{A,T_{Info}} + (1-\alpha)\mu_{B,T_{Info}} - \frac{(1-\alpha)^2}{2}R\sigma^2_{B,T_{Info}} + C$$

is maximized. For this reason, we use only this reduced form in the remainder of our analysis. Thus, after observing T_{Info} information signals, individuals can determine the optimal fraction α^* and the optimal expected conditional utility $\mathbb{E}_{\alpha^*}[U|I_{T_{Info}}]$ by solving the maximization problem

$$\max_{\alpha} \mathbb{E}[U|I_{T_{Info}}] = \alpha\mu_{A,T_{Info}} - \frac{\alpha^2}{2}R\sigma^2_{A,T_{Info}} + (1-\alpha)\mu_{B,T_{Info}} - \frac{(1-\alpha)^2}{2}R\sigma^2_{B,T_{Info}} + T_W\frac{w}{p}(\bar{T} - T_{Info}). \tag{MP}$$

Note that we have included the budget constraint in the objective function. Thus, after receiving information $I_{T_{Info}}$, it is optimal for the individual to adopt ideology A to the extent α^* and ideology B to the extent $1 - \alpha^*$. Consumption $\left[C = T_W\frac{w}{p}(\bar{T} - T_{Info})\right]$ is reduced with each additional piece of information, and marginal costs are equal to $T_W\frac{w}{p}$. In this way, we can solve the optimization problem sequentially, symmetrically to the consumer choice optimization.

Sequential Optimization

We can now describe how the individual's choice problem can be solved sequentially. Remember that the solution depends on the particular sequence of signals that is observed. We will see this again in the numerical examples at the end of this section.

Adopting an ideology requires more effort than choosing a product variation. Young adults, in particular, seek guidance through search and trial methods. In our model, this means that an ideology is adopted to the extent α^* after a few steps of information acquisition, but when more information is available, the fraction α^* may be adjusted. Thus, trial does not mean complete adoption and complete rejection of an ideology, but the degree of adoption may change. In fact, it is a chronological sequence of experiential steps until one finds one's own view, which may consist of a mixture of different ideologies and belief systems.

Again, the individual's decision problem is not only the choice of optimal ideologies but also an optimal stopping problem that can be formalized using the functional equation of dynamic programming

$$V(I_{T_{Info}}) = \max\{\mathbb{E}_{\alpha^*}[U|I_{T_{Info}}], V^{ant}(I_{T_{Info}+1})\}.$$

$\mathbb{E}_{\alpha^*}[U|I_{T_{Info}}]$ is the currently expected utility of stopping (the solution to (MP)), and $V^{ant}(I_{T_{Info}+1})$ is the value for continuation, i.e., the anticipated expected utility after observing an additional information signal. Again, we have to use the anticipated value because the individual cannot determine $\mathbb{E}_{\alpha^*}[u|I_{T_{Info}+1}]$ without performing, and thus "paying" for, an additional information step. Sequential information acquisition is stopped when for the first time additional information is not anticipated to increase the conditional expected utility, i.e., the optimal number of acquisition steps is

$$T^*_{Info} = \min\{T_{Info} \in \{0, \ldots, T\} : V(I_{T_{Info}}) = \mathbb{E}_{\alpha^*}[U|I_{T_{Info}}]\}.$$

As additional information can either increase or decrease the match value (see Chap. 3), it can also either increase or decrease the part of the current expected utility that is derived by the match, i.e.,

$$\mathbb{E}[\tilde{U}|I_{T_{Info}}] :=\alpha\mu_{A,T_{Info}} - \frac{\alpha^2}{2}R\sigma^2_{A,T_{Info}} + (1-\alpha)\mu_{B,T_{Info}} - \frac{(1-\alpha)^2}{2}R\sigma^2_{B,T_{Info}}.$$

We define $\mathbb{E}[\tilde{U}|I_{T_{Info}}]$ the "match utility". Thus, even though additional information brings the individual closer to the true match value, it does not necessarily increase the match utility. This also affects the individual's anticipation $V^{ant}(I_{T_{Info}+1})$. If the value derived from continuing is anticipated to be low, the information acquisition process may stop even though later signals might reveal high match values. Therefore, we want to ensure that additional information increases the current expected utility. In order to do so, we assume that individuals are risk averse with risk aversion parameter R that is sufficiently large[11] so that we obtain the standard positive and decreasing marginal expected utility with respect to the steps T^*_{Info}. The difference between two optimal match utilities between two acquisition steps is

$$\Delta_{T_{Info}} := \mathbb{E}_{\alpha^*_{T_{Info}+1}}[\tilde{U}|I_{T_{Info}+1}] - \mathbb{E}_{\alpha^*_{T_{Info}}}[\tilde{U}|I_{T_{Info}}].$$

Then, we assume that R is large enough so that

$$\Delta_{T_{Info}} > 0 \text{ and } \Delta_{T_{Info}} > \Delta_{T_{Info}+1} \text{ for all } T_{Info} \in \{0, \ldots, \bar{T}\}. \qquad \text{(R)}$$

[11] Again, we only consider the set of stochastic dynamic sequences that fulfill this criterion. The generality of our analysis is thus limited in this respect.

More details on this assumption can be found in Appendix A.6. As in the consumer choice problem described in Chap. 3, this assumption ensures that additional search steps, i.e., additional information, actually increase the expected utility from the match, $\mathbb{E}[\tilde{U}|I_{T_{Info}}]$. The more information one receives about an ideology, the better one knows one's match with it, and utility increases. High-risk aversion compensates for possible reductions in utility due to low signals. Further, the reduction in uncertainty is the most important effect of information. More certainty about one's match with an ideology reduces the risk of making the wrong decision. Making these assumptions, we can now return to the sequential information acquisition process. First, each individual forms prior beliefs about the match values of various ideologies under consideration. Second, they can update these beliefs by observing additional information in a Bayesian manner. However, because collecting additional information is time-consuming and costly, they must first decide whether to start the Bayesian Learning process and then when to stop.

Again, individuals start with a prior belief $\mu_{K,0}$ for each ideology K with prior variance $\sigma_{K,0}$. Before they can decide how to proceed, they need to determine the allocation of ideologies that yields the maximum expected utility from these prior beliefs. Thus, they must solve the prior maximization problem

$$\max_{\alpha} \mathbb{E}[U|I_0] = \alpha\mu_{A,0} - \alpha^2\frac{1}{2}R\sigma^2_{A,0} + (1-\alpha)\mu_{B,0} - (1-\alpha)^2\frac{1}{2}R\sigma^2_{B,0} + T_W\frac{w}{p}\bar{T},$$

which gives the optimal fraction α_0^* as its result, and we denote the corresponding optimal expected utility by $\mathbb{E}_{\alpha_0^*}[U|I_0]$. Note that at this point, $C = T_W\frac{w}{p}\bar{T}$ because no time is spent on information acquisition, and all the available time is spent on getting consumption. Without collecting any additional information, the individual adopts a mix of the two ideologies containing fraction α_0^* of ideology A and fraction $1-\alpha_0^*$ of ideology B. The maximum prior expected utility $\mathbb{E}_{\alpha_0^*}[U|I_0]$ is the reference point for deciding whether or not to start the Bayesian updating process. In doing so, $\mathbb{E}_{\alpha_0^*}[U|I_0]$ has to be compared with the anticipated expected utility after the first piece of additional information, $V^{ant}(I_{T_1})$, is acquired. But how can this value be anticipated? Individuals cannot know the next signal without performing search steps, which reduces consumption time. They know that additional information reduces uncertainty, but they do not know by how much. It must be anticipated.

In order to anticipate the value of the first search step, an individual must anticipate the parameters of its distribution. First, they need to know what signal will first be observed. Without any additional information, the prior belief $\mu_{K,0}$ is the best guess, because the individual needs new information to update their belief. Second, they need to know the precision of the signal to anticipate the reduction in uncertainty. This is indicated by the signal's variance, η_K^2, which can also only be known after conducting a search step. Thus, the individual has to make another guess $\tilde{\eta}_K^2$ for η_K^2. This guess $\tilde{\eta}_K^2$ reflects a subjective belief in the accuracy and usefulness of a signal. For example, a highly educated person may be very confident that they will only obtain very precise signals that can be interpreted well. This is reflected in a low $\tilde{\eta}_K^2$.

Then, the anticipated variance for the first step if information acquisition is

$$\sigma_{K,ant}^2 := \frac{\sigma_{K,0}^2 \tilde{\eta}_K^2}{\sigma_{K,0}^2 + \tilde{\eta}_K^2}.$$

Using these guesses about the first signal and its variance, the anticipated maximum expected value from the first piece of additional information can be determined solving the maximization problem

$$\begin{aligned}\max_{\alpha} \mathbb{E}[U|I_{0,ant}] &= \alpha\mu_{A,0} - \alpha^2\frac{1}{2}R\sigma_{A,ant}^2 + (1-\alpha)\mu_{B,0} \\ &\quad - (1-\alpha)^2\frac{1}{2}R\sigma_{B,ant}^2 + T_W\frac{w}{p}(\bar{T}-1),\end{aligned}$$

which returns the optimal fraction $\alpha_{1,ant}^*$ as a result. Now, total consumption $C = T_W\frac{w}{p}(\bar{T}-1)$ (consumption service including the time of enjoying this service) is reduced by one search step. Now the individual can determine

$$V(I_0) = \max\{\mathbb{E}_{\alpha_0^*}[U|I_0], V^{ant}(I_1)\}$$

to make a decision about the acquisition of new information. Assumption (R) ensures that additional information increases the match utility, but this has to compensate for the reduction in consumption caused by searching. Only if $V(I_0) = V^{ant}(I_1)$, information acquisition is started. If $V(I_0) = \mathbb{E}_{\alpha_0^*}[U|I_0]$, the process is not started. Note that this also depends on the subjective guess, $\tilde{\eta}_K^2$. For example, $\tilde{\eta}_K^2$ could be so high that the process is not started even though the signals are in truth very precise and indicate a completely different allocation than α_0^*. In this case, individuals never know whether more information yields a higher utility than $\mathbb{E}_{\alpha_0^*}[U|I_0]$.

So far, we have described the decision relating to the start of the process. Next, we look at further search steps. After each step, individuals have to decide whether additional information increases utility or whether they should stop information acquisition because the current information set already gives optimal utility. In doing so, they again have to anticipate the expected utility from continuation. Again, the parameters of the distribution of the match value after the following step are needed. We assume that after experiencing the first signal, individuals get to know the precision of the signal. So we assume that now their subjective guess is equal to the true variance η_K^2. This can be explained as follows: If the signal is very clear and focused, η_K^2 will be low. Conversely, if the signal is more diffuse or vague, η_K^2 will be high. We assume these observations to be correct. This is the ideal case. However, not every signal has to illustrate a true value of an ideology. False messages or "fake news" can influence the spread of information, and individuals may not perceive the true reality. This is discussed in detail in Sect. 8.2. At this point, we only consider the ideal case of true signals.

Thus, the variance of the match value, and thus the impact on uncertainty, can be determined for the second and all subsequent steps, $\sigma^2_{K,T_{Info}} = \frac{\sigma^2_{K,0}\eta^2_K}{T_{Info}\sigma^2_{K,0}+\eta^2_K}$ (see Eq. (6.9)). However, the expected match value after observing another piece of information still cannot be known without performing a search step. Therefore, the signal again has to be anticipated. One more time, the best guess for the signal $m_{K,T_{Info}}$ is the current expected value $\mu_{K,T_{Info}}$, which means that there can be no update without additional information. Thus, to decide whether to perform the search step $T_{Info}+1$, individuals must solve the following maximization problem:

$$\max_{\alpha} \alpha\mu_{A,T_{Info}} - \alpha^2\frac{1}{2}R\sigma^2_{A,T_{Info}+1} + (1-\alpha)\mu_{B,T_{Info}}$$
$$-(1-\alpha)^2\frac{1}{2}R\sigma^2_{B,T_{Info}+1} + T_W\frac{w}{p}(\bar{T} - T_{Info} - 1),$$

which gives the maximum anticipated expected utility $V^{ant}(I_{T_{Info}+1})$ as result. Comparing this to $\mathbb{E}_{\alpha^*_{T_{Info}}}[U|I_{T_{Info}}]$, individuals can determine $V(I_{T_{Info}})$ and decide how to proceed. As long as $V(I_{T_{Info}}) = V^{ant}(I_{T_{Info}+1})$, an increasing utility is anticipated and information acquisition continues. If $V(I_{T_{Info}}) = \mathbb{E}_{\alpha^*_{T_{Info}}}[U|I_{T_{Info}}]$, the search ends, and the optimal number of search steps T^*_{Info} is found. We can formulate the following:

Proposition 6.2 *Let assumption* (R) *hold. The dynamic maximization problem has a solution* T^*_{Info} *with corresponding fraction* $\alpha_{T^*_{Info}}$.

Consequently, the ideologies that are chosen with the incomplete information set $I_{T^*_{Info}}$ *lead to optimal expected conditional utility.*

Proof After observing each new piece of information, we solve (MP). Based on assumption (R), additional information increases expected match utility at a decreasing rate. Information acquisition stops as soon as the increase in the anticipated match utility does not compensate for the reduction in consumption, or when the maximum number of search steps $\bar{T} = T_{Info}$ is reached. ■

Note that such a solution $(\alpha^*_{T_{Info}}, T^*_{Info})$ is found for every sequence of signals that satisfies the assumption (R), and that this solution depends on the particular sequence of signals. Another sequence that also satisfies the assumption (R) may lead to a different solution $(\tilde{\alpha}^*_{T_{Info}}, \tilde{t}^*_{Info})$.

This proposition formally summarizes the fact that there is an optimal number of search steps and an optimal allocation structure of ideologies under consideration in our information acquisition process. Information can be collected about those ideologies that are available in an individual's sociocultural environment. At some point, the marginal cost of acquiring additional information exceeds its marginal benefit. Information acquisition then stops, and ideologies are adopted to the extent that they optimally serve the individual's needs and preferences. The fraction α^* of each ideology is between one and zero, but corner solutions ($\alpha^* = 0$ or $\alpha^* = 1$) are also possible. In this case, one ideology, either A or B, is fully adopted, while the other is fully rejected. In the case of an inner solution ($\alpha^* \in (0, 1)$), the individual adopts ideology A to the extent α^* and ideology B to the extent $1 - \alpha^*$. This means that the individual is attracted to a mixture of the values and norms of both ideologies A and B.

Numerical Examples

As in Sect. 3.2, we cannot give a general solution for (MP) but provide numerical examples of sequential solutions. This illustrates once again that the decision path depends on the specific sequence of signals observed. Again, consider two scenarios: Suppose an individual is considering two ideologies that seem very similar, i.e., the prior beliefs are $\mu_{A,0} = 5$ and $\mu_{B,0} = 5.2$ with $\sigma^2_{A,0} = 0.6$ and $\sigma^2_{B,0} = 0.8$.

The *first scenario* is an example where both ideologies A and B indeed have the same true match value. In this case, a balanced combination of the two ideologies ($\alpha^* = 0.5$) is the optimal choice. This ought to be revealed by the information acquisition process as more information is received. The *second scenario* illustrates a case where one ideology, namely B, has a higher true match value than the other. However, in our example, we see that the information acquisition process stops when it is optimal to adopt a mixture of both ideologies. Due to search costs, the process may not fully reveal that one ideology is the optimal choice.

Figure 6.7 sets out the first scenario. The expected conditional utility $\mathbb{E}[U|I_{T_{Info}}]$ is plotted as a function of T_{Info} and α. We see two examples with different observed signal sequences with all parameters held constant. The risk aversion parameter R is chosen large enough to satisfy the assumption (R). At each time step $T_{Info} = 0, 1, \ldots, T$, the maximization problem (MP) is solved to determine the optimal choice of α at that time. The corresponding optimal expected utility is

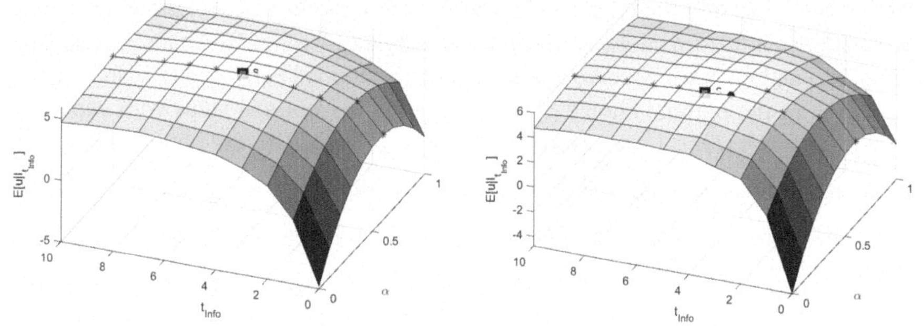

(a) (b)

Fig. 6.7 Two outcomes for $\mathbb{E}[u|I_{T_{Info}}]$ with $\mu_{A,0} = 5$, $\mu_{B,0} = 5.2$, $\sigma^2_{A,0} = 0.6$, $\sigma^2_{B,0} = 0.8$, $\eta^2_A = 1$, $\eta^2_B = 1$, $\mu_A = 6$, $\mu_B = 6$, $R = 30$, $w = 2$, $p = 10$, $T_L = 1$, $T = 10$ and $\tilde{\eta}_A = \tilde{\eta}_B = 0.1$

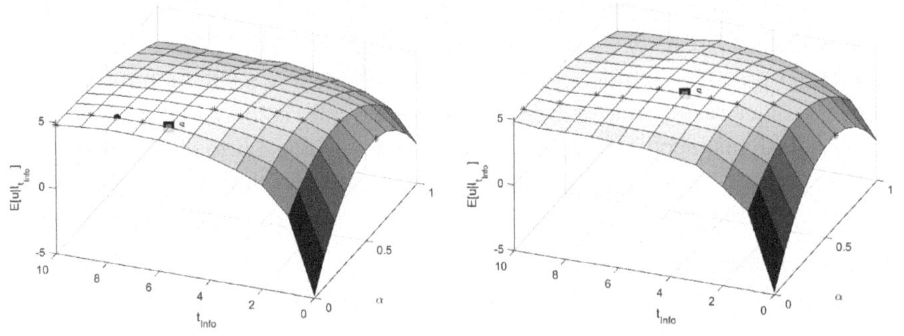

(a) (b)

Fig. 6.8 Two outcomes for $\mathbb{E}[u|I_{T_{Info}}]$ with $\mu_{A,0} = 5$, $\mu_{B,0} = 5.2$, $\sigma^2_{A,0} = 0.6$, $\sigma^2_{B,0} = 0.8$, $\eta^2_A = 1$, $\eta^2_B = 1$, $\mu_A = 4$, $\mu_B = 6$, $R = 30$, $w = 2$, $p = 10$, $T_L = 1$, $T = 10$ and $\tilde{\eta}_A = \tilde{\eta}_B = 0.1$

marked with an asterisk. In this first scenario, both true match values are equal to 6. In case 1(a), the optimal choice of α^* is 0.5 after five optimal steps, and the conditional expected utility is $\mathbb{E}_{\alpha^*_{T_{Info}}}[U|I_{T_{Info}}] = 5.900$. However, in case 1(b), the optimal choice of α^* is 0.4 after five optimal steps with expected utility $\mathbb{E}_{\alpha^*_{T_{Info}}}[U|I_{T_{Info}}] = 5.833$ (see Fig. 6.7). Thus, the signals in this sequence indicate that ideology B has a slightly higher match value than ideology A. More search steps are needed to find $\alpha^* = 0.5$, but the search stops earlier due to search costs.

Furthermore, in case 1(b), the black dot marks the maximum expected utility. In case 1(a), this is equal to the sequential solution. This shows that the solution to our sequential process is indeed an approximation of the optimal solution that could be determined if the sequence of signals were known prior to information acquisition, which is not realistic from the individual's point of view.

Figure 6.8 depicts two example processes for the second scenario. The only difference to the first scenario is that the true match value for ideology A is 4 instead of 6. The true match value for ideology B remains 6. Thus, the information acquisition ought to reveal that the optimal choice of α^* is 0. Again, in our two cases 2(a) and 2(b), we observe that the search is stopped early due to search costs. In case 2(a), the optimal choice of α^* is 0.1 after six optimal steps with expected utility $\mathbb{E}_{\alpha^*_{T_{Info}}}[U|I_{T_{Info}}] = 5.112$ (see Fig. 6.8). In case 2(b), the optimal choice of α^* is 0.4 after five optimal steps with expected utility $\mathbb{E}_{\alpha^*_{T_{Info}}}[U|I_{T_{Info}}] = 5.137$. In both cases, more steps are to be necessary to find out that ideology B is the true best choice and $\alpha^* = 0$ is the solution.

Again, we learn from these numerical examples that search costs lead to decisions with an imperfect information set and that this decision depends on the specific sequence of signals that is observed. More search steps would eventually reveal the best matching ideologies.

References

Bénabou, R. (2015). The economics of motivated beliefs. *Revue déconomie politique, 125*(5), 665–685.

Bénabou, R., & Tirole, J. (2016). Mindful economics: The production, consumption, and value of beliefs. *Journal of Economic Perspectives, 30*(3), 141–164.

Bentham, J. (1789). *An introduction to the principles of morals and legislation*. Clarendon Press.

Berry, S., & Pakes, A. (2007). The pure characteristics demand model. *International Economic Review, 48*(4), 1193–1225.

Burs, C., & Gries, T. (2022). Decision-making under imperfect information with Bayesian learning or heuristic rules. *Working Paper, Center for International Economics (CIE)*, Paderborn University, 149.

Burs, C., Gries, T., & Müller, V. (2022). The choice of ideology and everyday decisions. *Working Paper, APSA Preprints of The American Political Science Association*.

Caplin, A., & Nalebuff, B. (1988). On 64-percent-majority rule. *Econometrica, 56*(4), 787.

Caplin, A., & Nalebuff, B. (1991). Aggregation and social choice: A mean voter theorem. *Econometrica, 59*(1) 1–23.

Davis, O. A., Hinich, M. J., & Ordeshook, P. C. (1970). An expository development of a mathematical model of the electoral process. *American Political Science Review, 64*(2), 426–448.

Downs, A. (1957). An economic theory of political action in a democracy. *Journal of Political Economy, 65*(2), 135–150.

Golman, R., Loewenstein, G., Moene, K. O., & Zarri, L. (2016). The preference for belief consonance. *Journal of Economic Perspectives, 30*(3), 165–188.

Gries, T., Jost, J. T., & Müller, V. (2020). The market for belief systems: A formal model of ideological choice. *Working Paper, APSA Preprints of The American Political Science Association*.

Gries, T., Jost, J. T., & Müller, V. (2022). The market for belief systems: A formal model of ideological choice. *Psychological Inquiry, 33*(2), 65–83.

Hinich, M., & Munger, M. (2010). *Ideology and the theory of political choice*. Michigan Studies In Political Analysis. University of Michigan Press.

Hogg, M. A., Sherman, D. K., Dierselhuis, J., Maitner, A. T., & Moffitt, G. (2007). Uncertainty, entitativity, and group identification. *Journal of Experimental Social Psychology, 43*(1), 135–142.

Jackson, J. E. (2014). Location, location, location: the Davis-Hinich model of electoral competition. *Public Choice, 159*(1/2), 197–218.

Jost, J. T. (2006). The end of the end of ideology. *American Psychologist, 61*(7), 651–670.

Jost, J. T., Federico, C. M., & Napier, J. L. (2009). Political ideology: Its structure, functions, and elective affinities. *Annual Review of Psychology, 60*(1), 307–337.

Jost, J. T., Federico, C. M., & Napier, J. L. (2013). Political ideologies and their social psychological functions. In M. Freeden, L. T. Sargent & M. Stears (Eds.), *The Oxford Handbook of Political Ideologies* (pp. 232–250). Oxford University Press.

Jost, J. T., Stern, C., Rule, N. O., & Sterling, J. (2017). The politics of fear: Is there an ideological asymmetry in existential motivation? *Social Cognition, 35*(4), 324–353.

Kay, A. C., & Eibach, R. P. (2012). The ideological toolbox: Ideologies as tools of motivated social cognition. In *The SAGE handbook of social cognition the SAGE handbook of social cognition* (pp. 495–515). SAGE Publications.

Knight, K. (2006). Transformations of the concept of ideology in the twentieth century. *The American Political Science Review, 100*(4), 619–626.

Kruglanski, A. W., & Orehek, E. (2009). Toward a relativity theory of rationality. *Social Cognition, 27*(5), 639–660.

MacKenzie, M. J., & Baumeister, R. F. (2014). Meaning in life: Nature, needs, and myths. In *Meaning in positive and existential psychology* (pp. 25–37). Springer.
Schofield, N. (2007). The mean voter theorem: Necessary and sufficient conditions for convergent equilibrium. *The Review of Economic Studies, 74*(3), 965–980.

Chapter 7
Ideologies and Everyday Decisions

Up to this point, we have considered the fact that people have an information problem if they want to make good decisions for themselves. This information problem (see Chap. 2) can be mitigated by collecting real facts or by using heuristics. This was described for a household's consumption decision for a simple economic problem in Sect. 3.3.

In Chap. 4, we then left the standard framework of economic modeling and worked out that the human need set includes psychological needs in addition to physical consumption needs which we had already taken for granted in Chaps. 2, 3, and 6. Chapter 4 provides an overview of these psychological needs, which are also part of the economic scarcity problem that has to be solved. This means that humans have to handle two problems at the same time. They want to serve the entire spectrum of their needs, but because of the information problem they do not know how to do that.[1] In other words, humans wish for states of the world that meet their needs but initially have no real idea of what these states actually look like. Humans not only want a description of these conditions and states which match their needs, they also do not know how they can get to these states or which mechanisms actually lead them there.

Ideologies, belief systems, and their narratives provide an answer to these needs. They have important functions for people. For example, they address human needs and offer solutions to serving them. These functions are described in Sect. 5.1. Because ideologies, belief systems, and their narratives address and serve human needs, people are attracted to one or more ideologies, depending on their need

[1] When we describe this problem, we implicitly assume that people are aware of their needs and make decisions against this background. This assumption is not always given. Therefore, we have to argue again with Friedman's 'as if'. People make decisions, learn about their needs, and continuously improve their decisions through this learning. At the end of this learning process, they will then behave "as if" they had been aware of their needs.

T. Gries et al., *The Economics of Ideologies*, Springer Studies in Alternative Economics, https://doi.org/10.1007/978-3-031-93514-5_7

structure. They adopt those ideology or belief systems that match their needs (see Chap. 6).

Individuals hope that their ideology or belief system will give them advice on how their needs can be met. Ideologies and belief systems can thus provide guidance. This guidance can be very abstract, and ideologies and belief systems can provide general advice on values and evaluations. However, ideological narratives can also provide hints, explanations, and interpretations so that a person can understand and evaluate specific issues. This guidance can go as far as rules and instructions for action. In this chapter, we want to show that ideological narratives are present in everyday life. They help to understand and interpret everyday phenomena and influence decisions. They are used to alleviate our information problem, i.e., they give us an explanation, an interpretation, and a certain understanding of the conditions in which we find ourselves and how we can perceive and interpret reality (see Sect. 7.1).

As just mentioned, ideologies and belief systems can not only provide explanations but also formulate rules. These rules can be used in everyday decisions and serve as decision-making guidelines. They supplement the explanatory narratives of ideologies or belief systems, offering guidance on behaviors that align with the conditions promoted by the ideology and desired by its followers. These rules are designed to meet the needs of those who subscribe to the ideology, and they suggest that in decision-making situations, the individual comes closer to the desired states by following these rules. In Sects. 7.2 to 7.4, we will therefore describe how standard everyday decisions are made under these conditions. Everyday decisions are codetermined by ideological rules. We start with a classic consumption decision in Sect. 7.2, then present a workplace decision in Sect. 7.3, and finally model a political decision in Sect. 7.4. For all these decisions, we describe how ideological beliefs influence the decisions taken. As long as people have an information problem, and ideologies mitigate this information problem, ideologically codetermined decisions can ultimately be expected to be individually subjectively rational[2] decisions.

7.1 Facts or Ideologies? Optimal Orientation

People require information to make decisions, but they often lack the necessary information to make well-informed choices. In this discussion, we explore the concept of optimal orientation for understanding a decision problem. We will examine how we gather information, what information is accessible, and how we learn from it. We will also consider how we utilize the information to better understand the decision problem. Ultimately, we are faced with the decision of whether to rely on ideological narratives or on facts.

[2] Remember, a choice a is subjectively rational choice, if the decision-maker cannot do better under the subjective constraints and conditions. For this definition, see Chap. 1 and Sect. 3.2.

Information can be gathered from a variety of sources. Individuals can gather true facts and learn from this additional information in order to make decisions that best satisfy their subjective preferences. However, this can be costly and time-consuming. Although science is making huge progress, humans are still far from fully understanding their environment. As mentioned earlier (Chap. 3), the human information problem can be solved by incorporating beliefs. Even when individuals learn from facts, this remains an imperfect approximation of reality. As an alternative, individuals can rely on ideologies to make decisions. Ideologies and belief systems provide rules, norms, and values from which they can learn quickly and at low cost. This important function of ideologies was discussed in Sect. 5.1. But when do decision-makers rely on ideologies or belief systems instead of gathering facts themselves? In this section, we model the use of information from these two sources in a single decision situation. Logically, this choice problem has a similar structure to the sequential consumer decision process described in Sect. 3.1. Since the ideological narrative is a kind of heuristic, the decision-maker has to choose between the costly information fact and the ideological narrative that serves as a heuristic.

Let us therefore assume that the variable Z should have the highest possible value for this decision-maker, as Z is an important value that generates benefits. Z may be a match value, as in Chap. 2, but more generally, Z can be any other variable that generates utility with higher values and hence is important for decision-making.[3]

Let us look at an example. Consider a person for whom consumable wealth is important. Thus, in this example, Z represents consumable wealth. Based on the general match mechanism that was put forward in Chap. 6, this individual is an adherent of a particular ideology. This ideology promises that hard work on the scale of $\bar{T}_W$ will lead them to prosperity Z. This person now wonders whether they should follow this ideology's narrative or whether they should try to find out for themselves how the actual mechanisms work through which they can achieve wealth. Individuals must therefore decide whether they want to follow this ideology or whether they want to follow their own fact-based understanding. Again, in reality, this procedure is most often not a conscious and explicit procedure of rational search, so we again argue that this search for an optimal collection of information is more an "as if" optimization process. Hence, if they were to find out the actual mechanisms and these were not compatible with the ideological narratives, following the ideological recommendations would be unfavorable or even harmful. This decision – believing either in facts or ideological narratives – depends on the individual's uncertainty about the promises the ideology makes and the cost of gathering facts from other sources to form a fact-based belief (Bayesian Belief) about Z. Individual will choose the ideological narrative if their expected benefit from the ideology's promises (which have little or no information cost) is greater than the expected benefit from their own information gathering, which at the very least has a time cost.

[3] In the following, utility depends positively on this value. Therefore, the decision-maker should strive for a high Z. However, the other case is also possible by adjusting the utility function.

We now want to model this decision about facts vs. ideological narratives and establish that the decision to choose a guidance provided by an ideology is entirely subjectively rational. This means that it is subjectively rational to follow the belief in a (plausible) narrative because uncovering reality is currently too expensive. Beliefs thus guide human actions.

Formally, utility is derived from the value Z – in our example, consumable wealth (e.g., $Z = C$) – and as a second element, leisure time is T_L, such that the utility function in this model is

$$\mathfrak{U} = \mathfrak{U}(Z, T_L). \tag{7.1}$$

As the value Z is stochastic with expected value μ and variance σ^2, we chose a modeling similar to the approach used in Chap. 3. Hence, we can work with a specified and reduced utility function[4]

$$\mathbb{E}[U] = \mu - \frac{1}{2}R\sigma^2 + T_L,$$

with $R > 0$ denoting the risk aversion parameter.

Stochastic consumable wealth Z could be generated by a given working time $\bar{T}_W$. An individual has beliefs, there is some relation between hard work at $\bar{T}_W$ and the reward Z. However, that individual does not know the actual relationship or even causality. Since we want to focus on the information decision at this point, we assume a given working time $\bar{T}_W$ and only model the information acquisition decision, that is, the allocation between leisure time and information acquisition time. Thus, the total life time T_{total} can be allocated to working time $\bar{T}_W$, leisure time T_L, and info time T_{Info} [$T_{total} = \bar{T}_W + T_L + T_{Info}$]. Subtracting the given working time from the total lifetime leads to the given available time $\bar{T} = T_{total} - \bar{T}_W$ that is left over for leisure and information acquisition. Total leisure time is thus

$$T_L = \bar{T} - T_{Info}.$$

However, what is the consumable wealth this individual will receive? The value Z is stochastic, and μ and σ^2 are unknown. The individual has an information problem. He or she believes there may be a relationship between hard work and wealth. However, he or she does not know whether it is truly a close relationship or

[4] As in Chap. 3, we assume exponential utility, i.e.,

$$\mathfrak{U} = 1 - \exp(-R(Z + T_L)).$$

Then expected utility is

$$\mathbb{E}[\mathfrak{U}] = 1 - \exp\left(-R\left(\mu - \frac{1}{2}R\sigma^2 + T_L\right)\right).$$

whether this relationship is just a myth and does not actually exist. The individual has two options for solving this information problem: He or she can learn about this relationship by collecting facts or can follow the narratives suggested by the adopted ideology.

Information Through Facts and Bayesian Beliefs Again, learning through facts can be described by a Bayesian Learning process. As we discussed before (see Sect. 3.1), in a Bayesian Learning process, we collect signals about facts and use these signals to update our current belief as best we can. We learn more about reality with each information (signal) step we take, improve our beliefs about reality, and thus continuously approach reality. Our beliefs converge with true facts and reality. This is how we can proceed here as well.[5]

The ad hoc prior belief is the idea an individual initially has. In our example, an individual believes it to be a plausible idea that his or her work effort can actually lead to a certain level of prosperity μ_0 with a certain degree of uncertainty σ_0^2. It is a belief that serves as a kind of first piece of information in the information set $I_0 = \{\mu_0, \sigma_0^2\}$. This ad hoc prior belief can be used to determine the prior expected utility

$$\mathbb{E}[U|I_0] = \mu_0 - \frac{1}{2}R\sigma_0^2 + T_L.$$

The prior expected utility is the utility that would be obtained without acquiring any additional information. However, in order to make optimal decisions, individuals need information. Gathering facts involves search costs. Therefore, they must anticipate the expected utility of collecting a true fact before they take and thus pay for this step. This can be done as described in detail in Chap. 3: The best guess for the first fact is the prior belief μ_0. The variance σ_1^2 after receiving the first fact must be anticipated, since it can only be known after the first step of information acquisition. The parameter η^2 is needed to calculate σ_1^2, t. η^2 is the variance of the signal that gives information about the facts in question. It thus describes how precisely the perception and interpretation of the signal lead to an approximation of the individual's belief to the facts. In this first step, individuals must make a subjective guess about this parameter. This guess depends on how accurate they think a collected fact will be. We suppose that this belief varies across people. For example, the more educated a person is and the more confident they are that they can process an information signal correctly, the lower the guess $\tilde{\eta}^2$ for η^2 will be. Using this estimate, the anticipated variance after learning a first fact is

$$\sigma_{1,ant}^2 = \frac{\sigma_0^2\tilde{\eta}^2}{\sigma_0^2 + \tilde{\eta}^2}.$$

[5] While we assume here that the signals about the facts correctly reflect the facts, we will see later (Sect. 8.2) that such received signals can also be false signals about facts. A false statement is also a signal that, when we receive it, we initially process it on the assumption that it is correct.

Further, collecting true facts has a time cost. As each step of collecting real information about facts takes time ι_f, the total information time adds up with each information collecting step that is taken, such that the total time cost $T_{Info} = \iota_f N$. Thus, leisure time after collecting N facts is

$$T_L = \bar{T} - \iota_f N.$$

Then, the expected utility of collecting a first fact is

$$\mathbb{E}[U|I_{1,ant}] = \mu_0 - \frac{1}{2}R\sigma^2_{1,ant} + (\bar{T} - \iota_f).$$

This utility can be used as a reference point for deciding how to proceed. As already explained, decision-makers can use other sources of information or substitutes for information such as ideological narratives.

Information as an Ideological Narratives Simultaneously, individuals can also anticipate the expected utility of the ideological narrative. Again, the best guess for this ideologically determined information signal is the prior belief μ_0, and its variance $\hat{\eta}^2$ which must be anticipated. This variance depends on how much the individual trusts the narratives proposed by the ideology that is sending this information signal. The expected variance after using information from the ideology is

$$\hat{\sigma}^2_{1,ant} = \frac{\sigma_0^2\hat{\eta}^2}{\sigma_0^2 + \hat{\eta}^2}.$$

Thus, the anticipated expected utility of using information provided by the ideology is

$$\mathbb{E}[U|I_{Ideology}] = \mu_0 - \frac{1}{2}R\hat{\sigma}^2_{1,ant} + (\bar{T} - \iota_I),$$

where ι_I is the time cost for collecting the information from the ideology. Thus, the utility of the ideological narrative depends on the uncertainty about a piece of an ideological advice $\hat{\sigma}^2_{1,ant}$ and the cost ι_I of acquiring it. In this model, we assume that the ideology actively disseminates their narratives such that the individuals do not need to use time for information search. Hence, time cost is zero $\iota_I = 0$.

Choice of Source of Information These two anticipated expected utilities can be compared to the prior expected utility by determining the value function

$$V(I_0) = \max\{\mathbb{E}[U|I_0], \mathbb{E}[U|I_{1,ant}], \mathbb{E}[U|I_{Ideology}]\}.$$

The value $V(I_0)$ is high when the variance is low and the search cost is low. That is, it depends on how uncertain the individual is about the various sources

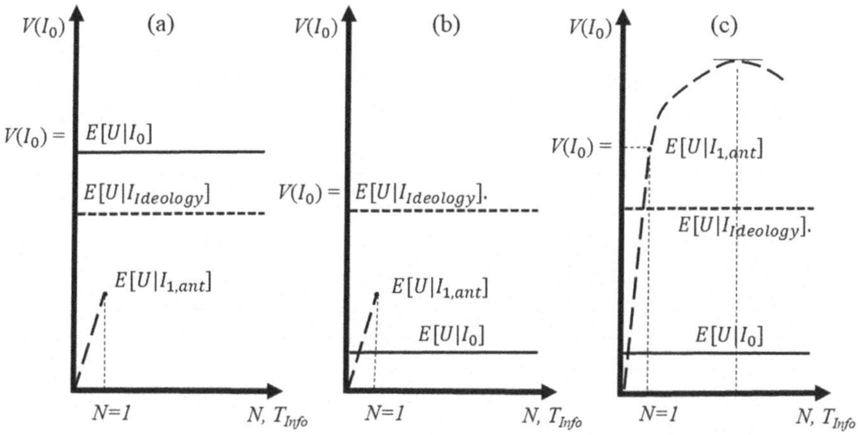

Fig. 7.1 (**a**) Dominance of prior beliefs, (**b**) Dominance of ideology, (**c**) Dominance of collecting facts

of information and on the cost of acquiring that information. We can discuss three cases that are also described in Fig. 7.1.[6]

(a) If $V(I_0) = \mathbb{E}[U|I_0]$, the individual is very certain about the personal prior, and so additional information is not expected to increase utility. Furthermore, the cost of collecting facts or using the ideological narrative may be high. Thus, the individual neither collects additional facts nor relies on the information provided by an ideology. This situation is described in Fig. 7.1, where $\mathbb{E}[U|I_0]$ generates the highest value.

(b) If $V(I_0) = \mathbb{E}[U|I_{Ideology}]$, the decision-maker does not collect facts but only relies on the ideology. The reasons can be high search costs ι_f or expected imprecise facts (high variance $\sigma^2_{1,ant}$). In this case (case b) in Fig. 7.1], the individual is convinced from the outset that their own search for facts and the development of their own understanding is too difficult. Particularly in the case of very complex topics or issues, it is conceivable that doing one's own research is very time-consuming and still not very enlightening.

Let us go back to our example. An ideological narrative suggests that a high work output $\bar{T}_W$ will lead to a very good level of prosperity. Its statement is "If you work hard and a lot, you will do well one day!" To find out whether this is true, the individual will have to carry out extensive research. They will have to find out whether the examples cited by the ideological narrative actually represent the expected value or whether they are stochastic exceptions. If it is difficult to approximate to this answer in a first research step, the expected

[6] To be reminded: N is the number of information collection steps and thus the amount of information collected. Since each step requires a fixed time to collect the information, the axis also describes the total information collection time T_{Info}.

benefit of this first step is very small. It is not worth research. However, since the narrative is one provided by the ideology that the individual has chosen and trusts, that individual will also follow the narrative at this point, as their own research does not have a high expected benefit. It is individually rational to follow the ideological narrative.

(c) If $V(I_0) = \mathbb{E}[U|I_{1,ant}]$, the individual believes that collecting facts will increase their prior expected utility more than trusting the ideology. And so they start collecting the first fact (Fig. 7.1c). As described in Chap. 3, the variance of the facts η^2 is known after the first fact is obtained. Thus, the variance σ^2_{N+1} can be determined for each fact $N \geq 1$. Again, the best guess for μ_{N+1} is the current expected value μ_N. Each time after a fact is collected, individuals compare the current expected utility from N facts and the expected utility from an additional fact $N + 1$ with the expected utility from relying on the ideology, i.e., determining the value of

$$V(I_N) = \max\{\mathbb{E}[U|I_N], \mathbb{E}[U|I_{N+1,ant}], \mathbb{E}[U|I_{Ideology}]\},$$

where

$$\mathbb{E}[U|I_N] = \mu_N - \frac{1}{2}R\sigma^2_N + (\bar{T} - \iota_f N)$$

$$\text{and } \mathbb{E}[U|I_{N+1,ant}] = \mu_N - \frac{1}{2}R\sigma^2_{N+1} + (\bar{T} - \iota_f(N+1)).$$

As long as $V(I_N) = \mathbb{E}[U|I_{N+1,ant}]$, the individual will continue to collect facts. At the first point in time N at $V(I_N) \neq \mathbb{E}[U|I_{N+1,ant}]$, the acquisition of facts stops. At $V(I_N) = \mathbb{E}[U|I_N]$, the expected utility of collecting facts is highest, and so the decision is made based on those facts, and no additional information is acquired. Collecting more and more facts leads to decreasing net benefits so that after a certain number of search steps continuing the search will no longer generate positive marginal benefits. The discussion here follows the same mechanism as described in Chap. 3. Accordingly, the search is optimally terminated after N^* steps (Fig. 7.1c). This again means that there is an optimal information acquisition, and all further considerations are made under incomplete information.

These three cases show that humans almost always have to act under incomplete information. They have to rely either on ad hoc ideas, ideological beliefs, or Bayesian Beliefs (BB). However, these are beliefs that sometimes reflect reality well but are often quite far removed from real facts and actual mechanisms. The consequence of this is that even "rational decisions" can and must lead to mistakes being made. Nevertheless, these errors only become apparent ex post and can only be corrected ex post. We already established this using the example of the consumption decision and the ex ante and ex post comparison in Sect. 3.4. Thus, we will not repeat the procedure here.

Whether individuals are more likely to gather their own facts or rely on the narratives and norms presented by ideologies and belief systems depends on the specific issue at hand. They may be more familiar with some topics than others, which is also reflected in the prior uncertainty σ_0^2. Furthermore, the propensity to rely on ideologies depends on a person's subjective trust in the respective narratives as well as subjective cognitive resources and the extent to which they are attached to their subjective beliefs. Thus, a person who has limited resources to understand all facts available may have subjectively high search costs ι_f for facts. By contrast, highly educated individuals may have low search costs ι_f when it comes to facts.

Nevertheless, this modeling shows that ideologies can always be a tool for mitigating the human information problem. Under complex conditions, individuals will not start gathering facts on their own but tend to rely on the narratives and norms presented by ideologies and belief systems. From a subjective point of view, this is rational because it is the best choice under the given circumstances. Individual behavior that is guided by ideologies is not necessarily irrational. Given the challenges humans face with imperfect information, adhering to beliefs and ideologies is a subjectively rational approach to navigating these limitations. We will return in Sect. 8.2 to this aspect and discuss how this mechanism can be used strategically by ideological organizations.

7.2 A Consumer Choice Model with Ideologies

Before[7] we move on to discuss how ideologies influence our everyday choices, we need to make a conceptual distinction. In the next sections, we explicitly want to distinguish between utilities derived from states and utilities derived from action flows. While peace or security, for example, are conditions or states that generate benefits for people, consumption in a period is a typical example of benefits from a flow.

The Two Dimensions of Utilities

Here an ideology is defined as a set of narratives that imply a possible state of the world. It interprets and evaluates the current state of the world and contrasts it with the possible other state that it describes in its narratives. This other state, however, is a vision of the world, albeit one that suits some individuals who long for such a fiction. Their needs are served by these narratives, at least in their imagination. If individuals are thus attracted to a certain ideology, it is their imagination and the prospect of having their needs served by the states proposed by the ideology. It is these prospects for positive development in terms of meeting one's own needs which we refer to as "need reconciliation". We therefore use the utility function to describe

[7] Parts of this chapter are based on Burs et al. (2022). A later variation of parts of this modeling can be found in Burs et al. (2023).

a match between the desired and promised states. Thus, this is a special dimension of the utility function that, unlike typical definitions of utility focused on material benefits, relates to narratives about real or imagined states rather than direct material goods or services as seen in conventional consumer utility.

In our notation, we thus denote states and utilities derived from states using uppercase letters,[8] and we describe utilities derived from a service flow, such as consumption services, using lowercase letters. Thus, the two relevant dimensions in Sect. 6.1 were the match value of an ideology M with respect to the intangible, psychological needs as a state variable and the level of consumable wealth C (an amount of tangible consumption goods) as promised by the narrative. Utility derived from state conditions thus is a function $U(M, C)$.We use the lowercase $u(c)$ for the standard utility flows.

In this chapter, we focus on daily decisions, illustrated by various, sometimes provocative examples of decision-making. We look at momentary periodic flow decisions such as simple consumption decisions, choices of occupation, or political decisions as momentary flow decisions. Of particular interest is the influence ideological orientation has on these decisions.

Ideological Guidance Through Rules and Recommendations

In Sect. 6.2, we learned how to use the information acquisition process described in Sect. 3.1 to search for ideologies and determine which mix of ideologies best suits our needs. Humans adhere to the norms, values, and rules of these ideologies to create consistency, certainty, and meaning in life. In addition, ideologies help process incoming stimuli and make decisions that serve an individual's subjective needs and preferences. In this section, we will examine how the chosen ideology can be used to make the "best" everyday decisions. Applying the rules, norms, and narratives proposed by ideologies has low information costs and helps individuals process and evaluate incoming information. In addition, ideologies are the base of a subjective evaluation of one's own norms, communication, and behavior. They form the basis of understanding, evaluation, perception, communication, and behavior.

Following the rules and norms of the chosen ideology implies consistent behavior because these ideologies serve the individual's need structure. Therefore, behaving, perceiving, and making decisions based on these ideologies increase utility. Such ideological rules, norms, and values can even serve as heuristics, facilitating information processing and decision-making. Individuals are confident that their chosen belief systems/ideologies represent the reality, and so they rely on them to make everyday decisions. They trust their beliefs because they are not able to process all the available information and, hence, use the narratives presented by

[8] In Sect. 6.1, a state with the value N_i^j was desired for each need category i. We were then able to measure the distance D_{Ki}^j between the desired state and the level of serving this need S_{Ki} which is determined by the fact that ideology K's narratives describe states that address this category of needs to a certain extent. In any case, as M_{Ki}^j is the match value that we finally measure, what is important is the benefit of the match between the desired states and the states depicted in the ideological narratives.

their adopted ideologies, sometimes without questioning them. When decisions are made on the basis of the best matching ideologies, information costs are reduced and subjective psychological needs are served. This creates consistency, certainty, and meaning in life. Furthermore, when people share their ideological perspectives with their social circles, it strengthens their sense of belonging and identity. This shared worldview also boosts self-efficacy and self-esteem by reinforcing the belief that their actions are not only in harmony with their personal needs and preferences but also with their social environment.

When we consider the implications of believing in an ideology or belief system as part of the decision-making process, it becomes clear that decision-makers strive to follow the rules, norms, and values of a particular ideology. Therefore, in this section, we examine how incorporating rules and norms in this way affects everyday decisions and how it increases subjective utility. In doing so, we use a standard model of rational choice.

However, even if we formally simplify to the rule-based model, we should be aware of the general mechanisms that are at work. Thus, we must include the general concept of decision-making using ideological guidance and fact collection as a general principal. In Fig. 7.2, we describe the complete interdependence of ideological guidance and individual information acquisition.

Figure 7.2 describes the structure and components of a decision problem. We start with the green boxes. They describe the three general components of the decision problem, objective, decision, and environment including constraints. The objective in this problem is to fulfill the needs of the decision-maker. To serve these needs, good decisions must be made. However, this is not easy, because the decisions have

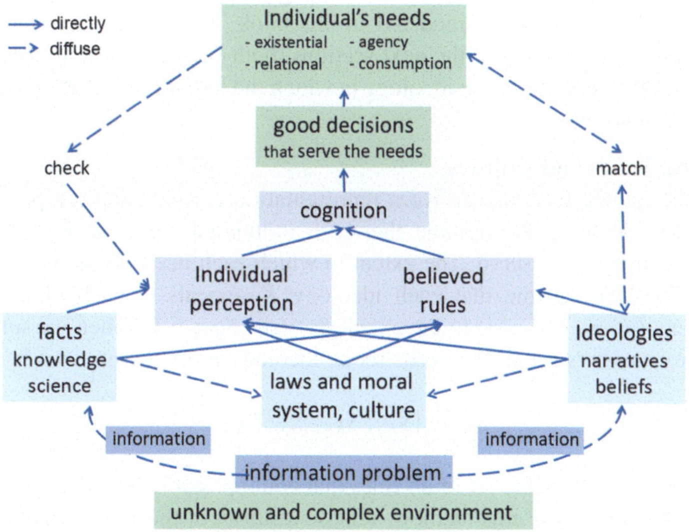

Fig. 7.2 Concept of decision-making with facts and ideologies

to be made in a complex environment that is in many ways not fully known. We have called this condition of incomplete information the information problem.

Since we are focusing on the information problem in this decision-making process, we must next look at the blue fields. The blue boxes describe that in a decision-making situation the decision-maker can tackle this information problem by a combination of (1) the actual facts and knowledge in the context of the decision; (2) the laws and moral and cultural rules that are currently observed and valid in society and which themselves were formed by facts, beliefs, and ideologies; (3) the narratives of the ideology of which the decision-maker is an adherent and that he or she trusts. These three components contribute to individual cognition and potentially lead to a subjectively rational and hopefully good decision. That is, this decision process uses rules as an inexpensive heuristic decision-making tool. These rules are either established by society in the form of laws or cultural rules or – and this is what we want to emphasize here – by the ideology or belief system the decision-maker follows. In other words, an individual's personal insights, combined with the principles of their chosen ideology, form a set of information and cognition that guides their decision-making. The individual hopes that this process will lead to decisions that effectively meet their needs.

After these decisions have been made, there is an ex post experience as to whether these decisions were actually good. This results in a feedback mechanism, which is represented in Fig. 7.2 using the term "check" as well as using a renewed review of the "match" value of the chosen ideology. If an individual repeatedly realizes over time that the ideology or belief system they follow does not in fact address their needs and that their living conditions are not moving in the desired direction due to the actions of this particular ideology, the match value may decrease. In the long term, this can lead to the individual abandoning their previous ideology. However, this is something that is not modeled in this book. Thus, Fig. 7.2 is intended to illustrate conceptually that in the next sections, both facts and real information, as well as rules that stem from the ideology in which the individual believes, contribute to decision-making.

Ideological Rules and Utilities

As a first step, we formally derive a representation of rules that are provided by an arbitrary ideology. We assume that each individual has a total number of n psychological needs to serve. The extent to which each need should be reconciled is subjective. We assume that each ideology K appeals to each of these need components i ($i = 1, \ldots, n$) to the extent S_{K_i} (see Sect. 6.1). Then we summarize these index numbers for all the needs for an ideology K in the set

$$S_K = \{S_{K_1}, S_{K_2}, \ldots, S_{K_n}\}.$$

Now suppose that $\mathfrak{R}$ is the set of all rules that could possibly be part of an arbitrary ideology. The leaders of this ideology choose a subset of these rules, and each rule addresses one or more needs. Thus, these leaders choose one or more index numbers from S_K to form rules $\mathfrak{r} \in \mathfrak{R}$. If we use $\mathcal{P}(S_K)$ to denote the set of all subsets of S_K

(also called the power set of S_K), we can define the relation

$$\mathcal{R}_K = \{(f, \mathfrak{r}) \in \mathcal{P}(S_K) \times \mathfrak{R} : f \text{ is the set of index numbers of served needs that create rule } \mathfrak{r}\}. \tag{7.2}$$

Note that using a relation makes it possible for a particular combination of needs – represented by a subset $f \in \mathcal{P}(S_K)$ – to give rise to multiple rules $\mathfrak{r} \in \mathfrak{R}$. Further, we use $\mathfrak{R}_K \subseteq \mathfrak{R}$ to denote the set of rules $\mathfrak{r} \in \mathfrak{R}$, such that $(f, \mathfrak{r}) \in \mathcal{R}_K$ for some set of need indices $f \in \mathcal{P}(S_K)$. Hence, an ideology K is characterized by its set of rules $\mathfrak{R}_K$, and adopting an ideology K means adhering to the rules and norms in this set.[9]

Let us now consider a consumption choice and assume that an individual can engage in two types of activities. The first type abides by the rules and norms of the chosen ideology, while the second type is not. We introduce ρ as an index that measures the extent to which an action and an individual's choice conform to the rules and norms of the adopted ideologies. Thus, ρ represents the match between the ideology's rules and the individual actions that serve subjective psychological needs. Consequently, ρ is included in the utility function for everyday decisions.

Parameter a_c denotes those activities that are inconsistent with the applicable rules of the ideology and purely related to consumption, and $\bar{c}_c$ denotes a standardized pure consumption unit. The total consumption flow that only serves consumption purposes is thus

$$c_c = \bar{c}_c a_c. \tag{7.3}$$

The other consumption activity which is rule consistent is referred to as a_ρ, and a standardized unit for this kind of consumption activity is referred to as denoted by $\bar{c}_\rho$. Total consumption for this kind is

$$c_\rho = \bar{c}_\rho a_\rho. \tag{7.4}$$

The important feature of activity a_ρ is that it not only serves pure consumption, it is also consistent with the rules and values of the adopted ideologies. Therefore, it serves the individual's subjective psychological needs and hence contributes one unit to the match with their belief-based rules ρ. Thus, the index value of ρ is directly determined by the number of activities that are consistent with the chosen ideologies and psychological needs

$$\rho = a_\rho. \tag{7.5}$$

[9] If an individual's choice after information acquisition is to adopt a combination of ideologies K, where each ideology is chosen at a fraction $\alpha_K \in (0, 1)$, they also choose the corresponding fraction of rules from $\mathcal{R}_K$ of the chosen ideologies K.

As a consequence, a_ρ generates a positive externality. This ideology-based activity not only serves consumption needs but also psychological needs. In other words, when the consumption choice is made and the ideological rules are applied, this also serves the psychological needs. It increases consumption of kind c_ρ as well as the index ρ. By combining (7.4) and (7.5), we obtain the fixed consumption ratio that addresses both consumption needs and psychological needs

$$\rho = \frac{1}{\bar{c}_\rho} c_\rho .$$

Since ρ appeals to psychological needs through ideology-consistent decisions, it is included in the utility function. Using two types of consumption goods, both of which satisfy consumption needs, we can describe the utility function with standard characteristics as[10]

$$u = u(\rho, c_\rho, c_c) \qquad \text{with } \frac{\partial u}{\partial x_i} > 0, \frac{\partial^2 u}{\partial x_i^2} < 0 \quad \text{for } x_i = c_c, c_\rho, \rho. \tag{7.6}$$

The standard assumption of positive and decreasing marginal utility with respect to both activities a_ρ and a_c holds.

Constraints and the Choice Problem

We introduce a price p_c for consumption c_c and a price p_ρ for consumption c_ρ. These prices differ because we are assuming two different types of consumption goods. To clarify, we assume that intangible, psychological benefits such as self-esteem or social belonging cannot be purchased directly.[11] Given an income $\bar{y}$, the budget constraint is

$$\bar{y} = p_c \bar{c}_c a_c + p_\rho \bar{c}_\rho a_\rho . \tag{7.7}$$

The choice problem is thus

$$\max_{a_c, a_\rho} u = u(c_\rho, c_c, \rho)$$

$$p_c \bar{c}_c a_c + p_\rho \bar{c}_\rho a_\rho - \bar{y} = 0,$$

with the system of first order conditions (FOCs)

$$\frac{\partial u}{\partial c_c} \bar{c}_c - \lambda p_c \bar{c}_c = 0 \tag{7.8}$$

[10] We illustrate this assumption using a standard Cobb-Douglas-type utility function in Appendix A.7.

[11] This assumption is made for the sake of simplicity. There may be products that directly satisfy psychological needs.

$$\frac{\partial u}{\partial c_\rho}\bar{c}_\rho + \frac{\partial u}{\partial \rho} - \lambda p_\rho \bar{c}_\rho = 0$$
$$-p_c\bar{c}_c a_c - p_\rho \bar{c}_\rho a_\rho + \bar{y} = 0.$$

We can apply the implicit functions theorem to this standard choice problem and obtain optimal activities[12]

$$a_c^* = a_c^*(p_c, \bar{c}_c, p_\rho, \bar{c}_\rho, \bar{y}) \qquad (7.9)$$
$$a_\rho^* = a_\rho^*(p_c, \bar{c}_c, p_\rho, \bar{c}_\rho, \bar{y})$$

that give optimal demand functions for c_c^* and c_ρ^* as well as an optimal level ρ^* of fulfilling the ideological rules.

Interpretation
While it is also important to find the optimal demand function, in this setting, it is more interesting to examine the first order conditions in order to understand the choice. From the first order conditions, we derive

$$\frac{\frac{\partial u}{\partial c_\rho} + \frac{\partial u}{\partial \rho}\frac{\rho}{c_\rho}}{\frac{\partial u}{\partial c_c}} = \frac{p_\rho}{p_c}. \qquad (7.10)$$

The fraction $\frac{\frac{\partial u}{\partial c_\rho} + \frac{\partial u}{\partial \rho}\frac{\rho}{c_\rho}}{\frac{\partial u}{\partial c_c}}$ on the left-hand side of Eq. (7.10) represents the willingness to pay for good c_ρ in terms of goods c_c. If $\bar{c}_\rho$ is comparable to $\bar{c}_c$ in serving the pure consumption preference $\left[\frac{\partial u}{\partial c_\rho} = \frac{\partial u}{\partial c_c}\right]$, condition (7.10) shows that individuals are willing to pay more for c_ρ due to the consumption externality. The purchase of an ideology-consistent consumption product not only fulfills the individual's material needs, it also serves their psychological preferences. Similarly, by rearranging Eq. (7.10), we obtain

$$\frac{\frac{\partial u}{\partial c_\rho} + \frac{\partial u}{\partial \rho}\frac{\rho}{c_\rho}}{p_\rho} = \frac{\frac{\partial u}{\partial c_c}}{p_c}.$$

This means that the marginal utility per unit of income must be equal, and each unit of currency must have the same effect on marginal utility. Consumption c_ρ through activity a_ρ has a positive externality because it generates both consumption-related utilities and ideology-related utilities. Therefore, the individual is willing to pay even more for the same amount of a consumption good. In fact, there is a growing body of literature that confirms the correlation between morals and

[12] For a short discussion, see Appendix A.7.

willingness to pay in markets, showing that people are willing to pay more for goods that conform to their moral standards, e.g., Bartling et al. (2014a).

Application: Environmentalist's Consumption Behavior
Let us illustrate this reasoning with an example. Suppose an individual subscribes to an environmentalist or green ideology, which advocates for consuming organic food whenever possible. Adhering to this rule, the individual meets their psychological needs for consistency, predictability, order, and control (among others). Although meals made with conventionally produced ingredients might be less expensive, individuals who follow this ideology are often willing to pay more for organic meals. Consuming organic products not only serves the individual's tangible needs (such as buying food to satisfy one's hunger), adhering to the rules, norms, and values of this green ideology also has positive psychological effects. Those activities that are consistent with the chosen ideology not only serve the individual's preferences, they also provide a positive self-image and facilitate coherent decision-making.

7.3 An Occupational Choice Model with Ideologies

We can model the occupational choice in the familiar way as a time allocation problem within a period of length $\bar{t}$. In each period, total time $\bar{t}$ can be allocated to working time t_w that generates income and consumption at the wage rate w, and leisure time t_l. As usual, both consumption and leisure time t_L generate utility. However, working time as well as leisure time can have different qualities. Let us start by discussing working time.

There are two sorts of occupations: conventional work on the one hand and work that is in line with an individual's beliefs and values on the other, which will thus have a different quality for that individual. In the case of conventional work, working time is denoted by t_{wc}, and the wage paid for this conventional work is w_c. If the choice of occupation leads to a job that matches the rules applicable in the individual's belief system or ideology, then working time not only generates income at wage rate w_ρ, working time $t_{w\rho}$ also makes that individual feel much better and appreciate this kind of job even more.

Take an individual who is a member of a belief system in which it is natural to support and care for people who need help. One rule in this belief system could be that those who need help must be helped. If an individual now has the choice between several occupational fields, they will see that there are professions that have nothing to do with this rule at all but also that there are those whose activities are directly linked to this rule. An administrative job, for example, has little to do with the principle of caring for those in need and is primarily an income-generating activity. However, the work of a nurse or doctor directly implements this rule. Such occupations serve both the desire to earn an income and the desire – in line with the rule applicable in the belief system – to help people in need. This means that both activities have a different quality for this individual, which will be taken into account when making decisions. Time engaging in occupation t_{wp} not only leads to more income and higher consumption utilities, it also serves psychological needs and hence has a positive effect on their utility.

As in the previous section, we again assume that an individual follows a belief system. Thus, they want to follow the rules and guidance provided by their belief system. We will now describe how an individual – on the basis of his belief system – evaluates two different activities and determines his working hours accordingly. As explained above, there is a conventional activity that has no relation to the belief system of the individual, and one that corresponds to the rules of the belief system of the individual. This difference is expressed by the individual preference parameter ρ_{wi}, which for the conventional activity is $\rho_{wc} \to 0$ and for the ideology-compliant activity is $\rho_{wp} > 0$. This job-specific preference parameter combines with the time spent working either in line with the ideology ($t_{wp} > 0$) or conventionally (t_{wc}) to give the total match value of the activity in line with the belief system, ρ. The variable ρ is thus the match value, the degree of compliance, between one's own activity and the rules prescribed by the belief system

$$\rho = \begin{cases} \rho_{wc} t_{wc} \to 0, & \text{for (i) } t_{wc} > 0 \\ \rho_{wp} t_{wp} > 0 & \text{for (ii) } t_{wp} > 0 \end{cases} . \tag{7.11}$$

As in the previous section, ρ enters the utility function such that the individual's utility function has three components: consumption utility, leisure time, and the extent to which the rules provided by the belief system are followed

$$u = u\left(c, t_l, \rho\right), \text{ with } \frac{\partial u}{\partial x} > 0, \frac{\partial^2 u}{\partial x^2} < 0\,, \frac{\partial^2 u}{\partial x \partial y} > 0 \text{ and } x, y = c, t_l, \rho. \tag{7.12}$$

Further, in our choice problem, the individual can choose between two kinds of occupations and has two job offers. Job offer (i) is a conventional job that is not related to his or her belief system. Time spend doing this job t_{wc} only generates income at wage rate w_c. Job offer (ii) is an occupation that relates to the individual's belief system such that time spend in this job increases the match value ρ as described in (7.11) and generates income at the wage rate w_ρ. For the sake of simplicity, we assume that individual can take only one of these jobs, and so the individual has to consider both options and decide which is the better choice. Thus, the two alternative time constraints are

$$\begin{aligned} (i) &: \bar{t} = t_{wc} + t_l, \\ (ii) &: \bar{t} = t_{wp} + t_l, \end{aligned} \tag{7.13}$$

and the resulting income and consumption ($c = y$) constraints are

$$(i) : c = w_c t_{wc}, \tag{7.14}$$

$$(ii) : c = w_\rho t_{w\rho}.$$

Choice Problem

With utility function (7.12) and time and income constraints (7.13) and (7.14), we can now describe the full choice problem

$$\max_{t_w, t_l} : u\left(c, t_l, \rho\right), \quad t_w = t_{wc}, \text{or } t_{w\rho}$$

$$s.t.(i) : \bar{t} = t_{wc} + t_l, \quad c = w_c t_{wc},$$

$$or\ (ii) : \bar{t} = t_{w\rho} + t_l, \quad c = w_\rho t_{w\rho}.$$

We start with case (i). Working time does not contribute to the match value such that $\rho \rightarrow 0$. Thus, the Lagrangian for this case is

$$\mathcal{L} = u^{\rho \rightarrow 0}\left(c, t, \rho \rightarrow 0\right) - \lambda\left(t_{wc} + t_l - \bar{t}\right),$$

and we obtain the FOCs for this problem

$$\frac{\partial u}{\partial c} w_c - \lambda = 0 \tag{7.15}$$

$$\frac{\partial u}{\partial t_l} - \lambda = 0$$

$$\bar{t} - t_{wc} - t_l = 0.$$

Based on the FOC, we can determine the conditions for an optimal time allocation for this standard problem

$$\frac{\partial u}{\partial c} w_c = \frac{\partial u}{\partial t_l}. \tag{7.16}$$

The standard interpretation is that the allocation is optimal if the marginal utility of using time for work to generate consumption is equal to the marginal utility of leisure time. This standard model is also described in Fig. 7.3a. Note that c^{sub} is the subsistence income which is externally provided.

At the point of optimal time allocation, point A, the wage rate is equal to the marginal rate of utility substitution

$$w_c = w = \frac{\frac{\partial u}{\partial t_l}}{\frac{\partial u}{\partial c}} = MRS = -\frac{dc}{dt_l}. \tag{7.17}$$

However, the standard decision is only the reference for the next more interesting case.

Case (ii), to assure that the two cases are as comparable as possible, we assume that all wages are identical for all occupations, i.e., $w_\rho = w_{c.}$ Also, the utility

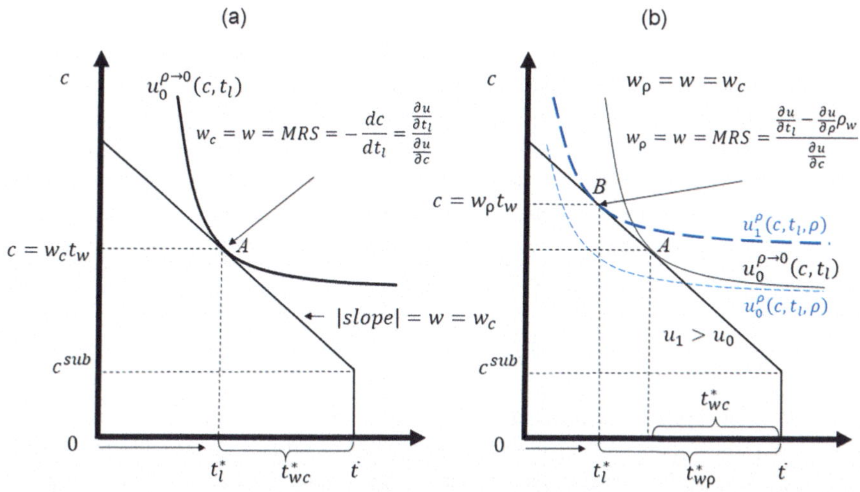

Fig. 7.3 Standard diagram of occupational choice: (**a**) case (i) conventional job offer, (**b**) case (ii) job offer that complies with the rules of the individual's belief system

function is identical because it is the same person who is choosing between two alternatives. However, the important difference is that working time in this occupation $t_{w\rho}$ significantly contributes to the match value related to the belief system

$$\rho = \rho_{w\rho} t_{w\rho}.$$

The Lagrangian for this problem is

$$\mathcal{L} = u^\rho (c, t_l, \rho) - \lambda \left(t_{w\rho} + t_l - \bar{t}\right).$$

The FOCs are now

$$\frac{\partial u}{\partial c} w_\rho + \frac{\partial u}{\partial \rho} \rho_{w\rho} - \lambda = 0, \tag{7.18}$$

$$\frac{\partial u}{\partial t_l} - \lambda = 0.$$

Based on the FOCs, we again obtain the interpretation in (7.19), namely that in optimum an additional time unit used as working time must generate the same marginal utility as an additional time unit used as leisure time

$$\frac{\partial u}{\partial c} w_\rho + \frac{\partial u}{\partial \rho} \rho_{w\rho} = \frac{\partial u}{\partial t_l}. \tag{7.19}$$

While leisure time still only generates leisure benefits, working time not only generates income and consumption benefits. Additionally, though, and simultaneously, working time also generates benefits from "correct" behavior as a kind of externality. Since working time in this case is a belief-compliant activity, an additional benefit arises that turns the previous condition (7.16) into the new condition (7.19). As the result, the new indifference curve changes shape, and the marginal rate of substitution along an indifference curve becomes flatter in Fig. 7.3b so that a different optimal time allocation is chosen in line with this new condition

$$w_{\rho} = -\frac{dc}{dt_l} = MRS = \frac{\frac{\partial u}{\partial t_l} - \frac{\partial u}{\partial \rho}\rho_{w\rho}}{\frac{\partial u}{\partial c}}. \tag{7.20}$$

Point B, new optimal allocation in Fig. 7.3b, shows that working time t_{wc}^* is extended at the expense of leisure time, as further benefits u_1^{ρ} are generated during this work that do not arise during leisure time. Again, we can apply the implicit function theorem and determine the functions for optimal time allocation

$$t_{wc}^* = t_{wc}(w), \qquad case(i) \tag{7.21}$$

$$t_{w\rho}^* = t_{w\rho}\left(w, \rho_{w\rho}\right), \quad case(ii) \tag{7.22}$$

$$t_{wc}^* < t_{w\rho}^*.$$

Unpaid Overtime in Care Work

Another example where the attitude shaped by a belief system plays a crucial role in executing work processes can be seen in the care work within various medical professions. Many people in these professions work overtime out of a sense of responsibility and compassion for those they are caring for but are paid hardly anything for that overtime. We can understand this decision more easily if we integrate it into our concept.

The reference point is again the idea that there is a standard job in the market that exclusively generates a wage income at wage rate w_c. For the individual in question, there is no relationship between this standard job and their belief and value system, meaning that it only leads to income and consumer benefits. The match value with the rules applicable in the individual's belief system is zero. In Fig. 7.4a) and b), this is again indicated by the point A, which represents the optimal working time at wage rate w_c under the condition of value-neutral working time (conventional job, see also reference point A in Fig. 7.3a). The resulting utility level is again $u_0^{\rho \to 0}$. To compare, let us now assume that this individual has a standard employment contract and that is identical to an optimal contract under value-neutral conditions. That is, the individual has a given wage rate w_c and a fixed working time t_w^A. Given such a fixed contract, the consumption level $\bar{c}$ arises in Fig. 7.4a.

In other words, we assume that the individual follows the rules of their belief system with their current type of work. This means that the ideology-compliance

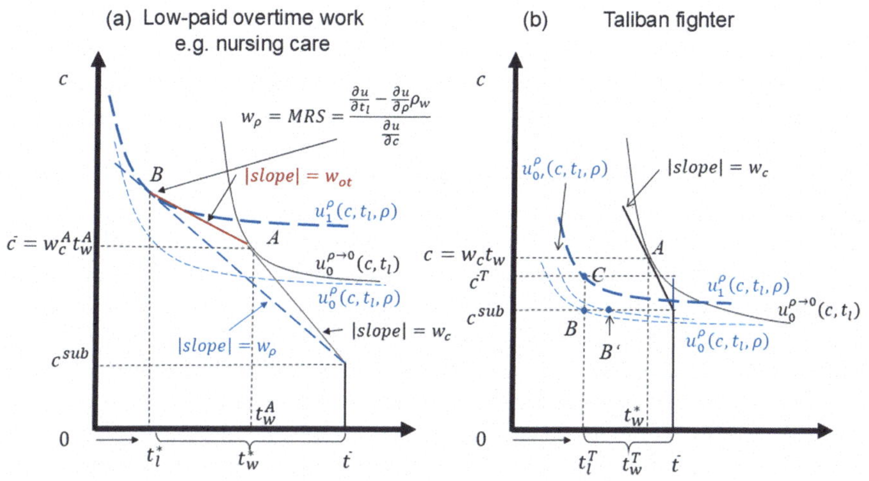

Fig. 7.4 More examples: low-paid overtime work and Taliban fighter

parameter $\rho_{w\rho}$ is high for this occupation, and the total match value with the rules of the belief system ρ may also turn high as time spent on this work increases.

As in the previous section, this externality of working time that generates a higher ρ leads to a different position and shape of the indifference curves u_0^ρ. The same level of utility is already achieved with less leisure time or less consumption, and the slope of the indifference curves becomes flatter.

In Fig. 7.4a, the utility level u_0 is already reached with the indifference curve u_0^ρ. Thus, the standard contract with working time t_w^A at the given wage w_c is not optimal and too rigid. Overtime could make this contract more flexible.

As, based on our assumption, overtime is paid only at a low rate w_{ot}, the income curve kinks at point A and shows only a very weak slope w_{ot}. However, this causes the average wage to fall overall, which leads to a new optimal choice of working hours at point B. This means that at the new optimal point B, the utility level is higher for value-addressing employment than for value-free employment (point A). Moreover, it is interesting to note that this is achieved even though the average wage in this job is lower $w_\rho < w_c$. The motivation to do something valuable and meaningful based on one's value system leads to additional hours being worked, even for a lower wage. The reward for working hours and for giving up leisure time is not only consumer benefits but also the serving of psychological needs and compliance with one's own belief and value system.

Becoming a Taliban Fighter

A completely different "occupational activity" but one that can still be related to the tools described in this chapter is the decision to join a group of "holy warriors". This may seem somewhat unconventional and surprising at first, but it is a way of identifying such a decision as a subjectively rational one. The example we choose here is that of the Taliban fighter, as he obviously adheres to a particular belief system.

In Müller and Gries (2024), we identified two channels that can be used to explain how new supporters or even active fighters can be recruited into an insurgent organization. Channel 1 describes the recruitment of new followers through the ideological organization's narrative. Channel 2 promises economic and social provision for the fighter and/or his relatives. We can identify both channels with the help of our simple formal modeling of choice of occupation.

The reference point is again a job that would exclusively give a wage income at wage rate w_c. This reference job bears no relation to the individual's belief and value system and thus only leads to income and consumer benefits. The match value with the rules provided by the belief system ρ is thus zero. In Fig. 7.4b, this is again indicated by the point A. In this figure, we assume that A even represents the optimal working time at wage rate w_c. Under the conditions in poor developing countries, where we often find such insurgent organizations, this assumption is already not realistic, since many people are unemployed, have very low wages, and often cannot realize their optimal time allocation due to a lack of job opportunities. Thus, for many people, the starting point when it comes to a discussion of indifference curves is the subsistence income c^{sub} in Fig. 7.4b. Subsistence income is paid by family support system. Under this condition, it were not too difficult to find cases in which even simple ideological narratives or small payments will entice people to join a rebel group or, in this case, a religious militant group. However, we choose the more difficult reference case that an individual can actually realize an optimal time allocation under the condition of a value-neutral working time at point A. The resulting utility level is again $u_0^{\rho \to 0}$.

However, after joining such a group (Taliban: T), we assume the allocation of a fixed amount of time to group activities and, in return, payment of a fixed amount of money that a group member can receive for themself or for his family. To relate to a benchmark, we assume that the payment initially considered is just the subsistence income level $\bar{c}^{sub}$. Thus, point B with consumption $\bar{c}^{sub}$ and working time for the Taliban $\bar{t}_w^T$ depicts this first consideration.

Channel 1: In channel 1, we assume that the individual believes in the ideological narrative provided by his organization and therefore tries to follow its rules and leadership. If a call goes out to join a group, the match value ρ will have a very high value if this individual joins the group and thus makes a very large predetermined amount of his time available to engage in group activities. For our analysis, we need to go back to condition (7.19) to consider an occupational choice driven by the organization's ideological narrative. Active membership of the group and engaging in activities that benefit the group fill the day. This means that the individual devotes the majority of the day to the rules of their belief system. The match value ρ is very high, and the utility value u_0, which was previously assigned to point A and the associated indifference curve $u_0^{\rho=0}$, can now already be realized on the indifference curve $u_0^{\rho}(c, t_l, \rho)$ in Fig. 7.4b. Thus, with a package of consumption and working time at point B $(\bar{c}^{sub}, \bar{t}_w^T)$ and the fact that working time serves their beliefs, this individual will – on account of high psychological rewards – be just indifferent $(u_0^{\rho \to 0} = u_0^{\rho})$, when considering giving up the normal income generation at point A and join the holy warriors. That is, at point B in Fig. 7.4b, the individual is indifferent in his choice even if he has less income available in B than in point A (only the subsistence income). With a little less labor obligation (point B'), he would change from a normal life to that of a fighter, and this decision will be taken entirely on the basis of high ideological motivations and not a consumptive reward, as consumption will fall from an appropriate level to the lower level at B. And so channel 1 is a relevant one.

Channel 2: The second channel is connected to standard economic thinking. The individual can be recruited if he or his family is offered material incentives or social security support.

While the individual is indifferent in his choice at point B and obtains utility level $u_0^{\rho \to 0} = u_0^{\rho}$), additional payments by the Taliban that lead to consumption level $\bar{c}^T$ would lead to point C with the package $[(\bar{c}^T, \bar{t}_w^T)]$. As utility at C is higher than that at points A and B $[u_1^{\rho} > u_0^{\rho \to 0} = u_0^{\rho}]$, we observe that more income motivates the individual to become a Taliban fighter.

Therefore, both channels are possible in real conflict parties because ultimately both channels address individuals' need structures. One channel addresses the need for certain states, which are addressed in the ideological narratives, while the other channel addresses the concrete material needs that individuals have.

7.4 A Political Choice Model with Ideologies

To analyze political decisions, we will return to the description of the activities of ideological organizations in Sect. 5.2. While in that section we modeled an organization's development, here we want to focus on individual political decisions. We will therefore move away somewhat from the model described in 5.2 and change the political decision-maker's objective system.

In Sect. 5.2, we described a full optimal intertemporal choice model. The objective was to maximize the organization's total benefit from the disposable income stream. In the current context, we reduce complexity. The organization has to make political decisions in a one-period model. This means that we move away from the long-term dynamic optimization process to a much more simple static decision. In this model, utility includes consumable wealth and ideological match values. We therefore assume a utility function that takes into account both the available wealth of the organization (and society) and the ideology of the organization by following the self-proclaimed ideological rules. The decision-makers therefore believe in their propagated ideology and its rules.

This means that we now also assume a utility function for the organization with two elements, consumption possibilities, and match values with respect to ideological rules. For the sake of simplicity, we assume additive utilities:

$$U = U(C, \rho) = U(C) + U(\rho). \tag{7.23}$$

In the following two sections, we look at two political games. In the first section, we show how ideological narratives can become the dominant element in the decisions of political organizations or governments. In the second section, we focus on the difference between individual, subjective rationality and collective, general rationality and reason.

An Example of an Imperialistic Narrative

In this section, we take the example of a political decision. As in all other models and examples, we must again emphasize that all these simplifications to simple economic rational model considerations should not imply that reality works that simply. These simplified models are intended to provide a clear and concise but also consistent argument. Of course, they cannot sufficiently take into account the real complexity, but perhaps they are an interesting part of this complex process that we may be able to understand better with the help of the model. Let us take a far-reaching political decision as an illustration. To put it particularly drastically, let us choose a decision between war and peace. Let us assume there are two countries. Both have resource endowments that either provide them with civilian goods or can be used for violent conflicts. The leaders of each country are considering how to behave toward the other country. In this example, only two forms of behavior are assumed to be possible. The countries can work peaceful, or even cooperatively, with the other country, or they can attack the other country and try to gain further resources by establishing their own rule in that country. Resources gained can then be used to increase domestic civilian prosperity as well as the ideological organization's income.

Figure 7.5 describes the payoff matrix for the benefits from all possible decisions. These benefits initially arise from the availability of goods (as resources) for both purposes. All entries of benefits generated from consumption are shown in entries a). Before we look at and interpret the table as a whole, however, we must first briefly explain the logic of the entries. Since we do not want to go through everything, we will focus on the perspective of country R. We start with the discussion purely of consumption benefits.

Field (1a) Both country R and country U behave peaceful and collaboratively. All the material resources in both countries can be used for civilian goods, and cooperative trade will allow for a maximum utility generated by consumption of $U_R(C) = 10$; $U_U(C) = 10$ for both countries.

Field (2a) describes a situation in which country R has attacked and conquered the other country, but it expends enormous resources on the attack and subsequent occupation. Therefore, although R can gain additional resources, many of these additional resources are consumed in maintaining the occupation. The net resource gain is therefore only $U_R(C) = 5$. Country U is deprived of some of its resources after the invasion. However, since it is peaceful and collaborative, this loss is limited to $U_U(C) = -10$, which is, therefore, not as high as if it were in a direct military conflict with R.

Field (3a) represents the benefit of continued military conflict. Country R attacks country U, which defends itself, resulting in a prolonged war that uses up a lot of

Country *U* \ Country *R*	peaceful behavior	aggressive with costs for occupation or continuous threatening behavior
peaceful behavior	1a) $U_R(C) = 10$ $U_U(C) = 10$ 1b) $U_R(\rho) = 0$ $U_U(\rho) = 5$ 1c) $U_R = U_R(C) + U_R(\rho) = 10$ $U_U = U_U(C) + U_U(\rho) = 15$	2a) $U_R(C) = 5$ $U_U(C) = -10$ 2b) $U_R(\rho) = 10$ $U_U(\rho) = -5$ 2c) $U_R = U_R(C) + U_R(\rho) = 15$ $U_U = U_U(C) + U_U(\rho) = -15$
aggressive with costs for occupation or continuous threatening behavior	4a) $U_R(C) = -10$ $U_U(C) = 5$ 4b) $U_R(\rho) = -10$ $U_U(\rho) = 0$ 4c) $U_R = U_R(C) + U_R(\rho) = -20$ $U_U = U_U(C) + U_U(\rho) = 5$	3a) $U_R(C) = -15$ $U_U(C) = -15$ 3b) $U_R(\rho) = 10;$ $U_U(\rho) = 10$ 3c) $U_R = U_R(C) + U_R(\rho) = -5$ $U_U = U_U(C) + U_U(\rho) = -5$

Fig. 7.5 Ideology and political decision

resources on both sides. The payoff for both is therefore $U_R(C) = -15; U_U(C) = -15$.

Field (4a) is like field (2a), except that country U is the aggressor.

First step of interpretation: Looking at consumption payoffs (entries a) in this example which are constructed symmetrically, we see that for the leaders in R, peaceful and collaborative behavior is the utility-maximizing choice, no matter what the other player does. When R considers their options and weighs peace and collaboration against aggression, the behavior of U must be taken into account: If U also collaborates $[U_R(C) = 10 \text{ (1a)} > U_R(C) = 5 \text{ (2a)}]$ and if U does not collaborate $[U_R(C) = -10 \text{ (4a)} > U_R(C) = -15 \text{ (3a)}]$. If we look at pure consumption, a war is not individually rational. Regardless of what the other country does, the benefit of aggressive behavior is lower than that of peace and cooperation. In this example, aggression ties up resources, and cooperation generates additional resources.

In the next step, we assume that the organizations leading the two countries follow different ideologies. To simplify, we assume that the ideology adopted by U's leadership (organization) sees its own sovereignty and freedom of action as central. A rule applied by U could be to ensure its own sovereignty and self-determination. The overall benefit for U is then not only determined by the use of resources for consumption purposes but also by the pursuit of the ideological requirement.

Country R's leadership, on the other hand, follows a clear nationalist-imperialist ideology of its own national supremacy. One of the rules adopted by this ideology could be to follow your nation's mission to rule and dominate. According to this ideology, a situation in which one's own leadership exercises dominance is preferred to a collaborative situation. The exercise of domination therefore generates an additional psychological benefit for supporters of this imperialist ideology. These ideology-related utility effects are reflected in further elements in Fig. 7.5. We can find them under the entries for (b). The entries for (c) give the total utility just by applying the additive utility function (7.23).

Entries (1b) and (1c) describe the fact that collaboration and cooperation only generate an ideological benefit for country U. Country U can collaborate with country R in a sovereign and self-confident manner and thus serve its ideology, $u_U(\rho) = 5$. However, country R has no additional ideologically induced benefit, $u_R(\rho) = 0$, since it does not exercise dominance and, according to R's ideology, only that would generate ideological utilities. The resulting total benefit for R is therefore 1c) $u_R = u_R(c) + u_R(\rho) = 10$. Total benefit for country U is 1c), $u_U = u_U(c) + u_U(\rho) = 15$.

Entries (2b) and (2c) describe the fact that country R now exercises domination in line with its imperialist ideology and thus realizes an ideological benefit. Since this has great significance for R's leadership, not only is the ideology-related benefit of exercising dominance high, at $u_R(\rho) = 10$ but so is the total benefit of this behavior, $u_R = u_R(c) + u_R(\rho) = 15$. Country U has no ideological benefit, even a loss of benefit as it is no longer a sovereign state, $u_U(\rho) = -5$. The overall benefit for country U as an occupied country that has to transfer resources to the occupying power and that loses sovereignty is thus $u_U = u_U(c) + u_U(\rho) = -15$.

Entries (3b) and (3c) indicate that country R again has an ideological benefit of $u_R(\rho) = 10$ due to its aggressiveness and the signaling that it wants to exercise dominance. However, warfare and the associated loss of resources then lead to an overall benefit for country R of (3c) $u_R = u_R(c) + u_R(\rho) = -5$. There is also an ideological benefit for country U, as its leadership signals that it is standing up for its freedom, $u_U(\rho) = 10$. The overall benefit for U is (3c) $u_U = u_U(c)+u_U(\rho) = -5$.

Entries 4(b) and (c) are discussed only with respect to the payoffs for country R, since we actually only want to interpret the decisions taken by country R. If country R were peaceful and collaborative, it would actually realize a particularly high negative ideological utility effect since it does not exercise domination but is even dominated, $u_R(\rho) = -10$. Therefore, the overall benefit effect for country R is now extremely negative $u_R = u_R(c) + u_R(\rho) = -20$. For country U, the result in (4b) is zero, since it has no ideological benefit from the conquest. In (4c), U does gain resources from R, but since there is no ideological benefit, it remains at this increase in utility [$u_U = u_U(c) + u_U(\rho) = 5$].

Second step of interpretation: In the first step of interpretation, we concluded that, considering only benefits of consumption, the best behavioral strategy from R's individual point of view is a peaceful and collaborative one.

This changes if R follows an imperialist ideology and the additional utility is added when it follows this ideological guidance. Given that U is peaceful and collaborative, the best total outcome for R is now the ideologically motivated aggressive action in entry (2c), $u_R = 15$, which is better than entry (1c), $u_R = 10$. Thus, aggressive behavior dominates in this case.

If U is aggressive and non-collaborative, R's collaborative behavior leads to entry (4c), $u_R = -20$, but aggressive behavior leads to entry (3c) $u_R = -5$. This means that aggressive behavior is also favorable. Aggressive behavior is therefore the dominant individual strategy for R no matter what the other country does. This applies even if this decision was made solely on the basis of ideological component in the generation of benefits. In this example, the nationalistic-imperialistic ideology guides the decision-maker into aggressive action. Country R will start a war because it follows its ideological narratives. This is the result we wanted to show. Important political decisions are often driven by ideological narratives, even if the ideological narrative is bad and leads to disaster. As long as people are guided by ideologies, disasters and dystopias are no less likely than utopias.

Individual Rationality Versus Collective Rationality and Reason

We have already talked a lot about subjective rationality in the previous sections. Subjective rationality refers to an individual's rationality, which involves making logically consistent and optimal decisions based on subjective conditions, such as incomplete or imperfect information. This section will explain why individual rationality alone is insufficient for effective social and collective decision-making. This will be illustrated with the help of a simple prisoner's dilemma game. We remain in the imperialist power game but drastically simplify our payoff matrix in Fig. 7.6 in order to get to the point quickly.

Justification of the payouts in the payout matrix Fig. 7.6: Both countries are assumed to be equal.

Field 1: Both countries are peaceful, do not threaten each other, cooperate, and require only limited defense resources. They trade technology and realize

Country *B* \ Country *A*	peaceful	aggressive with costs for occupation or continuous threatening
peaceful	**1** $U_A = 10$ $U_B = 10$	**2** $U_A = 12$ $U_B = 5$
aggressive with costs for occupation or continuous threatening	**4** $U_A = 5$ $U_B = 12$	**3** $U_A = 7$ $U_B = 7$

Fig. 7.6 Individual rationality versus collective rationality and reason

the benefits of cooperation together. This leads to high benefits in both countries, $U_A = 10$ and $U_B = 10$.

Field 2: A is aggressive and dominates the still peaceful country B, so that A can use some of B's resources for itself by dominating B. Higher expenditure on the armed forces reduces the net benefit to a certain extent, but A still gains a net benefit and B loses benefit, $U_A = 12$ and $U_B = 5$.

Field 3: A is aggressive and B is also aggressive, so that both threaten each other. This threat in turn costs resources, so that the payoffs for both are higher than that under foreign occupation but lower than that under cooperation, $U_A = 7$ and $U_B = 7$. Field 4 is symmetrical to Field 2.

Now let us go through the decision options again. Country A wants to make the best choice, given the activity of country B. If B is peaceful and cooperative, A has a higher payoff ($U_A = 12$) with aggressive behavior, than if it remains peaceful itself ($U_A = 10$). However, if B behaves aggressively and A remains peaceful, A only receives a very low payout $U_A = 5$, while it can still realize a moderate payout with its own aggressive behavior ($U_A = 7$). This means that, from A's individual perspective alone, the dominant strategy for all of B's behavior is to behave aggressively.

Since we have assumed a symmetrical scenario, the same considerations apply symmetrically to B. This means that it is rational for both to act nonpeacefully and noncooperatively from their individual perspective. From an individual perspective, this leads to the highest payout. In fact, however, it is not the highest possible payout if we look at the overall scenario. Field 1, the cooperative behavior, would be considerably better because both would not only receive a payout of 7 but 10 units of benefits. This would be better for both. However, the purely individual view prevents both from realizing these payouts. Only a collective mechanism could lead to the best possible overall result. This would then be the result of collective rationality and reason. Action guided by reason is therefore different from action from an individual perspective, even if it is individually rational.

This basic principle can easily be transferred to other social decision-making situations. The positions and narratives of individual ideology-representing organizations are often based on individual perspectives. If they act rationally from this individual perspective, this action is by no means necessarily rational, even if this is often claimed. Rational action only arises when an overall view is adopted and rational action is taken from this overall view.

7.5 Implications for Gathering Empirical Evidence

Given that individuals adhere to belief-based rules and principles to process information and make everyday decisions, we can conclude that there is a significant part of human cognition that seems to depart from traditional Bayesian inferences. Beliefs appear to play an important role in human existence. Forming one's own beliefs and values is an essential criterion for attaining adulthood (Arnett, 2000) and psychological well-being (Galek et al., 2015). Beliefs provide a mental guide to understanding and adapting to given environmental settings, to sharing reality with important others, and to processing information in a subjectively coherent way. The Evolutionary Threat Assessment Systems (ETAS) theory assumes that, in the first instance, beliefs serve some sort of a defensive or threat-relieving function.[13] Relying on certain belief-based ideals, rules, and norms to make decisions about what is right or wrong not only reduces anxiety and self-related uncertainty, it also provides a sense of security and greater self-esteem (Flannelly & Galek, 2009).

Although this implies that beliefs are a potent cause of action, this internal cognitive mechanism seems to be difficult to observe. The preference approach in economics postulates that individuals' (consumption) preferences can be revealed by observing their purchasing behavior under different price and income conditions. This means that individuals reveal their preference patterns through their market behaviors (Samuelson, 1948).

While this economic approach is based on observable behavior, the triggering source of this behavior can sometimes be difficult to identify. Making decisions in accordance with one's own norms and beliefs is sometimes difficult to observe, as there is often an inconsistency between these two aspects. This discrepancy between one's own values and sometimes contradictory behavior is also referred to in the literature as the attitude-behavior gap (Lehner et al., 2016) or value-action gap (Blake, 1999). This phenomenon has already been proven by several studies and refutes the theory that a lack of information is the reason for irrational or preference-independent behavior. Possible reasons for these behaviors include individual adaptation to social norms and the desire to belong (Akerlof & Kranton, 2010; Sinclair et al., 2005; Sechrist & Stangor, 2001).

However, recent neuroimaging and lesion studies suggest that beliefs are indeed "observable" in the form of neural underpinnings in the human brain. The choice of a particular belief system seems to be associated with individual differences in basic neurocognitive mechanisms (for a review, see Cristofori & Grafman, 2017). Such physiological measures are useful to assess implicit responses and infer subjective preferences. In neuroeconomics, it is assumed that if two different objects elicit neural activation of equal intensity, the two objects may be equally preferred. However, observing increased activation toward one object compared to another, the object that induces a higher neural reaction is likely to be preferred (Brosch & Sander, 2013). These studies show that individual differences in core values determine how much economic value is attached to different choices. Altruistic value-based choices, like donations or investments to restore distributive justice, activate stronger neural responses in some individuals, while self-related values induce greater rewards for others (Hare et al., 2010; Tricomi et al., 2010; Brosch et al., 2011). Individuals with fairly altruistic core values showed stronger activation

[13] The theory proposes "that the prefrontal cortex interacts with the basal ganglia and limbic system in making threat assessments and that the prefrontal cortex is the vehicle through which beliefs affect the assessment of threat" (Flannelly and Galek, 2009, p. 341).

in the dorsomedial prefrontal cortex (DMPFC) that, coupled with temporoparietal junction (TPJ) and precuneus, forms a social cognition network that is responsible for detecting the needs and beliefs of others. When making donations or altruistic choices, this social cognition network showed increased connectivity with regions representing economic value, implying that these choices had greater expected economic rewards. On the other hand, individuals with preferred hierarchy-based (self-centered) values make more selfish decisions and show stronger activation of the ventral striatum, which means that individuals with self-centered values may perceive selfish choices as more rewarding (Brosch et al., 2011).

These studies indicate that values have a direct impact on neural representations of economic rewards and an indirect impact on individual beliefs and norms. Conforming to our model, we suggest that an individual who assigns a high value to a certain need (like the need for benevolence or the call to restore social justice) will choose a belief system that best represents his or her values (and self-concept) and thus serves this particular need. The adopted belief system in turn provides behavioral norms, goals, and rules that allow that individual to make belief-consistent choices. Even in the absence of concrete economic rewards, adhering to one's own belief system tends to generate a higher belief-based utility.

Observing different neural correlates of various belief systems, subjective difference in responsiveness to complex and potentially conflicting information relates to the sensitivity of the anterior cingulate cortex (ACC) mechanism. Conservative beliefs are associated with lower conflict-related ACC activity, which implies lower neurocognitive sensitivity to cues for altering a habitual response pattern (Amodio et al., 2007). A similar study revealed that radical religious beliefs act as a buffer to reduce uncertainty, which is also associated with the reduced neural responses of an error-detection system centered on ACC (Kossowska et al., 2016).

A larger bilateral amygdala volume is positively correlated with the tendency to justify and support the existing social system and a reluctance to participate in social activities aimed at changing the status quo. The amygdala is linked to the processing of motivationally salient information concerning threat, uncertainty, or social groups (Nam et al., 2017). Psychological literature such as Jost et al. (2011) suggests that heightened physiological sensitivity to threat is associated with increased preferences for system-justifying (threat-reducing) conservative belief systems. Oxley et al. (2008) measured individuals' skin conductance response (SCR) to threatening images, considering their adopted belief systems. A high SCR reflects increased sweat gland activity associated with a sympathetic nervous system response to fear. The results show that participants who hold right-wing beliefs exhibited greater SCRs in response to threatening images. This would imply that those who feel more threatened tend to adopt rather conservative beliefs, which may serve some sort of defensive or anxiety-relieving function.

These studies find differential neurocognitive effects – after a decision, task, or stimulus – that are possibly linked to a previously adopted belief system or ideology. A next step could be to explore whether beliefs and ideologies are related to a differential weighting of the perceived rewards of different options before a decision is made. As we have seen, people not only derive utility from material goods and experiences but also from their beliefs and values. Adhering to a certain belief system, its rules and norms, and making decisions that are consistent with this belief system may induce high (psychological and economic) rewards for the subject.

In our model, we showed that belief-based consumption not only serves individuals' tangible or material needs but also their psychological requirements. Buying a good that resonates with one's own ideological values and rules generates a sense of consistency, control, and certainty, but it also enhances one's self-efficacy and self-esteem. We can thus make the assumption that making choices in line with one's own belief system or ideology implies greater rewards. Given all of the above, we can extend the classical preference approach by adding observable mental processes. Following the rules and principles of a belief system or ideology and making choices accordingly may reveal an individual's belief-based preferences – in the same ways as buying only vegetarian products reveals that a person has adopted ecological beliefs.

References

Akerlof, G. A., & Kranton, R. (2010). Identity economics. *The Economists' Voice, 7*(2).

Amodio, D. M., Jost, J. T., Master, S. L., & Yee, C. M. (2007). Neurocognitive correlates of liberalism and conservatism. *Nature Neuroscience, 10*(10), 1246–1247.

Arnett, J. J. (2000). Emerging adulthood. a theory of development from the late teens through the twenties. *The American psychologist, 55*(5), 469–480.

Bartling, B., Weber, R. A., & Yao, L. (2014a). Do markets erode social responsibility? *The Quarterly Journal of Economics, 130*(1), 219–266.

Blake, J. (1999). Overcoming the 'value-action gap' in environmental policy: Tensions between national policy and local experience. *Local Environment, 4*(3), 257–278.

Brosch, T., Coppin, G., Schwartz, S., & Sander, D. (2011). The importance of actions and the worth of an object: dissociable neural systems representing core value and economic value. *Social Cognitive and Affective Neuroscience, 7*(5), 497–505.

Brosch, T., & Sander, D. (2013). Neurocognitive mechanisms underlying value-based decision-making: from core values to economic value. *Frontiers in Human Neuroscience, 7*, 398. .

Burs, C., Gries, T., & Müller, V. (2022). The choice of ideology and everyday decisions. *Working Paper, APSA Preprints of The American Political Science Association.*

Burs, C., Gries, T., & Müller, V. (2023). The choice of ideology and everyday decisions. *Journal of Organizational Psychology, 23*(1), 134–153.

Cristofori, I., & Grafman, J. (2017). Neural underpinnings of the human belief system. In *Processes of believing: The acquisition, maintenance, and change in creditions* (pp. 111–123). Springer.

Flannelly, K. J., & Galek, K. (2009). Religion, evolution, and mental health: Attachment theory and ETAS theory. *Journal of Religion and Health, 49*(3), 337–350.

Galek, K., Flannelly, K. J., Ellison, C. G., Silton, N. R., & Jankowski, K. R. B. (2015). Religion, meaning and purpose, and mental health. *Psychology of Religion and Spirituality, 7*(1), 1–12.

Hare, T. A., Camerer, C. F., Knoepfle, D. T., O'Doherty, J. P., & Rangel, A. (2010). Value computations in ventral medial prefrontal cortex during charitable decision making incorporate input from regions involved in social cognition. *The Journal of Neuroscience, 30*(2), 583–590.

Jost, J. T., Liviatan, I., Van Der Toorn, J., Ledgerwood, A., Mandisodza, A., and Nosek, B. A. (2011). System justification: How do we know it's motivated? In D. R. Bobocel, A. C. Kay, M. P. Zanna & J. M. Olson (Eds.), *The psychology of justice and legitimacy* (pp. 173–203). Psychology Press.

Kossowska, M., Szwed, P., Wronka, E., Czarnek, G., & Wyczesany, M. (2016). Anxiolytic function of fundamentalist beliefs: Neurocognitive evidence. *Personality and Individual Differences, 101*, 390–395.

Lehner, M., Mont, O., & Heiskanen, E. (2016). Nudging—a promising tool for sustainable consumption behaviour? *Journal of cleaner production, 134*, 166–177.

Müller, V., & Gries, T. (2024). *Ideology and the microfoundations of conflict: From human needs to intergroup violence*. Oxford University Press.

Nam, H. H., Jost, J. T., Kaggen, L., Campbell-Meiklejohn, D., & Bavel, J. J. V. (2017). Amygdala structure and the tendency to regard the social system as legitimate and desirable. *Nature Human Behaviour, 2*(2), 133–138.

Oxley, D. R., Smith, K. B., Alford, J. R., Hibbing, M. V., Miller, J. L., Scalora, M., Hatemi, P. K., & Hibbing, J. R. (2008). Political attitudes vary with physiological traits. *Science, 321*(5896), 1667–1670.

Samuelson, P. A. (1948). Consumption theory in terms of revealed preference. *Economica, 15*(60), 243.

Sechrist, G. B., & Stangor, C. (2001). Perceived consensus influences intergroup behavior and stereotype accessibility. *Journal of Personality and Social Psychology, 80*(4), 645–654.

Sinclair, S., Lowery, B. S., Hardin, C. D., & Colangelo, A. (2005). Social tuning of automatic racial attitudes: The role of affiliative motivation. *Journal of Personality and Social Psychology, 89*(4), 583–592.

Tricomi, E., Rangel, A., Camerer, C. F., & O'Doherty, J. P. (2010). Neural evidence for inequality-averse social preferences. *Nature, 463*(7284), 1089–1091.

Chapter 8
The Quality of Ideological Guidance

Ideologies and belief systems play a crucial role in helping individuals and societies navigate decision-making for a better future. As coherent systems of narratives, they provide guidance toward making sound choices and achieving a good future.

But not every ideology or belief system is a good guide, which is why we need to ask ourselves which ideology or belief system is a good guide because it leads to "good" decisions and which is not. In doing so, we must take into account that there is a wide variety of ideologies and belief systems on offer and they can have different effects, especially on societal decision-making processes. Some ideologies and belief systems can help to promote positive societal developments, while others can lead to destructive and disastrous outcomes. It is therefore important to critically examine and analyze the different ideologies and belief systems to determine which are best suited to serve as a guide for good decision-making.

Which ideologies and belief systems in particular provide societies with "good guidance"? The quality of "ideological guidance" has many dimensions. We will only address and discuss three of them here: the normative dimension; the dimension of good information; and the question of the actual functionality of ideological instruments. Each of these dimensions is addressed in a separate section of this chapter. Our aim is to find out how the problem of good guidance manifests itself in each of these dimensions and how we can assess whether ideologies and belief systems provide good guidance.

8.1 The Normative Dimension of "good guidance"

When we talk about "good guidance" in this section, we cannot do without normative statements. We must therefore first postulate some normative axioms and use these as a basis for assessing what good guidance is. These normative axioms lead to fundamental principles that should then be used as a yardstick for the quality

T. Gries et al., *The Economics of Ideologies*, Springer Studies in Alternative Economics, https://doi.org/10.1007/978-3-031-93514-5_8

of ideological narratives. Even if we do not want to and cannot explicitly engage in a philosophical discussion here, we cannot avoid defining these principles for our normative discussion.

Basic normative axioms propose fundamental value statements that are supposed to be universally valid – or not if one does not agree with them. Normative axioms are thus specific fundamental assumptions and determinations that serve as a starting point for normative argumentation. We will see further below that all further arguments can be consistently deduced from these few normative axioms. They do not represent a typical belief system or ideology as a collection of narratives that may resonate to varying degrees with individuals; instead, they establish fundamental norms and principles that shape core social structures.

As the term "normative axiom" is important in the further argumentation, it should first be clarified and defined. An "axiom" is a fundamental assumption or unproven principle that is assumed to be true and serves as a starting point for deriving further conclusions in a logical system or theory. Axioms are often self-evident and require no further justification or proof, since they form the fixed framework within which logical reasoning takes place. They lay the foundation for mathematical, philosophical, or scientific theories. A "normative axiom" is thus a fundamental assumption, or a fundamental determination, that is assumed to be true or valid and serves as a starting point for normative arguments or ethical considerations and the development of ethical or legal theories.

However, before we argue further, let us define another term, the term "sovereign" that will be the focus of the following normative discussion.

The term "sovereign" refers to a person, an institution, or an entity that exercises supreme authority and unrestricted decision-making power over something or someone. In principle, a sovereign is not subject to any external authority.

Having defined these two terms, we can now start an argument that allows us to identify "bad guidance" as well as to identify the opposite, namely "good guidance".

Normative axiom 1 – sovereignty: As an autonomous being, every person is sovereign over his or her own person. Each person has full decision-making power over themself. This means that every person, being an independent and self-determined being, has the highest authority and control over themself. In principle, each person has the right and power to determine their own actions, decisions, and life.

The term "autonomous" is derived from the Greek word "autónomos", meaning "self-legislated". When referring to people or systems, "autonomous" means that they have the ability and the right to act independently and in a self-determined manner without being controlled by external influences or authorities. Autonomous persons or systems are able to make their own decisions, pursue their own goals, and direct their actions in line with their own beliefs and values. Autonomy is a fundamental principle in ethics, politics, philosophy, and other areas of human life and emphasizes the importance of individual freedom and self-determination. Axiom 1 thus describes every individual as being autonomous and sovereign, freeing them from limitations ranging from paternalism up to slavery.

Normative axiom 2 – equal rights: Equal rights refer to the principle that all individuals are endowed with the same rights without discrimination based on factors such as race, gender, ethnicity, religion, sexual orientation, or any other characteristic.

Normative axiom 3 – social relationality: As autonomous and sovereign beings, individuals are continuously interacting with one another. This places them within a social system where ongoing coordination with others is essential.

People can act freely, but they are part of a social structure in which their own sovereignty and their own actions may affect the sovereignty of other people. This brings us back to the well-known idea that each person can use their self-determination and freedom of action in their own best interests until they restrict the rights and freedom of action of others. Coordination of actions is necessary if different people want to use their fundamental freedom of action and encounter other individuals who want to do the same.

Recognizing the conflict – that one person's sovereign actions may limit another's – most people agree with the proposed solution: Individuals can exercise self-determination up to the point where it infringes on the rights and freedoms of others. However, many fail to realize that this limitation relies on a mutual agreement in which sovereign individuals voluntarily impose self-restraint. This inherently establishes a coordination principle to which sovereign individuals adhere. Why? The conflict of action between two autonomous individuals could also be ended by one of them (the stronger one) asserting his or her freedom of action and restricting the other individual, even to the point of complete subjugation (enslavement). However, this would mean depriving the inferior individual of his or her sovereignty, and he or she would not agree to the principle of "the stronger rules" because he or she does not want to be a slave. But even the currently stronger person would not agree to this principle as long as he or she did not know that he or she was actually the stronger of the two and could not in fact be enslaved. This leads to the fourth axiom that we need for our argument.

Normative axiom 4 – equality of perspective: For equal sovereign individuals to agree on coordination principles in a just manner requires conceptually equal starting positions, i.e., individuals having the same perspective of their position in the world. We refer to this as "equality of perspective". In the above example, this means that if the stronger person knows for certain that he or she is stronger, that person has a different perspective on the world than the weaker person. If the stronger person even knows that he or she will permanently remain the stronger of the two, he or she will prefer other coordination principals than if he or she had the possibility of becoming the weaker one of the two. We therefore postulate Rawls's "veil of ignorance" as a necessary prerequisite for making a universal decision on a coordination principle.

Rawls's "veil of ignorance" is a central concept in his political philosophy, especially in "A Theory of Justice" (Rawls, 1971). The "veil of ignorance" is a hypothetical notion that serves to develop just principles for the distribution of resources and rights in a society. The idea behind the "veil of ignorance" is that people can develop just principles if they do not know the conditions of the society into which they are born or in which they will live. When people are behind this "veil of ignorance", they do not know what position, social status, income, gender, race, or talents they will have in society. On this basis, they can develop just principles that treat all members of society fairly, regardless of their individual circumstances. Rawls argues that behind the veil of ignorance, people will tend to choose just principles based on fairness, equality, and mutual respect because they do not know whether they themselves will be in a privileged or disadvantaged position or not.

The "veil of ignorance" is a thought experiment that serves to develop just principles that apply regardless of individual preferences or interests. It serves as the basis for Rawls's theory of justice as fairness. For our discussion, this means that sovereign individuals need to find coordination principles that can be agreed upon by all those living under the same starting conditions ("veil of ignorance"). Only then, that is under the "veil of ignorance" and while maintaining one's own sovereignty, can one's own sovereignty be limited.

Simply put, such coordination of sovereign individuals can only occur through a mutual agreement on coordination rules established under conditions of initial equality. This requires sovereign individuals to limit their absolute freedom of action and either coordinate directly with others or temporarily delegate aspects of their sovereignty to coordinating institutions, which then organize this coordination. This idea was already anchored in Hobbes's proposal of a social contract (Hobbes, 1651).[1]

Apart from the idea of the social contract between sovereign individuals, however, our argument is clearly different to Hobbes. If sovereign individuals decide to transfer some of their sovereignty to a coordinating body, it is their sovereignty that gives them the power to determine how this body is structured. This includes deciding on the design of the institution and selecting the people responsible for finding the best ways to coordinate through the institution and implementing the coordination rules.

[1] Thomas Hobbes's social contract is a central idea in his political work Leviathan. Hobbes argues that humans inherently live in a state of nature that is characterized by war, conflict, and insecurity. In this state, everyone has the right to everything and is constantly in a state of mutual threat and violence. In order to escape this state of nature and to create a stable society, people enter into a "social contract". This contract involves people transferring their individual power to a central authority or government, the so-called Leviathan, which has absolute power. People give up their individual freedom and power in order to ensure security and peace in society.

It is interesting to note, however, that in Hobbes's theory this central authority is more of an autocratic ruler that safeguards the security interests of individuals but nothing more. Why the actions of an authoritarian ruler should be better than those of any other is unclear. Is the authoritarian ruler a better person? This is not thought through right to the end.

Essentially, at this point, the social contract as described by Hobbes creates the basis for forming a sovereign and authoritarian government that is responsible for maintaining law and order. Hobbes argues that this authoritarian government is necessary to protect people from the dangers of the state of nature and to ensure a stable society. However, as the following argument will show, we can in no way subscribe to the idea that an autocratic, authoritarian ruler is suitable for this purpose.

In this simplified argument, democracies can be understood as social systems designed to handle the necessary coordination among sovereign individuals while ensuring that each person relinquishes and delegates only the minimal amount of their sovereignty. Sovereign individuals temporarily transfer parts of their sovereignty to constitutional and democratic institutions (parliament, government, judiciary). Control over the sovereignty that has been transferred remains with the individuals and is not taken over by the country's institutions or their leaders. Sovereign individuals can always reappoint their representatives and governments, and the rule of law controls the implementation of legal rules.

These fundamental considerations can be used as the basis for developing various forms of democracy, which we can actually find in reality. Germany's democratic system, for example, functions somewhat differently than the French, British, U.S. or other democratic systems. However, they all have a similar constitutional structure that includes the separation of powers, meaning that the institutions control each other and can be kept under the control of the sovereign people.

Moreover, the four axioms outlined above can be used not only to justify democratic and social systems but also to establish fundamental minimum standards that define these systems. These standards guide coordination within democratic societies in a logically consistent way.

Let us return to the universal needs we identified in Chap. 4. Since they are universal, these needs can be found in every person, albeit at varying degrees of intensity. However, as in our discussion of sovereignty, if these needs are universal and part of human existence, individuals in the same starting position will agree that none of them should be completely disregarded. For if an individual agrees that a certain universal need is to be completely disregarded and later finds himself or herself to be the very individual for whom this need plays a particularly important role, he or she will suffer to a certain extent. Not even a minimum standard for serving this need will be guaranteed. The simplest example is again the need for security. Security, in its strict sense, means being free from direct threats, physical or psychological harm, or the risk of being killed. Since no one wants to face these possibilities, all sovereign individuals would agree on a social coordination rule that guarantees physical and psychological integrity as a minimum standard. This agreement could then be formalized as a fundamental right. In fact, the right to physical and psychological integrity, as well as the prohibition of torture, is explicitly recognized in the Universal Declaration of Human Rights. These rights represent the minimum standard that must always be upheld. While further coordination and adjustments to rules may be necessary beyond this point, falling below this standard is unacceptable. Many other legal norms (human rights) can also be justified on the basis of these very simple fundamental considerations. The minimum standard is defined by the presence of actual suffering. For example, those who are injured (existential needs, Sect. 4.1), those who are isolated (social-relational needs, Sect. 4.2), or those who are deprived of their self-determination (agency needs, Sect. 4.3) experience real suffering. The minimum standard to be ensured as a right is protection against the complete deprivation of fundamental needs and the resulting suffering.

Further discussion of these ideas and implications would be interesting and important but is not the task of this book. Here we want to look at ideologies and belief systems from an economic perspective. We have learned in the course of this book what functions and meanings ideologies and belief systems have. In this chapter, we explore when ideologies and belief systems offer good or bad guidance regarding our sovereignty and fundamental needs. Additionally, we seek to identify a normative standard that economists can agree upon and apply to evaluate ideological guidance.

Economic decision theory is based on the principle of individual sovereignty of action. This is a normative determination. This normative determination of human sovereignty not only applies to butter, jam, socks, and T-shirts, it is universal. Universal normative principles can be derived from individual sovereignty (Axiom 1) and equal rights (Axiom 2) together with – as discussed in the above – social relationality (Axiom 3) and equality of perspective (Axiom 4) and can be applied to social coordination and organizational structures. Such normative principles and norms can also be used to evaluate "ideological guidance". If we agree that all individuals possess equal dignity, rights, and sovereignty, interact with one another, and apply equality of perspective, evaluating "ideological guidance" from a normative standpoint becomes relatively straightforward. In fact, the normative principles listed below emerge directly from the three axioms. Examples of these principles include general nondiscrimination, equality before the law, individual political equality, inclusive participation in social, political, and economic spheres, fairness in negotiating coordination rules, democratic forms of political organization, preventing the concentration of political or economic power, rejecting authoritarianism, and ensuring equal opportunities in political and economic processes. People who live in democratic constitutional states are very familiar with these norms.

At this point, we can conclude that we have found normative principles as criteria for evaluating "good ideological guidance". To illustrate this, we can now try out which well-known ideologies and belief system that are also repeatedly found in reality do not stand up to these principles and therefore lead to "bad guidance". For example, all ideologies and belief systems that propagate fundamental discrimination and degradation or the systematic superiority of one's own group provide "bad guidance". As explained in (Müller & Gries, 2024), these types of ideologies also give rise to conflicts and, ultimately, violent confrontations and wars. Such ideologies providing "bad guidance" thus include racism, imperialism, colonialism, anti-Semitism, fascism, white supremacy, anti-feminism, any kind of autocratic ideology of rule, libertarian dogmatism, and many more. However, what are examples for good guidance? Narratives that demand and promote democratic institutions meet the normative criteria for good guidance just developed. Thus, ideologies and belief systems that emphasize democratic systems and the observance of human rights as the core message of their narratives are good examples of good guidance on a normative level.

Nevertheless, as described at the beginning of this chapter, there are other dimensions of good guidance that must also be taken into account in the search for ideologies and belief systems that are normatively good. Let us look at this aspect using the example of a democratic system. In the next two paragraphs, we will look at two further aspects of good guidance provided by ideologies: the information system and the instrument problem.

8.2 The Information Problem in Democracies

Ideologies based on democratic core statements in their narratives meet the criteria for good guidance described above. Democracy is the only form of government that attempts to coordinate individual sovereignty and create collective institutions that preserve individual's sovereignty as far as possible. However, democracies also face the information problem if they want to solve their coordination problem. Therefore, democracy cannot function on its own without solving the information problem.

Based on their information, individuals need to agree on a shared factual reality. What does this mean? A phenomenon that has been observed by all must be perceived as a fact by all and must be named in terms that reflect the phenomenon. For example, during the Covid pandemic, it was expected that more people would die than usual. With this in mind, statisticians used scientific methods to measure whether more people were actually dying than usual. Scientific studies are completely transparent, data sources can be checked, they can be repeated, and it can be verified that the results and findings obtained once can be obtained again. Therefore, the statement "there is excess mortality", derived using scientific methodology, has a different factual quality from the statement of an arbitrary person who claims that he cannot perceive more deaths than in other years. What would a common and shared reality look like? A common and shared factual reality would be that the measurement made by the best means and methods is accepted as fact, but that individual observations, while not necessarily wrong, do not reflect reality as a whole. A shared factual reality means that we have a common understanding of the facts that is shared by most people. This means that excess mortality is an actual fact and reality, that a Covid-19 infection is not the flu, that invading and occupying a neighboring country against its will is a war and not a "special military operation", that the moon landing was not a Hollywood staging, and that a false claim is not an "alternative reality". If we no longer have a shared and common factual reality in terms of fundamental facts, the balancing of different perspectives, interpretations, and interests in democracies becomes extremely difficult, if not impossible.

Democracy needs informed citizens and therefore a well-functioning information system. The education system must equip individuals with the skills to use the media effectively, while simultaneously understanding information in different contexts, and assessing its consistency and validity. Media holds the responsibility to clearly distinguish between credible information and fake news. However, as soon as there is clear identification of true and false and people turn to interpretations and explanations, they should also have learned to tolerate ambiguity, inconsistency, and divergent ideas. Decisions made based on superficial assumptions, incomplete or false information, or misinterpretations of reality often lead to distortions and poor outcomes, both individually and collectively. Populist ideological narratives, which offer oversimplified solutions to complex problems while ignoring or distorting facts, are a prime example of this issue.

Another and perhaps more far-reaching phenomenon is the strategy adopted by antidemocratic ideologies to systematically discredit the credibility of well-functioning information systems. While trust in the credibility of the reputably functioning media originally led to a reality that was shared by most people in a society, a loss of trust in a reputable information system leads to a change in the perceived reality of different groups. Those who continue to trust the credible information system develop a different perception of reality than those who no longer trust the interpretation of reality created in this way and follow other interpretations. This breach of trust, which occurs in the first step and can be generated by a propaganda system, makes it easier, in the second step, to establish other interpretations of reality with the help of these propaganda machines.

However, if a society's credible information system is destroyed, the basis of democracy is destroyed, as democracy needs the "informed citizen" if it is to function well. The information system is therefore a central element of social coordination. It is what leads to a shared, or divided, perception of reality within a society.

Authoritarian systems have understood this well. In authoritarian systems, we therefore often observe the censorship of media and the suppression of the free, pluralistic expression of opinions. Even more, in authoritarian systems, we often observe fake news and propaganda. Autocratic regimes are interested in dominating the information system because those whose narratives dominate the information system create the common perceived reality. The strategic destruction of a well-functioning information system means that only the information provided by those who dominate the system is disseminated. However, this not only applies to authoritarian regimes that exercise such control through state power. The concentration of "information power" can also occur through the corresponding use of resources in uncontrolled decentralized information systems. The dominance of resource-rich private actors with potentially a large amount of information power can also be a danger for a "good" functioning information system and thus for the functioning of a democratic system. Democracies must not relinquish their control of a well-functioning information system in favor of the business models and profit interest of private firms in the information generation and dissemination industry. Otherwise, they will allow the destruction of democracy with their eyes wide open.

From Fake News to Fake Realities

So how is it that individuals develop a perception of reality that is ultimately very different from factual reality? The answer is very simple. If the information they receive is often false, then over time "fake news" and propaganda create a false interpretation of reality that we call "fake reality". Generally speaking, people generate an image of reality from the information they receive. This image can be close to reality, but it does not have to be so. How close it is to reality depends on the quality of the information.

We will therefore now take a closer look at this mechanism of information reception and learning about reality. To do this, we will go back to Sect. 2.4 where we learned about the process of Bayesian Learning. As a reminder, Bayesian Learning describes an evolutionary process of learning. Let us take another brief look at such an evolutionary learning process and what it means for our perception of reality.

As we saw in Chap. 2, humans gather information by receiving information signals from various sources. They then use these information signals to update their subjective beliefs about reality. If these signals contain false information and the individuals do not notice this because they trust their sources, they incorporate these fake signals into their posterior beliefs. They will then not get closer to factual reality by obtaining more information. Instead, they will get a false perception of reality based on these false beliefs.

In the following very simple example, an individual wants to know why the sun rises each morning and makes its daily journey across the sky. How does this individual find the answer to this question? First, the person thinks about what might be happening. We have referred to this as "prior belief" because it is the belief in what might be happening before further information is obtained. The individual therefore starts with an initial belief about what might be happening. If his or her own explanation is not yet sufficient, the individual may ask his or her neighbor or read something about the matter. With each new piece of information, this individual will adapt his or previous belief about why the sun rises again every morning and runs its course. He or she will compare the next interpretation with observed reality, and if this allows a more plausible and empirically supported understanding, he or she will accept these new explanations to correct the previous explanations and beliefs about what mechanism is at work. In other words, the individual learns on the basis of more and more new information signals and uses what he or she learns to form a picture of the actual mechanism that is at work. This image of the actual mechanism defines what we believe about how the actual mechanism works. We believe that this is what reality is like. It is what we interpret as reality. What people perceive and learn from interpretations and subjective experience turns into their reality.

This means that people share a common reality precisely when the information signals (facts and interpretations) they receive are similar but above all not contradictory. All those people who receive similar signals throughout the process of learning about reality will also largely develop a similar picture from these signals and thus believe something similar about reality. They will share a similar reality.

This perceived reality can be very close to factual reality, but it can also be completely different to it. This can be seen in the example of the explanation of the course the sun runs in the sky. While in ancient times the reality individuals shared may have been that the sun rises because the sun god Helios is driving across the sky in a chariot to illuminate the world, today we know that this belief does not come close to factual reality. Factual reality works completely differently. The reason for this discrepancy lies in the quality of the information signals. None of the sources of information at that time were able to signal factual reality. The information signals were mythological, not scientific. The signaling was wrong and therefore led to a false perception of reality.

Therefore, we will now take a closer look at signaling as an important element of the Bayesian Learning process. In all our modeling so far, the signal comes directly from factual reality. It is stochastic, but the expected value of the information signal is identical to the expected value of factual reality, and the uncertainty about the current status compared to factual reality is thus reduced with each information signal. This brought us closer to factual reality – albeit stochastically, but nevertheless continuously over a longer period of time. Scientific progress can basically be described in exactly this way. If an attempt to measure reality actually captures it well, we can correct our previous knowledge with each new measurement signal and thus come closer to the expected value of factual reality. The same applies in our examples, which look at the real "match values" that we have approached using the information signals in order to make decisions after obtaining optimal information. Since these information signals were defined as factually correct in our modeling, the resulting learning processes also led to approximations to the actual match values.

This becomes even clearer when we look at another simple example, the Bayesian update procedure for a binary problem. In individual decision-making, this binary approach can be used to decide whether a hypothesis is factual or false. We further assume that information signals about these two potential outcomes can be observed repeatedly and contribute to the update process. To illustrate this Bayesian updating process, we use the example of propaganda of an Eastern European socialist state before the collapse of the Eastern Bloc. In these countries, the governments repeatedly signaled that socialism was 'on the right track' and claimed that these countries would develop better economically and socially than the capitalist West. The people in these countries had to decide for themselves whether they believed these claims to be true or false. They had a prior belief about the probability p that these statements were correct. If $p > 0.5$, they believed that the government statements were true. Each individual could collect information, i.e., receive signals that either supported or did not support the government statements. These signals were then used to update p, as described in Sect. 2.4.

The more propaganda was spread, the more these signals led to a polarization of beliefs. A larger group of supporters of the government ideology believed that the Eastern European countries were indeed on a more successful path than Western countries, while another group was convinced that Western European countries were economically more successful and that living conditions in the West were better. Ultimately, it turned out that the factual economic situation in Eastern Europe was characterized by deficiencies, frequent supply bottlenecks, and a shortage economy. Nevertheless, many people in Eastern Europe were still convinced of the "success of Soviet-style socialism" ($p > 0.5$). What happened? The government and the state apparatus spread false and, above all, embellished information signals. These were received by many supporters and led to repeated updates and a strengthening of their convictions. Individual Bayesian Belief depends on the signals received by each individual. However, if false messages (false signals) are spread, these beliefs about reality will be updated in a false way, which can lead to errors and a false interpretation of reality, i.e., a counterfeit reality. The reality of these people was that their system was more successful. False signals led to a false individual perception of reality, i.e., a nonfactual (fake) reality.

As a further example, we return to the Bayesian updating approach with normal distributions. Again, we can examine the impact of false messages (signals). Suppose that an individual wants to know a value μ. This can be the match value described in Chap. 2, 2, or a very different value, for instance, the rise in global temperatures due to climate change (see below). Another example is the number of people who died of COVID-19 and not from another disease with COVID-19. Again, individuals can learn about this value μ by observing signals and updating their prior beliefs in a Bayesian manner. They thus start by forming prior beliefs

$$\mu \sim \mathcal{N}(\mu_0, \sigma_0^2).$$

Since individuals are interested in factual reality in order to be able to make good decisions, they need information about μ. Thus, they can make observations of the value μ, i.e., they receive independent stochastic messages

$$M_i \sim \mathcal{N}(\mu, \eta^2).$$

The expected value of the messages is the desired value μ, but the messages can be ambiguous, so they are received with some uncertainty η^2. This is the ideal case that we already discussed in Chaps. 3 and 6. However, as the use of social media increases, so does the spread of fake news. This has been observed in various contexts, such as the fake news during the 2016 U.S. presidential election (Allcott & Gentzkow, 2017) or misinformation about the origin of the coronavirus (COVID-19) (Mian & Khan, 2020). Consequently, individuals may or may not receive the factual signal M_i but also a manipulated signal of the form

$$M_i^{\varepsilon} = M_i + \varepsilon_i.$$

Individuals receive a signal that is shifted by a certain value. This value varies depending on the source of the signal. Therefore, we can assume that ε_i is normally distributed

$$\varepsilon_i \sim \mathcal{N}(\mu_{\varepsilon}, \eta_{\varepsilon}^2).$$

In this case, M^{ε} is also normally distributed,

$$M^{\varepsilon} \sim \mathcal{N}(\mu + \mu_{\varepsilon}, \eta^2 + \eta_{\varepsilon}^2).$$

However, individuals do not know this. They think they are observing M, which has the factual expected value μ. Therefore, they update their beliefs as described in the above, and their posterior beliefs after receiving N signals are

$$\mu_N^{\varepsilon} = \frac{\sigma_0^2}{N\sigma_0^2 + \eta^2} \sum_{i=0}^{N-1} M_i^{\varepsilon} + \frac{\eta^2}{N\sigma_0^2 + \eta^2}\mu_0$$

$$= \frac{\sigma_0^2}{N\sigma_0^2 + \eta^2} \sum_{i=0}^{N-1} (M_i + \varepsilon_i) + \frac{\eta^2}{N\sigma_0^2 + \eta^2}\mu_0$$

$$\sigma_N^2 = \frac{\sigma_0^2\eta^2}{N\sigma_0^2 + \eta^2}.$$

The more manipulated signals M_i^{ε} the individual receives, the more μ_N^{ε} approaches $\mu + \mu_{\varepsilon}$ instead of the factual value μ. A proof of this idea is provided in Appendix "A.8".

We can illustrate this using an example. Consider the discussion about global warming. Let μ be the factual increase in global temperatures over a given period of time that can be measured and relate causally to greenhouse gas emissions. Various scientific institutions publish estimates of this value. They thus send signals M_i for μ, and individuals can use these signals to update their own beliefs. However, there are also some people who disagree with the calculations done by various scientific institutions and spread their own estimate of this rise in temperatures, for example, on social media platforms. Often these people are strong opponents of the hypothesis that global warming is being caused by humans. Therefore, they estimate μ to be higher or lower than the value published by scientific institutions. This means that these other people are spreading signals M_i^{ε} that are not based on best possible measurements. Individuals can then use these signals to determine their subjective posterior beliefs, resulting in a false perception of the factual value of the rise in temperatures caused by humans.

Figure 8.1 illustrates this example numerically. Suppose the factual temperature increase is $\mu = 0.2$. Consider a person who disagrees with the view that global warming indeed exists. Therefore, this person has a prior belief of $\mu_0 = 0.4$, with a prior uncertainty of $\sigma_0^2 = 0.04$. The factual signals are published by scientific institutions with variance $\eta^2 = 0.02$. However, our sample person follows other radical opponents of global warming on social media and uses their manipulated signals to update their subjective prior beliefs. We assume that this person receives 20 signals. The "fake signals" are manipulated by

$$\varepsilon_i \sim \mathcal{N}(-0.1, 0.1).$$

The evolution of posterior beliefs for μ is shown in Fig. 8.1. The blue dots illustrate an example sequence of posterior beliefs after receiving non-manipulated signals. The more of these signals are obtained, the closer the posterior beliefs approach the

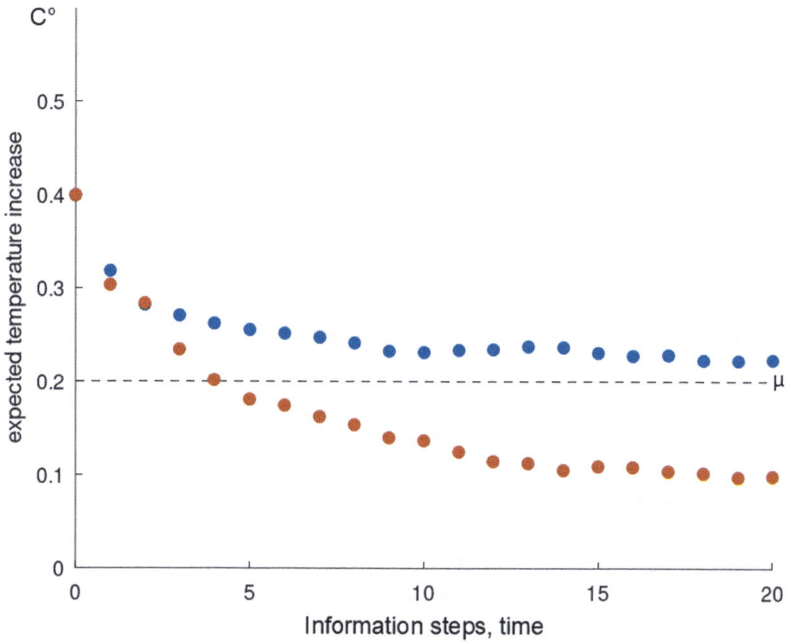

Fig. 8.1 Example sequence of posterior expected values after receiving scientific signals (blue) or "fake signals" (red)

factual value $\mu = 0.2$. The red dots show an example sequence of posterior beliefs after observing fake news with lower signals. We can see that these posterior beliefs are significantly lower than the beliefs following non-manipulated signals.

A group that is permanently supplied with fake information collects it as factual information about reality, and, thus, the fake information turns into a fake reality for these individuals. In their perceived reality, the development of average global temperatures is much less dramatic than in factual reality. In other words, they live nonfactual reality.

Let us go one step further and consider what this means when artificial intelligence (AI) is used in these information processes. With artificial intelligence, manipulated signals could be generated automatically and distributed on a massive scale. Artificial intelligence is trained. However, since this training process can be controlled by the AI operators, it opens the door to conscious manipulation. In the end, the machine only reproduces as information what it has learned, that is, the reality contained in the training material. If this training material consciously contains only certain sections of reality, then only this section is learnt by the AI and sent as a signal.

It could be even more drastic if the AI is even tasked with generating and sending masses of texts, photos, and videos according to certain wishes. It can then create a world of signals according to the wishes of the AI operators at the push of a button with automated mass signaling. The mass distribution of these manipulated fake signals is continuously absorbed by the recipients of these signals and is added to their image of reality. The representation of reality designed by the AI operators leads the recipients, through the massive signals from the AI, to a perception that then becomes a perceived reality. AI becomes a propaganda machine that works perfectly, more precisely and more efficiently than any analogue propaganda machine ever installed in history.

What are the implications of this model that describes the emergence of differently perceived realities and thus of different subjective realities? Basically, it is what we have already established in the above.

Subjective reality is what an individual perceives as reality. This perception is determined by the incoming flow of information. If a society's information system works, the vast majority of people in that society share a similar subjective reality, and this widely shared subjective reality becomes a social reality that forms the basis for joint social decisions. This is essential for a functioning democracy. In a functioning information system, fake news, disinformation, and propaganda are unmasked and labeled as such at an early stage. When it comes to the organization and design of our current information and media system, we must ask ourselves whether this requirement is still being met. In authoritarian regimes, it is clear that state power dominates the systems. But this is not the only threat to a functioning information system. The "good guidance" of our information system must be questioned most particular with a view to the business models of large companies in the Internet and social media sector. If this information system is clearly no longer functioning well, democratic societies must not hesitate to rate a well-functioning information system as more important for a democratic society than the business models of large Internet and social media groups. Other business models that are compatible with the requirements of a "good information system" must replace less compatible ones. The following questions must be answered in the affirmative in order for an information system to be classified as a system of "good guidance":

- Can the information system systematically detect and correct decentralized fake news, disinformation, and propaganda as such at an early stage and communicate this across the board?
- Is the reach and systematic dissemination of certain information and narratives (e.g., fake news, disinformation, and propaganda) independent of the use of resources and the wealth of resources that individuals in a society have? Is the system immune to the concentration of information and opinion power and – in the worst case – protected against being hijacked by a few resource-rich actors or the government?
- Are participants in debates in this information system protected from denigration, intimidation, or even threats, or can resource-rich users of the system or the government determine the extent to which other users are denigrated, intimidated, or threatened?

- Is there for all free access to reliable sources of information that are independent of economic and ideological perspectives and interests, whose research, data, and assertions are free of external influences and can be verified neutrally? Are these sources of information systematically and institutionally available to everyone, so that the required socially relevant information is always truthful, i.e., thoroughly and carefully researched, verifiable, and retrievable? Are these sources of information obliged and able to quickly correct mistakes and communicate them transparently?

If the answer to these questions is negative, there is no functioning "good information system" that is needed to create a shared, similar reality in a society. This also means that there will be no functioning democratic system based on sovereign citizens who are informed about reality.

The Deception Problem About Ideological Narratives and Organizations
In this short section, we want to take another look at how ideological organizations function. This was already done in Sect. 5.2, but now we want to establish in more detail how this functioning of the ideological organization affects good guidance.

In our discussion in Chap. 6, we describe how an individual decides to adopt an ideology, i.e., how he or she becomes a follower of a particular ideology. We will revisit this mechanism, as it can be directly combined with the mechanisms of disinformation addressed in the previous section.

We use the Bayesian Learning process as a universal description of learning processes. In Sect. 6.2,we also described the individuals' absorption of information about ideological narratives as a Bayesian Learning process about what these organizations stand for. However, we have just seen that information signals can shift. Since ideological organizations themselves determine which signals they send out, they can consciously shape their image and how they present themselves to the outside world differently to how they actually are.

In this way, an organization that actually represents an autocratic, antidemocratic, and violent ideology might pretend to accept democratic ideas in order to generate support from followers who have no preference for authoritarian forms of society. The signals sent by this organization then do not reveal its actual hostility to democracy; its supporters are deceived. However, this deception can lead to disaster. If the trivializing signals lead to the seizure of power by this organization and the implementation of its true ideology, then the result can be authoritarian tyranny. The deceived supporters can then say ex post that they neither knew nor wanted that to happen. However, it is then too late, and it may no longer be possible to correct the mistake.

The distinction between organizational goal and ideological narrative provides the starting point for another type of deception (see Sect. 5.2). In this case, an organization's ideological narrative solely serves as an instrument for acquiring followers. This distinction makes it possible to identify this additional problem of deception by ideological organizations. For example, if the organizational goal is solely to maximize power or resource availability, as assumed in Sect. 5.2, the ideological organization will not be very selective in choosing its narratives. It is not bound by any specific ideological narrative as the content of the narrative is only a means but not an end. As a result, it can always choose its narratives in such a way that its beliefs will reach a particularly large number of people and gain their approval based on its simple narratives. Populism is a good example. It is not interested in actually solving problems but in creating the perception that there is someone who can take on real problems and solve them. This already serves the needs of potential followers who join the ideology precisely for this reason (Sect. 6.2) and thus enables both the ideological organization and its significance to grow (see Sect. 5.2).

Hence, populist organizations and leaders often promise quick and easy solutions to complex problems without adequately considering the associated challenges or consequences. They also often rely on emotional messages and strong rhetoric to mobilize and polarize their supporters. In combination with disinformation and propaganda, this is a very effective strategy for mobilizing and acquiring supporters, especially when the actual goal is quite different (e.g., maximizing power or resources, see Sect. 5.2).

But it is not only populist narratives that can be used to characterize the deception problem, which always arises when narratives are generated that are ultimately intended to serve an interest group's specific purpose but conceal this purpose. In such cases, stories are invented that claim to be in the general interest of society but whose intention and narrative content ultimately serve the interests of a specific group. An example of this would be bans on advertising certain harmful substances such as tobacco. While the facts clearly indicate that tobacco consumption causes considerable harm to health and, therefore, at least restricting advertising for this harmful consumption would have a positive effect on the health of the population, there are some who would see this as detrimental to their business. And so a narrative is developed that suggests that banning tobacco advertising is paternalism and an inadmissible restriction of the general freedom of action. With the help of a libertarian ideology, almost any ban can be declared as the suppression of freedom of action and transformed into a corresponding narrative. What we are dealing with here is thus not disinformation but targeted manipulation and even misleading the interpretation of reality for the benefit of certain interests.

8.3 Implementing Narratives: The Instrument Problem

In this section, we address another issue that has to be considered in connection with ideological narratives. We call it the "instrument problem". As already noted in relation to our definition of "ideology" in Sect. 5.1, ideologies have several central aspects: First, they usually convey a particular set of goals and desired states, including a closely related system of values; second, they propose strategies and actions for achieving those desired states. These strategies and actions are what we call "instruments for achieving goals". Ideological narratives are not only interpretations of current reality and descriptions of a desired reality, they also suggest which measures should be taken that are consistent with one's interpretation of that narrative to achieve the desired conditions. But these measures are also part of an ideological belief. They may or may not work. Unfortunately, in most cases, there is no empirical evidence to support the vehemently held belief in the effectiveness of the proposed instruments.

We want to shed light on this issue by using a classic macroeconomic problem as an example. To clearly identify the instrument problem, we look at two ideologies for which we even assume an identical objective. Despite the same goals, the ideological interpretations and narratives, and the resulting political measures (instruments) to achieve them, are then by nature very different.

In our example, we look at the classic problem of underemployment in the presence of a fixed wage. The aim of our two ideologies is to increase employment by means of appropriate measures (instruments). The first ideology we have chosen for our comparison is a neoclassical narrative to explain this phenomenon and show that, under these neoclassical premises and interpretations, it is quite plausible and consistent to reduce the fixed wage to achieve a higher level of employment. This provides a consistent narrative and a coherent choice of instruments based on it.

In a next step, the same phenomenon (underemployment in the presence of a fixed wage) is interpreted based on a Keynesian narrative. We show that it is consistent under Keynesian premises not to lower the fixed wage but to raise it. That is, it is consistent under these ideological premises to implement the exact opposite measure to raise the level of employment.

The Neoclassical Narrative and Its Political Instrument

To keep the argument as simple as possible, we choose the simplest possible model for each ideology that allows us to present our argument. As regards the question of the effect of a minimum wage on underemployment, a partial neoclassical labor market model is the simplest one we can choose.

Labor demand can be derived from firms' profit-maximizing conditions, and labor supply can be determined based on households' optimization model. As a result, firms' labor demand decisions lead to the wage-dependent falling labor demand curve in Fig. 8.2. The narrative is simple: As wages rise, labor becomes increasingly more expensive, and producers use other production factors in place of labor. And so they use less and less labor the more wages rise. Labor supply is determined by household decisions. Households choose between work and leisure, and if they get more for their work, they work more because they can consume more for an additional hour of work. Household decisions thus lead to the upward-sloping, wage depending on labor supply curve in Fig. 8.2.

In an unregulated market, equilibrium is established when the market finds a wage for which the amount of labor firms demand is exactly the same as that offered by households. This equilibrium wage is represented by $\tilde{w}$ in Fig. 8.2. Where a fixed wage is introduced, for example, $\bar{w}$, which is higher than the equilibrium wage, then at this wage, firms will only employ the labor volume $L^D(\bar{w})$. At the same

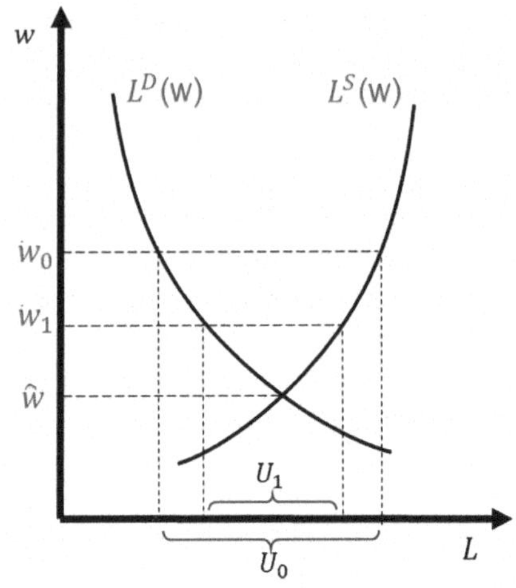

Fig. 8.2 Neoclassical labor market with fixed wages

time, however, the labor volume of $L^S(\bar{w})$ is available on the market, resulting in unemployment U_0. If we now believe this neoclassical narrative, we see that it is the excessively high fixed wage that is the cause of the unemployment.

If we now want to reduce unemployment, we only need to use the instrument of wage reduction and unemployment is eliminated. This line of argumentation as well as the recommendation to apply the political instrument are entirely plausible and consistent in this closed neoclassical narrative. The only question that remains is whether this narrative and the political instrument derived from it are a sufficient interpretation of reality. Does reality actually work in this way?

This may or may not be the case, because, as we will see, there is an alternative narrative that is equally consistent and plausible and leads to a completely different conclusion and to the use of completely different instruments.

The Keynesian Narrative and Its Political Instrument

The Keynesian narrative focuses on a completely different mechanism. According to this narrative, only what is in demand is produced. If not enough is produced and not as many workers as want to work can be hired, it is because the existing incomes, especially of poorer income groups who have a high consumption rate, do not earn enough to develop sufficient demand. If they earned more, mass income would rise, more would be consumed, and more consumer demand would be generated, creating more jobs.

We can also demonstrate this mechanism with a minimal macroeconomic Keynesian model.

Production and Input Factors

We start with firms producing with labor L and capital K at capital intensity, $k = K/L$, using a linear-homogeneous production function

$$Y = f(k)L.$$

For profit-maximizing firms and a given wage, $\bar{w}$, the optimal capital-labor ratio can be derived from the FOCs using the implicit function theorem (IFT).[2] Thus, optimal capital intensity is

$$\tilde{k} = k(\bar{w}).$$

With a fixed optimal capital intensity, we obtain a fixed relation between income Y and the labor L required for a given minimum wage

$$Y = f(\tilde{k}(\bar{w}))L.$$

Keynesian Demand Model In the simplest Keynesian demand model, the level of production and income Y is determined by the two demand components investment demand I and consumer demand C

$$Y = I + C$$

For the sake of simplicity, we assume that consumer demand is determined exclusively by the large number of working-class households and thus by earned income. Consumer demand is then

$$C = \bar{C} + c\bar{w}L.$$

Model Solution If we now solve this model directly in such a way that we can determine employment, we get [3] the employment multiplier

[2] Firms profit is

$$\pi = f(k)L - \bar{w}L - rK, \quad k = \frac{K}{L}.$$

Thus, the FOC with respect to labor is

$$\bar{w} = f(k) - f'(k)k,$$

which allows to apply the IFT.

[3] Insert and solve under the additional assumption that capital is sufficiently available or underemployed gives

$$\begin{aligned} Y &= I + C \\ f\left(\tilde{k}\left(\bar{w}\right)\right) L &= I + \bar{C} + c\bar{w}L \\ f\left(\tilde{k}\left(\bar{w}\right)\right) L - c\bar{w}L &= I + \bar{C} \\ \left(f\left(\tilde{k}\left(\bar{w}\right)\right) - c\bar{w}\right) L &= I + \bar{C}. \end{aligned}$$

$$L = \frac{I + \bar{C}}{f\left(\tilde{k}\left(\bar{w}\right)\right) - c\bar{w}}.$$

Change in Fixed Wages $d\bar{w}$ What will happen to employment if the fixed wage rate changes? We take the derivative of the employment multiplier and obtain

$$\frac{dL}{d\bar{w}} = -\frac{\left(I + \bar{C}\right)}{\left(f\left(k\left(\bar{w}\right)\right) + c\bar{w}\right)^2}\left[f'\frac{\partial k}{\partial w} - c\right] \gtrless 0.$$

The question of whether employment will rise or fall cannot be unambiguously answered. It depends on what sign $\left[f'\frac{\partial k}{\partial w} - c\right]$ takes. This, in turn, depends mainly on how large the change in capital intensity is when wages rise, and thus how strong a factor substitution between labor and capital technically is. If $\frac{\partial k}{\partial w} > 0$ is small and the factors labor and capital are relatively complementary, and thus $\left[f'\frac{\partial k}{\partial w} - c\right]$ turns negative. However, this means that $\frac{dL}{d\bar{w}}$ turns positive, and thus a higher minimum wage actually generates so much more purchasing power in line with the narrative that the surge in demand leads to higher overall employment despite the labor factor in production becoming more expensive. The Keynesian narrative can thus be consistently demonstrated using this simple model.

Implications Both narratives are plausible and have a theoretically consistent rationale. Both have proposals for policy instruments that can be directly derived from their theoretical arguments. Only the proposed instruments are diametrically opposite to one another. In one narrative, the proposal made to increase employment is to reduce the minimum wage, and in the other narrative, the proposal made is to increase in the minimum wage to increase employment. In reality, the two narratives, which are quite consistent in their respective worlds, would make contrasting but equally plausible proposals, and each group would demand one or the other policy, each trusting in their own narrative, and thus possibly propose exactly the wrong instrument. This is exactly what we call the instrument problem and why we wanted to raise an awareness of it. Only a good narrative whose explanations are close to reality can also make a good proposal for an instrument that can actually bring us closer to the desired state.

It is therefore crucial to find empirical evidence for both the explanatory narratives and the proposed instruments. Pure plausibility – as is repeatedly invoked in political debates – is by no means sufficient. However, this not only applies to the organizations that shape the ideologies and ultimately pursue their own interests, it applies all the more to the functioning of the information system as a whole. Dogmatism, extremism, and polarization based on the simplest ideological narratives should not be encouraged in a functioning information system. This applies to the functioning of the media (social media) as such, but it also applies to traditional analog journalism.

References

Allcott, H., & Gentzkow, M. (2017). Social media and fake news in the 2016 election. *Journal of Economic Perspectives, 31*(2), 211–236.

Hobbes, T. (1651). *Leviathan, or, the matter, form, and power of a common-wealth, ecclesiastical and civil.* Andrew Crooke.

Mian, A., & Khan, S. (2020). Coronavirus: the spread of misinformation. *BMC Medicine, 18*(1), 89.

Müller, V., & Gries, T. (2024). *Ideology and the microfoundations of conflict: from human needs to intergroup violence.* Oxford University Press.

Rawls, J. (1971). *A theory of justice.* Harvard University Press.

Chapter 9
Final Remark

Good decisions require good information about reality, how it is and how it works. This applies to individuals but also to societies as a whole. However, genuine and original factual information about facts and mechanisms, as collected in Bayesian Learning, is very expensive. Therefore, heuristics, which provide second-hand information and explanations of the world, can be a cost-effective alternative.

Ideologies and belief systems are a set of narratives that provide such cost-effective information, interpretations, and explanations of the present world, and, in addition, even offer values, evaluations, visions of the future, and suggestions for achieving them. They are therefore a heuristic alternative to Bayesian Learning and Bayesian Belief/knowledge. In this respect, their use can be a rational and optimal step in the shaping of reality. Which ideology or belief system a person adheres to depends on many things, but also on the psychological need structure of the individual. People believe, trust, and adopt the belief system with whose narrative they resonate most positively.

What does this ultimately mean for us? It means that we humans, even as rational beings, are dependent on what we believe. The subjective reality is what we believe it to be, whether true or not. This applies even if what we believe is coauthored by the narrative systems close to us.

Belief systems and ideologies are therefore important elements of human life because they provide people with orientation and guidance, for better or for worse. Since they are often led by organizations that shape these narratives, these organizations also provide orientation about which values are important and how we should behave. They develop rules for their followers from their various narratives and suggest what ethical behavior is.

While intense debates between the most diverse ideologies were still taking place in the last century, these discourses have waned in the breadth of society since the 1990s. However, with their loss of importance, orientation and guidance have also dwindled, helping people to evaluate what is good or bad for them in society, even in the longer term.

T. Gries et al., *The Economics of Ideologies*, Springer Studies in Alternative Economics, https://doi.org/10.1007/978-3-031-93514-5_9

To restore this orientation, we must relearn to identify ideologies and discuss them in order to determine what constitutes a "good" or "bad" ideology for our future. We must discuss how a society should be designed and what that means for the individual. We must clearly identify and evaluate the values that constitute an ideology.

To do this, however, we also need an information and communication system that enables a discourse about precisely these ideologies, beliefs, and values for everyone, without threat and on an equal footing – without an information power that is based on asymmetries of resources or direct power, neither by the state nor by social groups or individuals. It must be institutionally anchored in the best possible knowledge (Bayesian information) about reality and its mechanisms. We humans must shape society in the interplay between the narratives we believe in and the best possible knowledge (Bayesian information) so that as many people as possible can lead a good life.

Appendix

A.1 Solution for Maximization Problem (M)

We solve the maximization problem (M) after N steps using the Lagrange function

$$\begin{aligned} L(x_1, x_2, \lambda) = & x_1\mu_{1,N} - \frac{1}{2}Ax_1^2\sigma_{1,N}^2 + x_2\mu_{2,N} - \frac{1}{2}Ax_2^2\sigma_{2,N}^2 + \bar{T} - N \\ & + \lambda(y - x_1 p_1 - x_2 p_2). \end{aligned}$$

The first order conditions are

$$\begin{aligned} \frac{\partial L}{\partial x_1} &= \mu_{1,N} - Ax_1\sigma_{1,N}^2 - \lambda p_1 = 0 \\ \frac{\partial L}{\partial x_2} &= \mu_{2,N} - Ax_2\sigma_{2,N}^2 - \lambda p_2 = 0 \\ \frac{\partial L}{\partial \lambda} &= y - x_1 p_1 - x_2 p_2 = 0. \end{aligned}$$

From the first equation, we obtain

$$\lambda = \frac{\mu_{1,N} - Ax_1\sigma_{1,N}^2}{p_1},$$

and from the second equation, we obtain

$$\lambda = \frac{\mu_{2,N} - Ax_2\sigma_{2,N}^2}{p_2}.$$

T. Gries et al., *The Economics of Ideologies*, Springer Studies in Alternative Economics, https://doi.org/10.1007/978-3-031-93514-5

Consequently, we have

$$\begin{aligned}
\frac{\mu_{1,N} - Ax_1\sigma_{1,N}^2}{p_1} &= \frac{\mu_{2,N} - Ax_2\sigma_{2,N}^2}{p_2} \\
\Leftrightarrow \mu_{1,N} - Ax_1\sigma_{1,N}^2 &= \frac{p_1(\mu_{2,N} - Ax_2\sigma_{2,N}^2)}{p_2} \\
\Leftrightarrow -Ax_1\sigma_{1,N}^2 &= \frac{p_1(\mu_{2,N} - Ax_2\sigma_{2,N}^2)}{p_2} - \mu_{1,N} \\
\Leftrightarrow x_1 &= \frac{\mu_{1,N}}{A\sigma_{1,N}^2} - \frac{p_1(\mu_{2,N} - Ax_2\sigma_{2,N}^2)}{A\sigma_{1,N}^2 p_2} \\
&= \frac{\mu_{1,N}}{A\sigma_{1,N}^2} - \frac{p_1\mu_{2,N}}{A\sigma_{1,N}^2 p_2} + \frac{x_2\sigma_{2,N}^2 p_1}{\sigma_{1,N}^2 p_2}.
\end{aligned}$$

We plug this into the third equation

$$y = p_1\left(\frac{\mu_{1,N}}{A\sigma_{1,N}^2} - \frac{p_1\mu_{2,N}}{A\sigma_{1,N}^2 p_2} + \frac{x_2\sigma_{2,N}^2 p_1}{\sigma_{1,N}^2 p_2}\right) + x_2 p_2.$$

Solving for x_2, we obtain

$$\begin{aligned}
y - \frac{\mu_{1,N}p_1}{A\sigma_{1,N}^2} + \frac{p_1^2\mu_{2,N}}{A\sigma_{1,N}^2 p_2} &= \frac{x_2\sigma_{2,N}^2 p_1^2}{\sigma_{1,N}^2 p_2} + x_2 p_2 \\
\Leftrightarrow y - \frac{\mu_{1,N}p_1}{A\sigma_{1,N}^2} + \frac{p_1^2\mu_{2,N}}{A\sigma_{1,N}^2 p_2} &= x_2\left(p_2 + \frac{\sigma_{2,N}^2 p_1^2}{\sigma_{1,N}^2 p_2}\right) \\
\Leftrightarrow \frac{yA\sigma_{1,N}^2 p_2 - \mu_{1,N}p_1p_2 + p_1^2\mu_{2,N}}{A\sigma_{1,N}^2 p_2} &= x_2\frac{\sigma_{1,N}^2 p_2^2 + \sigma_{2,N}^2 p_1^2}{\sigma_{1,N}^2 p_2} \\
\Leftrightarrow \frac{yA\sigma_{1,N}^2 p_2 - \mu_{1,N}p_1p_2 + p_1^2\mu_{2,N}}{A} &= x_2\left(\sigma_{1,N}^2 p_2^2 + \sigma_{2,N}^2 p_1^2\right) \\
\Leftrightarrow \frac{yA\sigma_{1,N}^2 p_2 - \mu_{1,N}p_1p_2 + p_1^2\mu_{2,N}}{A\left(\sigma_{1,N}^2 p_2^2 + \sigma_{2,N}^2 p_1^2\right)} &= x_2.
\end{aligned}$$

Now we can determine x_1,

$$x_1 = \frac{\mu_{1,N}}{A\sigma_{1,N}^2} - \frac{p_1\mu_{2,N}}{A\sigma_{1,N}^2 p_2} + \frac{x_2\sigma_{2,N}^2 p_1}{\sigma_{1,N}^2 p_2}$$

$$= \frac{\mu_{1,N}}{A\sigma_{1,N}^2} - \frac{p_1\mu_{2,N}}{A\sigma_{1,N}^2 p_2} + \frac{yA\sigma_{1,N}^2 p_2 - \mu_{1,N}p_1p_2 + p_1^2\mu_{2,N}}{A\left(\sigma_{1,N}^2 p_2^2 + \sigma_{2,N}^2 p_1^2\right)} \frac{\sigma_{2,N}^2 p_1}{\sigma_{1,N}^2 p_2}$$

$$= \frac{yA\sigma_{2,N}^2 p_1 - \mu_{2,N}p_1p_2 + p_2^2\mu_{1,N}}{A\left(\sigma_{1,N}^2 p_2^2 + \sigma_{2,N}^2 p_1^2\right)}.$$

A.2 Derivation of Assumption (A)

We assume

$$\tilde{\Delta}_N = \mathbb{E}^*[\tilde{u}|I_{N+1}] - \mathbb{E}^*[\tilde{u}|I_N] > 0,$$

which is equivalent to

$$x_1^{N+1}\mu_{1,N+1} - \frac{1}{2}A(x_1^{N+1})^2\sigma_{1,N+1}^2 + x_2^{N+1}\mu_{2,N+1} - \frac{1}{2}A(x_2^{N+1})^2\sigma_{2,N+1}^2$$
$$- \left(x_1^N\mu_{1,N} - \frac{1}{2}A(x_1^N)^2\sigma_{1,N}^2 + x_2^N\mu_{2,N} - \frac{1}{2}A(x_2^N)^2\sigma_{2,N}^2\right) > 0$$

and

$$\frac{1}{2}A\left((x_1^N)^2\sigma_{1,N}^2 - (x_1^{N+1})^2\sigma_{1,N+1}^2 + (x_2^N)^2\sigma_{2,N}^2 - (x_2^{N+1})^2\sigma_{2,N+1}^2\right)$$
$$> x_1^N\mu_{1,N} + x_2^N\mu_{2,N} - x_1^{N+1}\mu_{1,N+1} - x_2^{N+1}\mu_{2,N+1}.$$

We obtain

$$A > 2\frac{x_1^N\mu_{1,N} - x_1^{N+1}\mu_{1,N+1} + x_2^N\mu_{2,N} - x_2^{N+1}\mu_{2,N+1}}{(x_1^N)^2\sigma_{1,N}^2 - (x_1^{N+1})^2\sigma_{1,N+1}^2 + (x_2^N)^2\sigma_{2,N}^2 - (x_2^{N+1})^2\sigma_{2,N+1}^2} \tag{A4}$$

if we assume that x_i^N and x_i^{N+1} fulfill

$$(x_i^N)^2\sigma_{i,N}^2 - (x_i^{N+1})^2\sigma_{i,N+1}^2 > 0. \tag{A0}$$

This means that the adjustments in quantities in one time step are not large enough to dominate the reduction in uncertainty. We assume that (A0) also holds for x_i^N and x_i^a, which becomes clear in the proof of proposition 3.2. Additionally, we assume

$$\tilde{\Delta}_N - \tilde{\Delta}_{N+1} > 0.$$

This means

$$\tilde{\Delta}_N - \tilde{\Delta}_{N+1} = \mathbb{E}^*[\tilde{u}|I_{N+1}] - \mathbb{E}^*[\tilde{u}|I_N] - \mathbb{E}^*[\tilde{u}|I_{N+2}] + \mathbb{E}^*[\tilde{u}|I_{N+1}]$$
$$= 2\mathbb{E}^*[\tilde{u}|I_{N+1}] - \mathbb{E}^*[\tilde{u}|I_N] - \mathbb{E}^*[\tilde{u}|I_{N+2}] > 0.$$

This is equivalent to

$$2\left(x_1^{N+1}\mu_{1,N+1} - \frac{1}{2}A(x_1^{N+1})^2\sigma_{1,N+1}^2 + x_2^{N+1}\mu_{2,N+1} - \frac{1}{2}A(x_2^{N+1})^2\sigma_{2,N+1}^2\right)$$
$$- \left(x_1^{N+2}\mu_{1,N+2} - \frac{1}{2}A(x_1^{N+2})^2\sigma_{1,N+2}^2 + x_2^{N+2}\mu_{2,N+2} - \frac{1}{2}A(x_2^{N+2})^2\sigma_{2,N+2}^2\right)$$
$$- \left(x_1^{N}\mu_{1,N} - \frac{1}{2}A(x_1^{N})^2\sigma_{1,N}^2 + x_2^{N}\mu_{2,N} - \frac{1}{2}A(x_2^{N})^2\sigma_{2,N}^2\right) > 0$$

and

$$A\begin{pmatrix} -(x_1^{N+1})^2\sigma_{1,N+1}^2 - (x_2^{N+1})^2\sigma_{2,N+1}^2 + \frac{1}{2}(x_1^{N+2})^2\sigma_{1,N+2}^2 \\ +\frac{1}{2}(x_2^{N+2})^2\sigma_{2,N+2}^2 + \frac{1}{2}(x_1^{N})^2\sigma_{1,N}^2 + \frac{1}{2}(x_2^{N})^2\sigma_{2,N}^2 \end{pmatrix}$$
$$> -2x_1^{N+1}\mu_{1,N+1} - 2x_2^{N+1}\mu_{2,N+1} + x_1^{N+2}\mu_{1,N+2} + x_2^{N+2}\mu_{2,N+2} + x_1^{N}\mu_{1,N} + x_2^{N}\mu_{2,N}.$$

Therefore, we assume

$$A > \frac{\begin{matrix} -2x_1^{N+1}\mu_{1,N+1} - 2x_2^{N+1}\mu_{2,N+1} + x_1^{N+2}\mu_{1,N+2} \\ +x_2^{N+2}\mu_{2,N+2} + x_1^{N}\mu_{1,N} + x_2^{N}\mu_{2,N} \end{matrix}}{\begin{matrix} -(x_1^{N+1})^2\sigma_{1,N+1}^2 - (x_2^{N+1})^2\sigma_{2,N+1}^2 + \frac{1}{2}(x_1^{N+2})^2\sigma_{1,N+2}^2 \\ +\frac{1}{2}(x_2^{N+2})^2\sigma_{2,N+2}^2 + \frac{1}{2}(x_1^{N})^2\sigma_{1,N}^2 + \frac{1}{2}(x_2^{N})^2\sigma_{2,N}^2 \end{matrix}} \tag{A5}$$

and slightly adjust assumption (A0) to

$$\begin{bmatrix} -(x_1^{N+1})^2\sigma_{1,N+1}^2 - (x_2^{N+1})^2\sigma_{2,N+1}^2 + \frac{1}{2}(x_1^{N+2})^2\sigma_{1,N+2}^2 \\ +\frac{1}{2}(x_2^{N+2})^2\sigma_{2,N+2}^2 + \frac{1}{2}(x_1^{N})^2\sigma_{1,N}^2 + \frac{1}{2}(x_2^{N})^2\sigma_{2,N}^2 \end{bmatrix} > 0. \tag{A0'}$$

Thus, if we assume (A0), (A0'), and that A is larger than the maximum of the right-hand sides of (A4) and (A5), we obtain assumption (A).

A.3 Proof of Proposition 3.2

Proof Information acquisition is stopped after N steps as soon as

$$\mathbb{E}^*[u|I_N] - V^a(I_{N+1}) \geq 0.$$

This is equivalent to

$$x_1^N \mu_{1,N} - \frac{1}{2}A(x_1^N)^2\sigma_{1,N}^2 + x_2^N \mu_{2,N} - \frac{1}{2}A(x_2^N)^2\sigma_{2,N}^2 + \bar{T} - N$$
$$- \left(x_1^a \mu_{1,N} - \frac{1}{2}A(x_1^a)^2\sigma_{1,N+1}^2 + x_2^a \mu_{2,N} - \frac{1}{2}A(x_2^a)^2\sigma_{2,N}^2 + \bar{T} - (N+1) \right)$$
$$=(x_1^N - x_1^a)\mu_{1,N} - \frac{1}{2}A\left((x_1^N)^2\sigma_{1,N}^2 - (x_1^a)^2\sigma_{1,N+1}^2 + (x_2^N)^2\sigma_{2,N}^2 - (x_2^a)^2\sigma_{2,N}^2 \right)$$
$$+ (x_2^N - x_2^a)\mu_{2,N} + 1 \geq 0.$$

We derive the left-hand side with respect to A and obtain using the envelope theorem

$$-\frac{1}{2}\left((x_1^N)^2\sigma_{1,N}^2 - (x_1^a)^2\sigma_{1,N+1}^2 + (x_2^N)^2\sigma_{2,N}^2 - (x_2^a)^2\sigma_{2,N}^2 \right) < 0$$

according to assumption (A). To be precise, we need assumption (A0) to hold for anticipated quantities.

Thus, $\mathbb{E}^*[u|I_N] - V^a(I_{N+1})$ is smaller when A is increased. This implies that at least as many or even more steps N are necessary until $\mathbb{E}^*[u|I_N] - V^a(I_{N+1}) \geq 0$ and the process is stopped. The number of steps cannot be decreased. ■

A.4 Proof of Proposition 3.3

Proof Information acquisition is stopped after N steps as soon as

$$\mathbb{E}^*[u|I_N] - V^a(I_{N^*+1}) \geq 0.$$

This is equivalent to

$$x_1 \mu_{1,N} - \frac{1}{2}Ax_1^2\sigma_{1,N}^2 + x_2 \mu_{2,N} - \frac{1}{2}Ax_2^2\sigma_{2,N}^2 + \bar{T} - N$$
$$- \left(x_1^a \mu_{1,N} - \frac{1}{2}A(x_1^a)^2\sigma_{1,N+1}^2 + x_2^a \mu_{2,N} - \frac{1}{2}A(x_2^a)^2\sigma_{2,N}^2 + \bar{T} - (N+1) \right)$$
$$=(x_1 - x_1^a)\mu_{1,N} - \frac{1}{2}A\left(x_1^2\sigma_{1,N}^2 - (x_1^a)^2\sigma_{1,N+1}^2 + x_2^2\sigma_{2,N}^2 - (x_2^a)^2\sigma_{2,N}^2 \right)$$
$$+ (x_2 - x_2^a)\mu_{2,N} + 1 \geq 0,$$

where $x_i = x_i^N$ is the optimal quantity after N information acquisition steps and x_i^a the anticipated quantity for an additional step. In the following, we only use N instead of N^* for simplicity.

We derive the left-hand side with respect to η_i and obtain using the envelope theorem

$$(x_i - x_i^a)\frac{\partial \mu_{i,N}}{\partial \eta_i} - \frac{1}{2}A\left(x_i^2\frac{\partial \sigma_{i,N}^2}{\partial \eta_i} - (x_i^a)^2\frac{\partial \sigma_{i,N+1}^2}{\partial \eta_i}\right)$$

with

$$\frac{\partial \sigma_{i,N}^2}{\partial \eta_i} = \frac{2N\sigma_{i,0}^4\eta_i}{(N\sigma_{i,0}^2 + \eta_i^2)^2} > 0 \text{ and}$$

$$\frac{\partial \mu_{i,N}}{\partial \eta_i} = \frac{2\sigma_{i,0}^2\eta_i}{(N\sigma_{i,0}^2 + \eta_i^2)^2}\left(N\mu_{i,0} - \sum_{s=0}^{N-1} m_{i,s}\right).$$

Thus, the derivative is

$$\begin{aligned}
&(x_i - x_i^a)\frac{\partial \mu_{i,N}}{\partial \eta_i} - \frac{1}{2}A\left(x_i^2\frac{\partial \sigma_{i,N}^2}{\partial \eta_i} - (x_i^a)^2\frac{\partial \sigma_{i,N+1}^2}{\partial \eta_i}\right)\\
=&(x_i - x_i^a)\frac{2\sigma_{i,0}^2\eta_i}{(N\sigma_{i,0}^2 + \eta_i^2)^2}\left(N\mu_{i,0} - \sum_{s=0}^{N-1} m_{i,s}\right)\\
&- \frac{1}{2}A\left(x_i^2\frac{2N\sigma_{i,0}^4\eta_i}{(N\sigma_{i,0}^2 + \eta_i^2)^2} - (x_i^a)^2\frac{2(N+1)\sigma_{i,0}^4\eta_i}{((N+1)\sigma_{i,0}^2 + \eta_i^2)^2}\right).
\end{aligned}$$

In order to determine the sign of this derivative, we need to make the additional assumptions (3.2), (3.3), and (3.4). We can use assumption (3.2) together with (2.11) and obtain

$$N\mu_{i,0} - \sum_{s=0}^{N-1} m_{i,s} \leq N\mu_{i,0} - Nm_{i,min} \leq 3N\sigma_{i,0},$$

where $m_{i,min}$ is the smallest signal that the consumer has received after N steps. Furthermore, we determine the derivative of reduction in variance with one step with respect to η_i,

$$\begin{aligned}
\frac{\partial \sigma_{i,N}^2}{\partial \eta_i} - \frac{\partial \sigma_{i,N+1}^2}{\partial \eta_i} =& \frac{2N\sigma_{i,0}^4\eta_i}{(N\sigma_{i,0}^2 + \eta_i^2)^2} - \frac{2(N+1)\sigma_{i,0}^4\eta_i}{((N+1)\sigma_{i,0}^2 + \eta_i^2)^2}\\
=&\frac{2\sigma_{i,0}\eta_i(N(N+1)\sigma_{i,0}^4 - \eta_i^4)}{(N\sigma_{i,0}^2 + \eta_i^2)^2((N+1)\sigma_{i,0}^2 + \eta_i^2)^2},
\end{aligned}$$

which is positive for every step $N \geq 1$ if we assume $2\sigma_{i,0}^4 \geq \eta_i^4$, which is assumption (3.3). Now we can calculate

$$x_i^2 \frac{2N\sigma_{i,0}^4\eta_i}{(N\sigma_{i,0}^2+\eta_i^2)^2} - (x_i^a)^2 \frac{2(N+1)\sigma_{i,0}^4\eta_i}{((N+1)\sigma_{i,0}^2+\eta_i^2)^2}$$

$$=(x_i^2-(x_i^a)^2)\frac{2N\sigma_{i,0}^4\eta_i}{(N\sigma_{i,0}^2+\eta_i^2)^2} - (x_i^a)^2 \frac{2(N+1)\sigma_{i,0}^4\eta_i}{((N+1)\sigma_{i,0}^2+\eta_i^2)^2} + (x_i^a)^2 \frac{2N\sigma_{i,0}^4\eta_i}{(N\sigma_{i,0}^2+\eta_i^2)^2}$$

$$=(x_i^2-(x_i^a)^2)\frac{2N\sigma_{i,0}^4\eta_i}{(N\sigma_{i,0}^2+\eta_i^2)^2} + (x_i^a)^2 \underbrace{\left(\frac{2N\sigma_{i,0}^4\eta_i}{(N\sigma_{i,0}^2+\eta_i^2)^2} - \frac{2(N+1)\sigma_{i,0}^4\eta_i}{((N+1)\sigma_{i,0}^2+\eta_i^2)^2}\right)}_{\geq 0 \text{ from the assumption for the derivative (3.3).}}$$

$$\geq (x_i^2-(x_i^a)^2)\frac{2N\sigma_{i,0}^4\eta_i}{(N\sigma_{i,0}^2+\eta_i^2)^2}.$$

Returning to the derivative, we can estimate

$$(x_i - x_i^a)\frac{2\sigma_{i,0}^2\eta_i}{(N\sigma_{i,0}^2+\eta_i^2)^2}\left(N\mu_{i,0} - \sum_{s=0}^{N-1} m_{i,s}\right)$$

$$-\frac{1}{2}A\left(x_i^2 \frac{2N\sigma_{i,0}^4\eta_i}{(N\sigma_{i,0}^2+\eta_i^2)^2} - (x_i^a)^2 \frac{2(N+1)\sigma_{i,0}^4\eta_i}{((N+1)\sigma_{i,0}^2+\eta_i^2)^2}\right)$$

$$\leq (x_i - x_i^a)\frac{2\sigma_{i,0}^2\eta_i}{(N\sigma_{i,0}^2+\eta_i^2)^2} N 3\sigma_{i,0} - \frac{1}{2}A\left((x_i^2-(x_i^a)^2)\frac{2N\sigma_{i,0}^4\eta_i}{(N\sigma_{i,0}^2+\eta_i^2)^2}\right)$$

$$= \frac{N\sigma_{i,0}^3\eta_i}{(N\sigma_{i,0}^2+\eta_i^2)^2}\left(6(x_i - x_i^a) - A\sigma_{i,0}(x_i^2-(x_i^a)^2)\right),$$

which is negative if

$$6(x_i - x_i^a) - A\sigma_{i,0}(x_i^2-(x_i^a)^2) < 0.$$

This is equivalent to

$$6(x_i - x_i^a) < A\sigma_{i,0}(x_i^2-(x_i^a)^2), \tag{A3}$$

which is assumption (3.4). Note that the sign of $(x_i - x_i^a)$, respectively $(x_i^2-(x_i^a)^2)$, can be both positive and negative. Therefore, at this point, we need to both assume that A is large enough, so that (3.4) holds, and, if necessary, that $\sigma_{i,0}$ is small enough.

Thus, if we assume that (3.4) holds (together with (3.2) and (3.3)), then the difference between the current expected utility and anticipated utility for one more search step, $\mathbb{E}^*[u|I_N] - V^a(I_{N+1})$, is decreased when η_i is increased, because the assumptions form sufficient conditions such that the derivative with respect to η_i is negative. Thus, it is not possible that search stops with less steps. Therefore, N^* is either increased or remains unchanged.

We also take a look at the case, where $N = 0$. Information acquisition is only started if

$$\mathbb{E}^*[u|I_0] - V^a(I_1) < 0.$$

The left-hand side is equal to

$$(x_1 - x_1^a)\mu_{1,0} - \frac{1}{2}A\left(x_1^2\sigma_{1,0}^2 - (x_1^a)^2\sigma_{1,ant}^2 + x_2^2\sigma_{2,0}^2 - (x_2^a)^2\sigma_{2,ant}^2\right)$$
$$+ (x_2 - x_2^a)\mu_{2,0} + 1.$$

The derivative with respect to $\tilde{\eta}_i$ is

$$\frac{1}{2}A(x_i^a)^2\frac{2N\sigma_{i,0}^4\tilde{\eta}_i}{(N\sigma_{i,0}^2 + \tilde{\eta}_i^2)^2} > 0.$$

Thus, the difference $\mathbb{E}^*[u|I_0] - V^a(I_1)$ is increased with an increase in $\tilde{\eta}_i$, which can mean that $\tilde{\eta}_i$ is so large that this difference becomes positive and information acquisition is not started. ■

A.5 Organizations

Equations (5.8) and (5.9) form a two-dimensional system of autonomous differential equations. Therefore, we can perform a qualitative analysis using a phase diagram. However, the variables in Eqs. (5.8) and (5.9) are F and μ. Since Eq. (5.7) is a function of $\mathfrak{d}$, we want to draw the phase diagram in $(F, \mathfrak{d})$ space. Therefore, we need to eliminate μ. From (5.7), we know that $\mu = \frac{\mathfrak{d}^{-\sigma}}{\varphi\bar{\mathfrak{M}}^b}$. We can differentiate this and get $\dot{\mu} = \frac{-\sigma\mathfrak{d}^{-\sigma-1}}{\varphi\bar{\mathfrak{M}}^b}\dot{\mathfrak{d}}$. Then we can set this equal to the expression from (5.9) and get the organization's Ramey rule:

$$\dot{\mu} = -\mu\left(\varphi\alpha F^{\alpha-1}\bar{\mathfrak{M}}^b - \delta - \rho\right)$$
$$\frac{-\sigma\mathfrak{d}^{-\sigma-1}}{\varphi\bar{\mathfrak{M}}^b}\dot{\mathfrak{d}} = -\frac{\mathfrak{d}^{-\sigma}}{\varphi\bar{\mathfrak{M}}^b}\left(\varphi\alpha F^{\alpha-1}\bar{\mathfrak{M}}^b - \delta - \rho\right)$$
$$\frac{\dot{\mathfrak{d}}}{\mathfrak{d}} = \frac{\varphi\alpha F^{\alpha-1}\bar{\mathfrak{M}}^b - \delta - \rho}{\sigma}.$$

A.6 Choice of Ideologies

Derivation of Assumption (R) To simplify, let us replace $T := T_{Info}$. Our first assumption is

$$\Delta_T = \mathbb{E}_{\alpha^*_{T+1}}[\tilde{u}|I_{T+1}] - \mathbb{E}_{\alpha^*_T}[\tilde{u}|I_T] > 0,$$

which is equivalent to

$$\alpha^*_{T+1}\mu_{A,T+1} - \frac{(\alpha^*_{T+1})^2}{2}R\sigma^2_{A,T+1} + (1-\alpha^*_{T+1})\mu_{B,T+1} - \frac{(1-\alpha^*_{T+1})^2}{2}R\sigma^2_{B,T+1}$$
$$-\alpha^*_T\mu_{A,T} + \frac{(\alpha^*_T)^2}{2}R\sigma^2_{A,T} - (1-\alpha^*_T)\mu_{B,t} + \frac{(1-\alpha^*_T)^2}{2}R\sigma^2_{B,T} > 0$$

and

$$\frac{1}{2}R\left(-(\alpha^*_{T+1})^2\sigma^2_{A,T+1} - (1-\alpha^*_{T+1})^2\sigma^2_{B,T+1} + (\alpha^*_T)^2\sigma^2_{A,T} + (1-\alpha^*_T)^2\sigma^2_{B,T}\right)$$
$$> \alpha^*_T\mu_{A,T} + (1-\alpha^*_T)\mu_{B,T} - \alpha^*_{T+1}\mu_{A,T+1} - (1-\alpha^*_{T+1})\mu_{B,T+1}.$$

So we have to assume that

$$(\alpha^*_T)^2\sigma^2_{A,T} - (\alpha^*_{T+1})^2\sigma^2_{A,T+1} + (1-\alpha^*_T)^2\sigma^2_{B,T} - (1-\alpha^*_{T+1})^2\sigma^2_{B,T+1} > 0 \tag{R0}$$

so that

$$R > 2\frac{\alpha^*_T\mu_{A,T} + (1-\alpha^*_T)\mu_{B,T} - \alpha^*_{T+1}\mu_{A,T+1} - (1-\alpha^*_{T+1})\mu_{B,T+1}}{(\alpha^*_T)^2\sigma^2_{A,T} - (\alpha^*_{T+1})^2\sigma^2_{A,T+1} + (1-\alpha^*_T)^2\sigma^2_{B,T} - (1-\alpha^*_{T+1})^2\sigma^2_{B,T+1}}. \tag{R1}$$

Moreover, we assume

$$\Delta_T - \Delta_{T+1} = 2\mathbb{E}_{\alpha^*_{T+1}}[\tilde{u}|I_{T+1}] - \mathbb{E}_{\alpha^*_T}[\tilde{u}|I_T] - \mathbb{E}_{\alpha^*_{T+2}}[\tilde{u}|I_{T+2}] > 0,$$

which is equivalent to

$$2\alpha^*_{T+1}\mu_{A,T+1} - 2\frac{(\alpha^*_{T+1})^2}{2}R\sigma^2_{A,T+1} + 2(1-\alpha^*_{T+1})\mu_{B,T+1}$$
$$-2\frac{(1-\alpha^*_{T+1})^2}{2}R\sigma^2_{B,T+1} - \alpha^*_T\mu_{A,T} + \frac{(\alpha^*_T)^2}{2}R\sigma^2_{A,T}$$

$$- (1-\alpha_T^*)\mu_{B,T} + \frac{(1-\alpha_T^*)^2}{2} R\sigma_{B,T}^2 - \alpha_{T+2}^*\mu_{A,T+2} + \frac{(\alpha_{T+2}^*)^2}{2} R\sigma_{A,T+2}^2$$
$$- (1-\alpha_{T+2}^*)\mu_{B,T+2} + \frac{(1-\alpha_{T+2}^*)^2}{2} R\sigma_{B,T+2}^2 > 0$$

and

$$\frac{1}{2}R(-2(\alpha_{T+1}^*)^2\sigma_{A,T+1}^2 - 2(1-\alpha_{T+1}^*)^2\sigma_{B,T+1}^2 + (\alpha_T^*)^2\sigma_{A,T}^2$$
$$+ (1-\alpha_T^*)^2\sigma_{B,T}^2 + (\alpha_{T+2}^*)^2\sigma_{A,T+2}^2 + (1-\alpha_{T+2}^*)^2\sigma_{B,T+2}^2)$$
$$> -2\alpha_{T+1}^*\mu_{A,T+1} - 2(1-\alpha_{T+1}^*)\mu_{B,T+1} + \alpha_T^*\mu_{A,T}$$
$$+ (1-\alpha_T^*)\mu_{B,T} + \alpha_{T+2}^*\mu_{A,T+2} + (1-\alpha_{T+2}^*)\mu_{B,T+2}.$$

Hence, we must assume that

$$R > 2\frac{\begin{array}{c}-2\alpha_{T+1}^*\mu_{A,T+1} - 2(1-\alpha_{T+1}^*)\mu_{B,T+1} + \alpha_T^*\mu_{A,T} \\ +(1-\alpha_T^*)\mu_{B,T} + \alpha_{T+2}^*\mu_{A,T+2} + (1-\alpha_{T+2}^*)\mu_{B,T+2}\end{array}}{\begin{array}{c}-2(\alpha_{T+1}^*)^2\sigma_{A,T+1}^2 - 2(1-\alpha_{T+1}^*)^2\sigma_{B,T+1}^2 + (\alpha_T^*)^2\sigma_{A,T}^2 \\ +(1-\alpha_T^*)^2\sigma_{B,T}^2 + (\alpha_{T+2}^*)^2\sigma_{A,T+2}^2 + (1-\alpha_{T+2}^*)^2\sigma_{B,T+2}^2\end{array}} \tag{R2}$$

and slightly adjust (R0) to

$$- 2(\alpha_{T+1}^*)^2\sigma_{A,T+1}^2 - 2(1-\alpha_{T+1}^*)^2\sigma_{B,T+1}^2 + (\alpha_T^*)^2\sigma_{A,T}^2 + (1-\alpha_T^*)^2\sigma_{B,T}^2$$
$$+ (\alpha_{T+2}^*)^2\sigma_{A,T+2}^2 + (1-\alpha_{T+2}^*)^2\sigma_{B,T+2}^2 > 0. \tag{R0'}$$

So if we assume (R0), (R0'), and that R is greater than the maximum of the right-hand sides of (R1) and (R2), we get the assumption (R).

A.7 Everyday Decisions

Consumer Utility Function Example for a Cobb Douglas utility function, derivatives:

$$u = c_c^\alpha c_\rho^\beta \rho^{1-\alpha-\beta}$$

$$\frac{\partial u}{\partial c_c} = \alpha c_c^{\alpha-1} c_\rho^\beta \rho^{1-\alpha-\beta} > 0, \quad \frac{\partial^2 u}{\partial c_c^2} = -(1-\alpha)\,\alpha c_c^{\alpha-2} c_\rho^\beta \rho^{1-\alpha-\beta} < 0$$

$$: \frac{\partial^2 u}{\partial c_c \partial c_\rho} = \beta\alpha c_c^{\alpha-1} c_\rho^{\beta-1} \rho^{1-\alpha-\beta} + (1-\alpha-\beta)\,\alpha c_c^{\alpha-1} c_\rho^\beta \rho^{1-\alpha-\beta-1} > 0$$

$$\frac{\partial u}{\partial c_\rho} = \beta c_c^\alpha c_\rho^{\beta-1} \rho^{1-\alpha-\beta} > 0, \quad \frac{\partial^2 u}{\partial c_\rho^2} = -(1-\beta)\,\beta c_c^\alpha c_\rho^{\beta-2} \rho^{1-\alpha-\beta} < 0$$

$$: \frac{\partial^2 u}{\partial c_\rho \partial c_c} = \alpha\beta c_c^{\alpha-1} c_\rho^{\beta-1} \rho^{1-\alpha-\beta} > 0$$

$$\frac{\partial u}{\partial \rho} = (1-\alpha-\beta)\, c_c^\alpha c_\rho^\beta \rho^{-\alpha-\beta} > 0, \quad \frac{\partial^2 u}{\partial \rho^2} = \begin{bmatrix} -(\alpha+\beta)(1-\alpha-\beta) \\ c_c^\alpha c_\rho^\beta \rho^{-\alpha-\beta-1} \end{bmatrix} < 0.$$

Optimization Problem Optimization for consumer choice with ideologies leads to the Lagrange function

$$\mathcal{L} = u(c_\rho, c_c, \rho) - \lambda\left(p_c \bar{c}_c a_c + p_\rho \bar{c}_\rho a_\rho - \bar{y}\right).$$

The FOCs are

$$F\left(a_c, a_\rho, \lambda, \ldots, p_\rho\right) = \frac{\partial \mathcal{L}}{\partial a_c} = \frac{\partial u}{\partial c_c}\bar{c}_c - \lambda p_c \bar{c}_c = 0$$

$$F\left(a_c, a_\rho, \lambda, \ldots, p_\rho\right) = \frac{\partial \mathcal{L}}{\partial a_\rho} = \frac{\partial u}{\partial c_\rho}\bar{c}_\rho + \frac{\partial u}{\partial \rho} - \lambda p_\rho \bar{c}_\rho = 0$$

$$F\left(a_c, a_\rho, \lambda, \ldots, p_\rho\right) = \frac{\partial \mathcal{L}}{\partial \lambda} = \bar{y} - p_c \bar{c}_c a_c - p_\rho \bar{c}_\rho a_\rho = 0.$$

From the implicit function theorem, we know that if the second order conditions for a maximum hold (bordered Hessian $\left|\bar{H}\right| > 0$), this equation system defines a system of optimal values for

$$a_c^* = a_c^*(p_c, \bar{c}_c, p_\rho, \bar{c}_\rho, \bar{y})$$
$$a_\rho^* = a_\rho^*(p_c, \bar{c}_c, p_\rho, \bar{c}_\rho, \bar{y})$$
$$\lambda = \lambda(p_c, \bar{c}_c, p_\rho, \bar{c}_\rho, \bar{y}).$$

In order to show this, we take the derivatives of the system of FOCs. The second order sufficient condition for a maximum requires the bordered Hessian $\left|\bar{H}\right|$ to be positive. Consequently, the respective Jacobian of the equation system $|J|$ is also positive, and since $|J| \neq 0$, we can apply the implicit function theorem:

$$|J| = \det\begin{vmatrix} \frac{\partial^2 u}{\partial c_c^2}\bar{c}_c^2 & \frac{\partial^2 u}{\partial c_c \partial c_\rho}\bar{c}_c & -\lambda p_c \bar{c}_c \\ \frac{\partial^2 u}{\partial c_\rho \partial c_c}\bar{c}_\rho + \frac{\partial^2 u}{\partial \rho \partial c_c} & \frac{\partial^2 u}{\partial c_\rho^2}\bar{c}_\rho^2 + \frac{\partial^2 u}{\partial \rho^2} & -\lambda p_\rho \bar{c}_\rho \\ -p_c \bar{c}_c & -p_\rho \bar{c}_\rho & 0 \end{vmatrix} = \left|\bar{H}\right| > 0$$

$$|J| = -p_\rho \bar{c}_\rho p_\rho \bar{c}_\rho \lambda \frac{\partial^2 u}{\partial c_c^2} \bar{c}_c^2 + p_\rho \bar{c}_\rho p_c \bar{c}_c \lambda \left[\frac{\partial^2 u}{\partial c_\rho \partial c_c} \bar{c}_\rho + \frac{\partial^2 u}{\partial \rho \partial c_c} + \frac{\partial^2 u}{\partial c_c \partial c_\rho} \bar{c}_c \right]$$
$$- p_c \bar{c}_c p_c \bar{c}_c \lambda \left(\frac{\partial^2 u}{\partial c_\rho^2} \bar{c}_\rho^2 + \frac{\partial^2 u}{\partial \rho^2} \right) > 0.$$

A.8 The Quality of Ideological Guidance

Proof of the Impact of Fake News The individuals do not know that the signals are being manipulated. Therefore, they think that they are receiving N independent signals $\underline{M} = (M_1, M_2, \ldots, M_N)$ such that

$$M_i|\mu \sim \mathcal{N}(\mu, \eta^2).$$

In reality, individuals receive signals $\underline{M}^\varepsilon = (M_1^\varepsilon, M_2^\varepsilon, \ldots, M_N^\varepsilon)$ such that

$$M_i^\varepsilon|\mu \sim \mathcal{N}(\mu + \mu_\varepsilon, \eta_\varepsilon^2).$$

The posterior density is

$$f(\mu|\underline{m}) = \frac{f(\mu) f(\underline{m}|\mu)}{f(\underline{m})} \propto f(\mu) f(\underline{m}|\mu).$$

However, since the signals are correct from the individual point of view, they determine their posterior density

$$f(\mu|\underline{m}^\varepsilon) \propto f(\mu) f(\underline{m}^\varepsilon|\mu)$$

believing that they are calculating $f(\mu|\underline{m})$. Therefore, the Bayesian formula is used as if the signals were not manipulated, but the observations m_i^ε were used. The density becomes

$$f(\mu) f(\underline{m}^\varepsilon|\mu) = f(\mu) f(m_1^\varepsilon|\mu) f(m_2^\varepsilon|\mu) \ldots f(m_N^\varepsilon|\mu)$$
$$= \frac{1}{\sqrt{2\pi\sigma_0^2}} \exp\left(\frac{-(\mu - \mu_0)^2}{2\sigma_0^2} \right) \prod_{i=0}^{N} \frac{1}{\sqrt{2\pi\eta^2}}$$
$$\times \exp\left(\frac{-(m_i + \varepsilon_i - \mu)^2}{2\eta^2} \right)$$

$$= \frac{1}{(2\pi)^{\frac{N+1}{2}}\sqrt{\sigma_0^2\eta^{2N}}} \exp\left(\frac{-(\mu-\mu_0)^2}{2\sigma_0^2} + \sum_{i=1}^{N} \frac{-(m_i+\varepsilon_i-\mu)^2}{2\eta^2} \right)$$

$$= \frac{1}{(2\pi)^{\frac{N+1}{2}}\sqrt{\sigma_0^2\eta^{2N}}} \exp\left(\begin{array}{c} \frac{-\mu^2+2\mu\mu_0-\mu_0^2}{2\sigma_0^2} + \\ \sum_{i=1}^{N} \frac{-(m_i+\varepsilon_i)^2+2(m_i+\varepsilon_i)\mu-\mu^2}{2\eta^2} \end{array} \right)$$

$$\propto \exp\left(\frac{\left(\begin{array}{c} -\mu^2\eta^2 + 2\mu\mu_0\eta^2 - \mu_0^2\eta^2 - \sum_{i=1}^{N}(m_i+\varepsilon_i)^2\sigma_0^2 \\ + \sum_{i=1}^{N} 2(m_i+\varepsilon_i)\mu\sigma_0^2 - N\mu^2\sigma_0^2 \end{array} \right)}{2\sigma_0^2\eta^2} \right)$$

$$= \exp\left(\frac{\begin{array}{c} -\mu^2(\eta^2+N\sigma_0^2) + 2\mu(\mu_0\eta^2 + \sum_{i=1}^{N}(m_i+\varepsilon_i)\sigma_0^2) \\ -\mu_0^2\eta^2 - \sum_{i=1}^{N}(m_i+\varepsilon_i)^2\sigma_0^2 \end{array}}{2\sigma_0^2\eta^2} \right)$$

$$= \exp\left(\frac{-\mu^2 + 2\mu\frac{\mu_0\eta^2+\sum_{i=1}^{N}(m_i+\varepsilon_i)\sigma_0^2}{\eta^2+N\sigma_0^2} - \frac{\mu_0^2\eta^2+\sum_{i=1}^{N}(m_i+\varepsilon_i)^2\sigma_0^2}{\eta^2+N\sigma_0^2}}{2\frac{\sigma_0^2\eta^2}{\eta^2+N\sigma_0^2}} \right)$$

$$\propto \exp\left(\frac{-\left(\mu - \frac{\mu_0\eta^2+\sum_{i=1}^{N}(m_i+\varepsilon_i)\sigma_0^2}{\eta^2+N\sigma_0^2}\right)^2}{2\frac{\sigma_0^2\eta^2}{\eta^2+N\sigma_0^2}} \right).$$

Thus, we can define

$$(\sigma_N^\varepsilon)^2 = \frac{\sigma_0^2\eta^2}{\eta^2+N\sigma_0^2}$$

$$\mu_N^\varepsilon = \frac{\eta^2}{\eta^2+N\sigma_0^2}\mu_0 + \frac{\sigma_0^2}{\eta^2+N\sigma_0^2}\sum_{i=1}^{N}(m_i+\varepsilon_i).$$

The posterior distribution is

$$\mu | m^\varepsilon \sim \mathcal{N}(\mu_N^\varepsilon, (\sigma_N^\varepsilon)^2).$$

Index

T. Gries et al., *The Economics of Ideologies*, Springer Studies in Alternative Economics, https://doi.org/10.1007/978-3-031-93514-5

The manufacturer's authorised representative in the EU is Springer Nature Customer Service Centre GmbH, Europaplatz 3, 69115 Heidelberg, Germany. If you have any concerns regarding our products, please contact ProductSafety@springernature.com

Printed and bound by CPI Group (UK) Ltd, Croydon, CR0 4YY
01/10/2026
02225954-0016